Is There a Latin American Text in This Class?

Bernard McGuirk

London

Spanish, Portuguese and Latin American Studies in the Humanities

Is There a Latin American Text in This Class? by Bernard McGuirk
Collected Essays, vol. 3

The right of Bernard McGuirk to be identified as author of this work
has been asserted by him in accordance with the Copyright, Designs
and Patents Act, 1988.

ISBN 9781912399154

Cover illustration by Gradiva:

> *Mola* from Panama. The cloth has multiple layers, each
> superimposed on the other, slit and pulled through. When Kuna
> women tire of a particular blouse they deconstruct it and sell the
> *molas*.

> Y a-t-il de hors-*mola*?

> Il n'y a pas de hors-*molas*...

Cover design by Francesca Pasciolla.

Note

To mark the elevation to the title of Professor Emeritus of Bernard McGuirk, distinguished holder of the Chair of Romance Literatures and Literary Theory at the University of Nottingham, SPLASH Editions publishes a series of his essays collected from the various fields of his writings over four decades. The first volume, *Erasing Fernando Pessoa*, appeared in 2017, the second, *Latin American Literature and Post-Structuralism*, in 2018. This companion volume, *Is there a Latin American Text in this Class?*, takes up the challenge of revisiting the diverse contexts of the numerous international lecture or teaching invitations received following the publication by Routledge, in 1997, of *Latin American Literature: Symptoms, Risks and Strategies of Post-structuralist Criticism*. The texts explored in each chapter are thus preceded by a short pre-text, included in recognition and acknowledgment of critics, whether from Latin America or elsewhere, who responded variously to a decade or more of the interaction of deconstruction and the so-called cultural turn in literary studies. Critical responses to his published work include:

'McGuirk is well known for introducing poststructuralist theory to Latin American Studies, and he does not attempt to flatten out his writing style, which remains playful and inventive. Yet he is also acutely aware of a broad audience that might approach this work not for meta-textual analysis, but for his engagement with a social text. This is deeply engaged and political work, which does manage "to achieve accessibility without diminishing the literary critical edge"' (John King).

'Timely and appropriate, precisely when deconstruction seems ready for a vigorous return to the scene of public discussion, McGuirk's [writing] is a lesson in defusing the sunny paranoias of mimetic culturalism. [He] interrupts every one of the critical categories the book deploys in order to undermine the ostensible investments transactional geo-cultural inequalities would seem to promote. The book's very form is the (im)proper deconstructive machine' (Alberto Moreiras).

'Humour is a prerequisite of the play of readings – an inescapable antidote to appropriations by those, old and new, who assume themselves to be in charge – in McGuirk's inscription of timbres, affections and variations that render such writing necessary' (Silvina Rodrigues Lopes).

'Did I mention that we are talking about a great teacher? And critic, too. With a supervisor like this, who needs an education? [T]hat, of course, was Critical Theory, that which Bernard *is* and which, in many different formats, underpins what he thinks and writes. One has to work hard at it. Is it worth it? "Valeu a pena? Tudo vale a pena, se a alma não é pequena"' (Maria Manuel Lisboa).

Until his retirement, in 2014, from the University of Nottingham, Bernard McGuirk had been Head of the Postgraduate School of Critical Theory and Cultural Studies, recipient in 1999 of the Inaugural Lord Dearing Award for Distinction in Learning and Teaching, and is a former President of the Association of Hispanists of Great Britain and Ireland. In 2002, he was created Commander of the Order of Merit, Portugal. In 2013, he received the Brazilian International Press Awards Board of Directors' Special Award for the promotion of Portuguese and Brazilian Studies, including African literature in Portuguese on the 'Black Atlantic'. As Director of the International Consortium for the Study of Post-Conflict Societies, he has addressed representations of the 1982 South Atlantic conflict and its aftermath in *Falklands-Malvinas: An Unfinished Business*, 2007, and its recent sequel, *It Breaks Two to Tangle: Political Cartoons of the Falklands-Malvinas War*. The joint Anglo-Argentine initiative on the plight of ex-combatants and PTSD sufferers was the subject of his plenary presentation, 'Veteranos nunca más olvidados', in 2018, to the *First World Forum of Critical Thinking* and subsequently to the Honourable Chamber of Deputies of the Argentine Parliament. At postgraduate level, he supervised some 40 Ph.D. theses to completion. His former research students have gone on to gain posts and to pursue with distinction academic careers across five continents.

In 1997 everybody knew: McGuirk was 'doing deconstruction'. A *tour de force*, his is one of the most accomplished and consistent books of literary deconstruction produced during the latter's heyday – as such, it marks an epoch of criticism in the Latin American field.

Alberto Moreiras

Contents

Foreword
Else R. P. Vieira

Even by the standards set over four decades of writing, ever ingeniously, and often in a characteristically provocative style, on literatures in the romance languages, this the latest book by Bernard McGuirk proves to be a distinctively original undertaking. *Is there a Latin American Text in this Class?* turns out to be a far from just teasingly rhetorical or echoingly nostalgic title; for the challenge posed afresh is not to seek an answer, or answers, rather to join in, to participate, in speculating on how texts may be re-approached in an era too readily deemed post-theoretical.

It is a particular pleasure to offer a Foreword to essays chosen to reflect, or respond to, generational concerns long shared if ever irresolvable. For the eavesdropping Brazilian other hearkens here, where the contested term 'Latin American' echoes loud, much as the Hispanic ear of Alberto Moreiras had done in listening to the transatlantic voice of a critic who never ducks the outside/inside complexities nor avoids the risk of undermining 'the ostensible investments transactional geo-cultural inequalities would seem to promote'. In his own Foreword to the companion volume *Latin American Literature and Post-structuralism*, of 2018, Moreiras recognized, in introducing the philosophically grounded expressions of a thoroughly practised post-structuralism at work, that critical *'tour de force* in deconstructive performance' which is here replicated albeit with a new and welcome slant. In this instance, the plural voices of international classroom experiences are invited to resonate, across languages and other frontiers, with a calculatedly de-hierarchizing energy.

In another era, McGuirk used to take by surprise, either by fresh and often disconcerting insights into the texts of established major authors, and this via the application of instrumental devices taken from the 'new', the controversial, the polemical, theorists of the structural and post-structural quarter century; or, thereafter, when invited to lecture internationally as a result of his reputation as a challenging but always meticulously attentive-to-text close reader, recognized too as a seeker out, a disseminator, of the works of overlooked, lesser-known or neglected writers.

Not the least benefit of the publishing initiative of SPLASH Editions, the first volumes of which enterprise have appeared regularly since the series launch in 2017, is the recapturing of seminal out-of-print critical writings of earlier generations of subject specialists from mediaeval to contemporary. Diligent searches for appropriate contributions to the range of disciplines signalled in the imprint's title have rendered available again key texts, updated and added to where possible, authored by pioneer thinkers from across the historical, methodological and, in the case of this volume, theoretical spectrum of critical practices. The years are rolled back in the decade of chapters here, elaborately reworked and craftily juxtaposed sorties into a recent yesteryear of journal publications ever with a conjoining thread. If ever there were exemplary demonstrations of Roland Barthes's shift of emphasis from *lisible* to *scriptible* they could hardly be bettered than here displayed as enhanced in cultivated classroom asymmetries; expectations changed, changing, via the shuttle agency of the texts' shifting across the weft and warp of languages re-woven within and between inescapably political contexts.

The architecture of McGuirk's construction will require the reader to grasp the workings of deconstruction as analysis, as an instrumental strengthening of modes of access to multiple reconstructions, strong whilst never guaranteeing the permanence of any edifice; of any formative, let alone solid, verity. As a comparatist with a notable command of both the languages and the variants thereof uncovered in even the most experimental expressions of culturally grounded differences in literary production, he operates at the intra-colonial borders, fissures, gaps, repairs and graftings of Latin American and, of course, other texts; yet never alone. Any teacher-learner, learner-teacher relation is time and again re-inverted; thereby, the learner is the sharer and the text might even be said to 'learn' in the very acts of dialogical re-writing. *Voilà*, Barthes *encore*:

> When the solidarity of the old disciplines breaks down – perhaps even violently [...] performances, 'limit works', exist [...] at the limits of 'enunciation, rationality, readability etc.' [...] Texts are radically symbolic, 'off-centre, without closure', playful, offering *jouissance* [...] Texts help us glimpse a 'social utopia'... [a] transparency of linguistic relations if not social ones, a 'space where no language has a hold over any other'. (Barthes, 'From Work to Text')

This insight is re-deployed explicitly in the pulling off of the improbable trick of addressing, in chapter VI, a little-known short text by Federico Andahazi via a cross-reading with an over-visited poem by Jorge Luis Borges – evocative of some of the remarkable tones and nuances of McGuirk's landmark work, of 2007, on literary representations of the

Malvinas-Falklands conflict.

Area specialists might readily detect in Moreiras's phrase 'ostensible investments' a hardly veiled reference to those cultural turns in critical approaches to Latin American literature over the last four decades or more that, it might be said, arose predominantly from US-derived institutional preoccupations. Aware as he obviously is of the brouhaha that has accompanied any and all dipping of toes into the troubled water of those polemics, McGuirk gets on with what he does best; a nod, or nods, in many a such direction whilst remaining consistent to the enduring tenet of his 1997 *Latin American Literature: Symptoms, Risks and Strategies of Post-Structuralist Criticism*. His original project's defining claim can be shown to apply, as reiterated, in 2018, in the first of the new companion volumes: 'the studies collected and updated or expanded here seek, still, to highlight the differences at play in literature which cultural studies may, might, continue to explore'.

The deconstructive framing of the late twentieth century is evinced in the tell-tale terminology deployed in the chapter headings; each and all, I suggest, might be heard as resonances of the opening salvo of far from rhetorical questions: 'Interventions. Who put the Latin in Latin America? Who put the post- in post-colonial? Who patrols the borderlines?' As a spectrum of threshold expressions arising at and from borders north to south, and from frontiers never allowed to escape their status as signposts to colonial, post-colonial and intra-colonial re-investments, cultural specificities are confronted and acknowledged as aporetic locations; spaces both porous and, still, stubborn obstacles erected only to be confronted and challenged.

Whereas *Latin American Literature and Post-structuralism* comprised post-structural engagements with works by Pablo Neruda, Brazilian modernists of the 1922 *Semana de Arte Moderna*, Rubén Darío, César Vallejo, Jorge Luis Borges, Juan Rulfo, João Guimarães Rosa, Gabriel García Márquez, Julio Cortázar, Carlos Fuentes, Augusto Monterroso and Susana Thénon, its sequel, *Is there a Latin American Text in this Class?*, develops a broadly comparatist's no less theory-driven engagement with the tensions arising from the proponents of Cultural Studies' oft-times fraught relationship with the close reading of primary texts. In the process, and with moments of calculated echo and overlap (García Márquez, Thénon, Borges, Rosa), analysis covers a range of writers and performers in various genres and artistic modes, from Tato Laviera, John Agard and Merle Collins, Guillermo Gómez-Peña and Coco Fusco, Haroldo de Campos and Frei Betto, Néstor Perlongher, Federico Andahazi, María Luisa Bemberg, and Chico

Buarque de Hollanda. Methodologically, the ease with which, in both volumes, he moves across whilst pointedly interrogating the often dense discourses of numerous post-structuralist high priestesses and priests will be all the more welcome to a new generation of readers. They will appreciate how McGuirk uses ever instrumentally the reading and writing tools of a long from bygone register; in short, they open up only to invite re-openings. Symptomatically so, especially, when his own challenging style of writing – not least in the wryness of his dexterous word play – is juxtaposed with such as the revisited Derrida's 'Speculations on Freud'. Unforetellably, he reveals, in one of the single-page 'Pretexts' that contextualize each chapter, that is where it all started; *that* being the shift from a late 'seventies Paris to a first teaching post in the ever empirical and soon-to-be-Thatchered dis-United Kingdom.

The then shock to the system of a – largely male – critical establishment of what would soon be a successful generation of trained and theoretically-informed researchers in such as the addressing of putative responses to Freud's unanswered interrogative 'What does a woman want?' can but be imagined. No loss of contemporaneity then in the return to the institutional circumstance of 'Free play of foreplay' in the chapter enabling a *cherchez la femme* sexual/textual political appropriation of *Crónica de una muerte anunciada* as 'fiction of non-consummation'. Nor, at various junctures, in the re-staging of Thénon's 'ball-breaking' of machismo in her 1987 *Ova Completa* which, in the 1990s, McGuirk effectively introduced to a broader international readership. And today? No easy task, it must be conceded, for any reader reluctant to admit that complex literary writings demand never other than challenging critical readings; that the former discourses imply, indeed, implicate the latter. He knows as much and from the outset assumes responsibility for concomitant discontinuities and often non-matching pluralities. Aesthetic and political urgencies are rendered inseparable in any and all the approaches purveyed in the book, with the pedagogical as but an albeit seminal factor in the dissemination of meditations on topics such as: cultural memory; the 'task of the trans(at)l(antic)ator'; the problematic cross-cultural transfer of 'Truth and Reconciliation'; the literature of war steeped in violent racial prejudice; torture, murder and State criminality; censorship and the implausible silencing of *Obediencia Debida*; the incommensurate relationship of justice to injustice; and, pervasively, intra-colonialisms; all through the filter of textuality. Even the notorious 'locus of enunciation' requirement is fulfilled, but far from *de rigueur*, in a remarkable tail-piece dating from 2002, the indelibly personal 'A response *d'après* W. G. Sebald to Alberto Moreiras on Deconstruction', itself a challenge to any distinction between critical and creative writing.

Amidst the discursive prestidigitation long recognized as his signature by specialists, whether of theoretical persuasion or of more traditional area studies preferences, he shows that deconstruction cannot occur without the intervention of both agency and the imperative that the reader locate and identify that agency as such. In short, one does not have to think let alone read or write like Bernard McGuirk, much less agree with the underpinning deconstructive tenets and ploys, when conceding the overall effect of his wholly original performative and often dazzlingly revelatory insights. Even before a surprise tawny rabbit is pulled by a transatlantic tale right out of the Coda's teaching hat. Yet I should warn of the sting in the tail-piece: 'Is there a transatlantic class in this text?'. The provocative inversion of the volume's title is the daring finale to the meditations – the lessons – on intra-colonialisms that suffuse this most arresting of books.

Preface

> The place of *aporia* is at the border,
> before a door, threshold line, or the
> approach of the other as such.
>
> Jacques Derrida

Agency may, or may not, operate at the borders, the thresholds, the approaches signposted potentially in and by literary texts; for there can be no guarantee of meeting any other as such. Interventions will occur in the act of reading not via the superimposition of a given view – extraneously or intrinsically pre-determined – but voluntarily, even wilfully, in re-writings that seize the occasion to perform in the knowledge that literatures are to be approached as already and always border texts, as themselves putative agencies of encounters with others; certainly not as corroborators of self-held pre-conceptions. As for deconstructions, they never just occur; they are performed.

In the two decades and more since the publication of *Latin American Literature Symptoms, Risks & Strategies of Post-structuralist Criticism*, I have been invited time and again to address the relationship of literary and cultural studies in an era often termed post-theoretical and characterized by the so-called cultural turn in Latin American Studies. It has never been a question of either literary or cultural but rather of the different inflections that have symptomized the expectations of the various national audiences and traditions in which I have shared the insights developed in that series of readings recently republished, in revised form, in *Latin American Literature and Post-structuralism*. The present book is thus projected as a companion volume in which the primarily instrumental strategies of a post-structuralist bent are again applied and explored inseparably from the preoccupations of both creative writers and literary critics concerned to highlight socio-political urgencies without the loss of complexity demanded by and expressed in the challenging texts of a cultural production deemed, categorically, to be Latin American.

If the title of the volume seems to be pitched for or against any alternative practice or practices, then so be it. *For* reading; *Against* criticism in which practitioners want students, colleagues, or the general reader to focus on them and on their debates rather than on the literary or the cultural text... overlooking the ostensible fact that there is no cultural study that is not always already textual, too. Thus inviting, requiring, no lesser attention, or re-reading, than the often supposedly superannuated fictions, poetry, theatre, or film texts of some scorned yesteryear; of an era that, under close scrutiny, has itself survived the more persistently for having been revitalized by the near half-century of critical and cultural theories that abounded initially within institutions yet resonated well beyond them.

Is There a Latin American Text in This Class? is a choice of title that might have triggered the subtitle *Literature at the Limits of Cultural Studies*, not only archly – deliberately echoing shibboleths or credos of the last and first decades of the change of centuries – but also strategically; still riskily, and, why not?, symptomatically. For, while much has changed politically, socially, culturally and institutionally in the ways in which Latin American Studies are conceived of and delivered, a consistent encounter of reader with texts throws up questions that the companion essays – with moments of calculated overlap and, in the present selection, chapter by chapter, orienting contextualizing Pretexts – have sought and still seek to address if not answer. Challenges, too, to the many presumptive purveyors of courses ostensibly pitched exclusively on Latin American Cultural Studies.

Presumption? You must know *that* before, or worse, rather than, addressing *this* (where this is the literary text and that is my/our/their self-interested discourse). The issue of what to say or think about one's own reading and writing practices is often experienced but not so easily confronted in the transition from one culture to another. For instance, the advocate of close reading might flounder in an unfamiliar system where all thinking and statements are grounded – and thus the more promptly recognized – in social commentary or in the views and opinions of arbiters who tend to overlook, by-pass or relegate the literariness of cultural expression. Or vice versa; for the latter category of thinker, teacher, student, performer, might encounter, conversely, a perceived over-attention to text that can seem to eschew context. Only when the two, text and contexts – ever plural – are shown to interact instrumentally in the mutual highlighting or interrogating of inseparable and, indeed, urgent concerns is the critical act convincingly performed. To this end, it will always have been necessary to identify and respect the place and space of the other. Of the interlocutor – as well as those of the self; even if then to say: 'I understand... but I don't do that. I do this. Do you, are you willing to, understand?'.

> This is life lived on high alert [...]
> Never again will a single story be
> told as though it were the only one.
> *Reality Hunger: A Manifesto*
> David Shields

Ova completa, Susana Thénon's subversive *tour de force*, was revealed to me shortly after its publication in 1987 by the indomitable multi-lingual literary critic, theorist and inspirational mentor of generations of Latin Americanists, Susana Reisz. The context of the revelation spoke and speaks volumes, for it was at the University of Michigan during a semester spent teaching there during a seminal phase of so many area specialists' crucial encounter with the cultural turn in the discipline's engagement with post-colonial studies. Subjecting to a renewed and originally-voiced stress the categorizing of the aesthetic and the political, the literary and the cultural, and indulging radical untranslatability ('struss'), Thénon's still neglected text became a mainstay in my classroom practice and lecture tours from the 1990s to this day. At venues in Latin America, Europe, Asia and Africa, its subversions of mono-ethnic language and neolithic nationalisms prompted juxtapositions with too-often overlooked or marginalized performances at, within and beyond national borders as in the poems of Tato Laviera, John Agard and Merle Collins. In my companion-volume chapter of 2018, *Latin American Literature and Post-Structuralism*, 'On ball-breaking *machismo* and choreographed *intra*-colonialism: Susana Thénon's *Ova completa*', too-long-standing engenderings were exposed – pre-post-eros – as giving rise to poetry's potential to weigh, measure and again display readily-to-be deconstructed instances of the perduring and perjuring discourses of stubbornly inseparable post- and intra-coloniality.

I. INTERVENTIONS
Who put the Latin in Latin America?
Who put the post- in post-colonial?
Who patrols the borderlines?

On intra-colonialisms

Who interred invention in interventions?
Who put the late in translate?
Who turns difference into *différance*?
Who conspires?

Conspiracy theory – perhaps. Creative literature in the Latin Americas
has consistently engaged with, and in, critical discourses more readily
associable, in some cultures, with the traditions of philosophy, political
theory or even literary criticism. Contemporary texts also often deal
differently with colonial imprints highlighted by territorial and border
relations, as in the performance-poems to be analyzed in the contexts of
these opening salvos. Treatments of the colonial, the post-colonial and,
here, intra-colonialism, will be shown to emphasize how pervasive
differences between are represented inseparably from no less invasive
differences within societies. Whether the tensions provoked by
discursively as well as geographically shifting boundaries arise, in the
first instance, from the Malvinas-Falklands conflict of 1982, within
Nuyorican expression of the 1980s and its diasporic transatlantic
counterparts or, immediately thereafter, across the Mexican-US border
of the 1990s, resonantly unresolved in subsequent and current re-
visitations, a strongly performative strain will ever characterize the
staging of often raw, day-to-day, contacts-cum-confrontations. Here, in
the first instance, strategic interventions of Susana Thénon, Tato
Laviera and, in the following chapter, of Guillermo Gómez-Peña, Coco
Fusco and, eventually, in a dialogical gesture, my own, are addressed in
a critical discourse which exploits the subversively ludic language and
disruptive play of the performances under review.

The term 'Latin America' operates ever as a project, a projection, and
for many Latin Americans there is no such place, let alone a common
language, a common literature. Yet, whether utopian or atopian, any
emphasis on difference can never be just linguistic or literary and the
differences to be confronted by critics will be always also ideological.
Wherever they – or I – speak and write from, and in whichever language,
any outside-inside distinction, never viable, ever falsifiable, in the never-

to-be patrolled borderlines of each and all critical *paroles*, will be undone in and by the pluri-lingual encounters exploited alike by mutually porous creative and critical interventions.

Re-pondering the Pond

At the then time of writing, for the 2000 Special Topic issue of the journal *Interventions* on 'Latin America: Brazilian Postcolonialisms in Dialogue with Hispano-America', a *hic et nunc* marker of the discourses of cultural studies intruded. On this 'other side of the pond' or, in the erstwhile-fashionable and *de rigueur* declaration of the *locus* of my enunciation, it was the very week of the 1999 British Conservative Party Conference. Margaret Thatcher, Prime Minister of the UK from 1979-1990, had been indulging in an opportunist's attempt to sequester the past. The revivalist strategy of her Wednesday 6 October Blackpool harangue was to appropriate the very terms used, internationally, over the last quarter-century, against the Chilean regime of Augusto Pinochet, calculatedly inverted on his behalf. 'International lynch-law' had caused her 'outrage at the callous and unjust treatment of Senator [*ipsa dixit*, demilitarizing her zone of political intervention] Pinochet'. A Labour government, ungrateful for the 'essential intelligence information', provided to the UK during the Falklands conflict, and in a 'judicial kidnapping' which would 'do credit to a police-state', had made the General 'Britain's only political prisoner'. 'What the left cannot forgive is that Pinochet undoubtedly saved Chile and helped save South America'. However, what the right does not, and Thatcher did not, mention is the contemporary Chile-Argentina hostilities over the Beagle Channel (1977-1984). This skirmish, coinciding with the Malvinas war of 1982, was then still awaiting the decisive Papal intervention of John Paul II... another in the series initiated by Pope Alexander VI who, in 1494, negotiated the Treaty of Tordesillas, calculated to avoid a conflict of Spanish and Portuguese interests in the New World, and splitting Latin America into separate, controllable, spheres of colonial interest.

While Thatcher's conference speech had again drawn attention to differences *between* – 'in my lifetime all the problems have come from mainland Europe, and all the solutions have come from the English-speaking nations across the World' – subversion continues to come, too, from *within* Latin America. The Tory Conference meeting was paid for by the Chilean Reconciliation Movement (*sic*), with funds raised by businessmen in Chile. Thatcher was openly supported on the platform by Fernando Barros, Chair of that movement, and by two Chilean senators. Democracy was overt. Less so was the timing of a judicious attempt to influence the judicial. Forty-eight hours after her speech, a London metropolitan magistrate was to decide whether Pinochet was to be extradited to Spain on thirty-five counts of torture; an excess of discourse versus excessive facts? On this occasion, The Iron Lady's off-shore rigging had struck crude but, not as yet, oil. The magistrate had recommended extradition to Spain. Yet even the most stage-managed performance can be seen to have had other, unintended though ever excessive, effects of sight and of sound. Hair *bouffant*. Her? *Bouffonne*. But she faced the music. Ennio Moricone's score from Roland Joffé's 1986 *The Mission* was the prelude to her speech, obviously chosen by an impresario unaware that the sequence in question had accompanied the film's representation of a massacre of the pre-Conquest tribes over whose different borders latter-day Argentina, Chile, Paraguay and Brazil had been drawn (and quartered). Even Thatcher's earlier visit to the General, temporarily 'at home' in England's Home Counties, for a 'tea-party', had borne echoes of Albion's ill-judged New World adventurism. Bossed on, and ever on, it would seem, were flag-waving patriots, *hic et illic*, interchangeably. Santiago... St George; Moor-killer... more killing? The capital interventions of Amnesty International in the region might be seen, again, in the Pinochet case, to have involved urgencies only hinted at in the rhetorical questions of my overture.

In her 'Postcolonialisms and the Latin Americas', in the previous number of *Interventions* (1999, 274), Else Vieira had made the point that 'a heightened awareness of the postcolonial condition' is 'brought to visibility' by a textual practice whereby creative and political writing co-exist as, for example, in the 'Colombian meditation on transnational colonialism' of Gabriel García Márquez. The legacy of meta-critical literary writing is still strong and I wish to focus now on several contemporary instances of the phenomenon from that contingent, continent-(un)bound, category called Latin America.

Two to tangle?

My first re-reading of political, no less than of literary, interventions – always in excess of themselves – is the closing sequence of a poem, from her 1987 collection *Ova completa*, by the Argentine writer Susana Thénon (my translation). It might, indeed, take but two to tangle, yet multiple (p)layers of post-colonial discourse come together in the text's re-staging of the Malvinas-Falklands war:

17

Poema con traducción	Poem with Simultaneous
simultánea Español-Español	Translation Spanish to Spanish

[...]	[...]
desembarcaron	they disembarked
en 1492 a. D.	in 1492 AD
(pisaron	(they trod
en 1982 a. D.)	in 1982 AD)
jefes esperaban	chiefs were waiting
en pelota	stark naked
genuflexos	genuflecting
(mandamases aguardaban	(bosses waited
desnudos	stripped
de rodillas)	kneeling)
Cristóforo gatilló el misal	Cristóforo triggered the missal
(Christopher disparó el misil)	(Christopher fired the missile)
dijo a sus pares	said to his peers
(murmuró a sus secuaces)	(whispered to his followers)
coño	coño
(fuck)	(fuck)
ved aquí nuevos mundos	see here new worlds
(ved aquí estos inmundos)	(see here these unwashed)
quedáoslos	keep them
(saqueadlos)	(sack them)
por Dios y Nuestra Reina	for God and our Queen
(por Dios y Nuestra Reina)	(for God and our Queen)
AMÉN	AMEN
(OMEN)	(OMEN)
(Thénon, 1987: 28)	

The somewhat less than celebratory pre-quincentenary gift from British Prime Minister Thatcher to the regime of the Argentine President General Leopoldo Galtieri came, in 1982, ten years too early. At least the unseemly rush across the South Atlantic, again to see and sack new worlds, allowed Thénon the time (she died in 1990) to situate the translatability of inseparably monarchic, ecclesiastical and military rhetoric. She treats it as not only a clichéd North-South, English-Spanish, relation but also as an effect shown to be operative between Spanish and Spanish, between Spanish American and Spanish Americans. Here, Thénon shows up the virtual taboo-subject of *intra*-colonialism. Within the political/ideological frontiers of Spanish America, there would appear to be a need not (only) for translation of the message of resistance against cyclical colonizing aggression into the language (English) of its latest perpetrators but (also) for its repetition, in difference, to the often indifferent (Spanish American) other.[1]

The very title of the poem broaches (humorously?) the problematic issue of difference *within* as opposed to the more conventional difference *between* languages. However many millions the United Nations might spend on the provision of simultaneous translation, its peace-making services will always founder amidst an excess of history and an excess of language. The official version will ever be shadowed by the parenthetic (trace of) supplementarity. Moreover, a *traduttore/traditore* view of translation need not be confined to language; the question of history as repetition, as action replay, is posed only to be deposed; 'source' is mined only to be undermined; 'target' will be gauged by missal *and* missile… intertextuality *qua* infra-red brutality. Playing the translation game, Thénon's poem indulges an illusory binary of past versus present, 1492 versus 1982, (West-seeking) aetiology versus (heat-seeking) teleology. Written dates here perform in excessive relation one to the other, highlighting the limitations of the frame of history. *Un*repeatability, *un*translatability, allows particular perceptions of political events to resist such blanket rallying calls to imperial adventurism as that of a Churchill-echoing demagogue. It is as if the brackets which represent, visually, the simultaneous translator's version were, auditively, ear-phones conveying the message of a constant, and sardonic, interference. The archetypal primal scene of North-South/East-West encounter is re-enacted in rapid-fire rhythms as the tread-mark of post-Freudian as well as of post-colonial imprinting is trans-scribed. Christopher Columbus, Bernal Díaz del Castillo, Pêro Vaz da Caminha, scriptors all, whether as conquistadors or chroniclers, shadow an official résumé of colonists' arrivals: hierarchy held in suspense, naked exposure of the local, religious submission, occupation by force (1982 version: Argentine despots on tenterhooks, stripped, on their knees, sacked). And who are the phantom-scribes in the translation from fifteenth-century Santo Domingo to twentieth-century Port Stanley? Always 'our' own correspondents. Never un-author-ized versions. An excess of language, in relation not only to its self but also to its other, is revealed. The possibility of colonial/post-colonial equivalence

---

[1] I take up but briefly here the poetry of war, explored extensively in my *Falklands-Malvinas. An Unfinished Business* (2007), a volume deemed unsuitable (unsaleable?), I have been, glacially, informed, and thus unavailable in either library or bookshop – *d'après* Jorge Luis Borges – 'en unas islas demasiado famosas'. Too famous, it would seem, to countenance further interventions…

is posed, but simultaneously deconstructed by the poem's performative translation. An excess of history, too, is revealed in the surplus moral (re-) armament of the missal (missile). Christ is borne on the tracer-bullet-points of binary bearers, preached (hissed) to peers (or followers)... apostles all. And who are these disciples to punish? The expletive, somewhat unusually in the documenting of history, remains *un*deleted in official and unofficial versions. Translation intervenes only as an intensifier, of force, contempt, sex, obscenity, transgression. Behold new worlds/Go forth and multiply possession. (Behold these unwashed 'Argies'/*Gotcha!*). Thus ran the populist tabloid headline when, outside the unilaterally declared 'exclusion zone' of the hostilities, the Argentine light cruiser ARA *General Belgrano* was hit, on 2 May 1982, by two of three torpedoes launched from the British nuclear-powered hunter-killer submarine *Conqueror*, with the loss of 323 of the Argentine crew. It was, thenceforth, to be *The Sun* which ever (type) set on the British (post-) Empire.

The intonation would appear to be univocal as the text approaches its Vespers. For the only time in the poem, the ear-phone parentheses apparently contain the self-same locution in the translation as in the original: 'por Dios y Nuestra Reina' (encore). Faithful? Where linguistic and historical differences disappear is in *cliché*, language emptied of particularity, that unquestioning imprecation which carries us once more onto the breach of all nations at war. Fateful? Or perhaps avoidable, as soon as a differential reading is allowed? For the boomed imperative of faith-*full* resignation, 'AMÉN', faces a faith-*less* future as '(OMEN)'. It is (mis)translated with the inclusion of a supplementarity borrowed, perhaps, from the most bedevilling of paper Concordats. If the question of history, if the question of language, if all questions of representation are, indeed, always already excessive with respect to histories, languages and representations, then the 'So be it' of Church and State conformity will always be the least digestible of imperatives. The slippage from AMÉN to (OMEN) supplements South-to-North vassalage with a warning of resistance to all unquestioned assumptions regarding translation and translatability. In the politicization of deconstructive practices, the necessary supplementarities, in any case, are to be traced not only between the lines and between the cultures, but also within. My claim that Susana Thénon's poem confronts *intra*-colonialism inseparably from its uncompounded progenitor needs be re-addressed now by re-posing the question of the repeatability of AMÉN within Latin America. So be it?

To any and every Latin American who has said, since 1982, 'What *we* need is a Margaret Thatcher', the poem pleads 'coño' (and only in brackets '(fuck)' for the Anglo-Saxons who never listen until it suits them). For in the wings, always opportunist, are the listeners – on the inside as well as on the outside – who will (mis)interpret the plea, hear differently the same words. For those who still regard their own history and language as subordinate to their business enterprise, prayer will easily be (mis)read as imprecation, invitation... '(ved aquí estos inmundos)' [...] '(saqueadlos)' [...] '(OMEN)'. From within, too, comes the subversion, the ominous call for outside intervention by those who have always (ever ready) been poised to pounce, and to sack – '(fuck)' – their fellow nationals. Echoes less of the benighted Chilean Reconciliation Movement of a 1999 Blackpool-Tory jamboree than of a 1973 Santiago de Chile delighted junta-in-waiting, long-complicit, inviting the menacing protection of the US-backed naval blockade of Valparaiso. Far from taboo was the overt, the cyclical, *intra*-ference: Kissinger–Pinochet, Pinochet–Thatcher; marriages of illegal 'Havens', *pace* William Blake, made in (between post- and intra-)... a re-colonizing Hell.

The body *politic*?

The interplay of physical, linguistic and political aggression operating between and within sovereign states and their peoples, so blatant in the Malvinas-Falklands conflict and in its post-colonial after-effects, may be shown by other cartographies, spoken in other accents. Usually the 'state of conflict', while no less overt, has not been officially declared, though its expression can be just as powerful. For all the distance and differences between a nationally identifiable Argentine literature and that shuttle-space of Latino writing from which I take my second example, the performative construct still derives from persistent colonial insistencies and resistances. On display will be a body politic, certainly, but also a body erotic. At issue, this time, will be the excessive (body) language of racial stereotyping and ethnic *un*translatability. How, and by whom, is the emigrant-cum-immigrant to be viewed, photographed, classified... entered?

Border crossings will be shown to entail considerably more than geographical, economic, political and cultural events. When, under pressures of globalization, travelling theory runs the risk of turning into travelling *cliché*, the commentator on Latin American literary and cultural studies will ask, again: what happens to representation on the other side? What further confrontations and (lack of) negotiations await migrants often forced, and reluctant, to supplement the already precarious term of their mobility by the ever-problematic prefix *in*-? How are the tariffs of *im*migration from language to language to be levied and paid? And at what (inter-)personal cost?

Perhaps the most celebrated representation of the dilemmas broached by such questions is 'Asimilao', from *AmeRícan* (1985), written by the Puerto-Rican Santurce-born New York resident Jesús Abraham, or 'Tato', Laviera. The poem performs, re-embodies, moves beyond, choreographs, updated sights and sounds of the ever-staged but far from one-sided West's *I* story. New *Yo* Rican eyes like to see in America, ears like to hear in America. *I* shall be seen in America, *Yo* shall be heard in Ame-Ríc-ah.

Asimilao

    assimilated? que assimilated,
    brother, yo soy asimilao,
    asi mi la o si es verdad
    tengo un lado asimilao.
    You see, they went deep... Ass
    oh.........they went deeper........SEE
    oh, oh,... they went deeper...ME
    but the sound LAO was too black
    for LATED, LAO could not be
    trans*lated*, assimilated,
    no, asimilao, melao,
    it became a black
    spanish word but
    we do have asimilados
    perfumados and by the
    last count even they
    were becoming asimilao
    how can it be analyzed
    as american? así que se
    chavaron
    trataron
    pero no
    pudieron
    con el AO
    de la palabra
    principal, deles gracias a los prietos
    que cambiaron asimilado al popular asimilao
                                (Laviera, 1985: 54)

I shall now stretch appropriation beyond the limit of the semi(er)otic necessity of (un)translatability. On display will be another body politic, posing; re-posing the challenge for a no-longer capitalizable, culture-free, strictly – merely – textual 'Semiotics'. How is the sign, constructed not on the (im)possibility but rather on the (un)necessity of inter-lingual translation to be (uncomfortably) accommodated *within* the other('s) culture?

In an unapologetic writerly intervention of de/re/*requete*/de-constructive appropriation – approaching the text from the left (the Left) and nudging the lines to refit/befit my (will it be yet another, already and always, re-colonizing?) reader's desire to revisit the margin(s), I project a further embodiment, a distortion, an appropriation – in short, an unsolicited viewing, without (trust me?) re-possessing... for, *d'après* Emmanuel Levinas, nothing could be further from Eros than possession.

Dis/play – dis-respect? Such re-embodiment draws overtly and mischievously on the resources of the calligrammatic genre in general and deploys, in particular, its post-colonial palimpsest upon the outline configuration of a body political, subsumed into a complex dynamics of race, rape, resistance and pride. But to what effect?

Asimilao

assimilated? que assimilated,
brother, yo soy asimilao,
asi mi la o si es verdad
tengo un lado asimilao.
You see, they went deep... Ass
oh.........they went deeper........SEE
oh, oh,... they went deeper...ME
but the sound LAO was too black
for LATED, LAO could not be
trans*lated*, assimilated,
no, asimilao, melao,
it became a black
spanish word but
we do have asimilados
perfumados and by the
last count even they
were becoming asimilao
how can it be analyzed
as american? así que se
chavaron
trataron
pero no
pudieron
con el AO
de la palabra
principal, deles gracias a los prietos
que cambiaron asimilado al popular asimilao

(Laviera, 1985: 54)

Can poetry ever capture a photographic (or mirror) state without providing a stage on which are performed not only the exoticisms but also the eroticisms – indeed the strange pathologies – of an inherited Eurocentrism and a gendered gaze? The process of self-realization, in poetry, as distinct from the narcissistic construction which fixes self in a mirror-state, will divulge a restless, unfulfilled, performative subject strutting its identity on a mirror-stage – inseparably from a constructed (or is it deconstructed?) gendered identity for the reader.

Teasing theatrics produce in the ogler an illusion which is self-delusion. The rising temperature of any voyeurism momentarily threatening to melt down the implicit differences of gender, colour, class and economies of a post-colonial relation is suddenly turned *inside* out. What is being framed and – as every reading is a re-reading – self-framed, is never captured; only, *in camera*, aperture-d; clicked, as a 'mode of presentation of otherness' (Bhabha, 1983, 19). As the shapely text shoulders responsibility, a left-to-right scan traces aporia at the heart:

You see	Ass
oh	SEE
oh, oh	ME
but	black

Inserted, inserted again, re-inserted, pushed, pushed hard, pushed harder, is the scandalously repressed history of male – as well as of female – rape. And not only on the ships. For, as long since reported, one of the highest incidences of rape recorded in the USA is that of young black males in prison (Ladipo, 2001). A scream of pain – inside – scandalously unheeded – outside – seeks to fill that space of judicial recognition, and action, which legislation and its history have rendered excessive. 'Too' hot to handle for a mere cultural study?

they went deep
they went deeper
they went deeper
the sound LAO was too...

Yet mine is no *mere* deconstructive appropriation. Laviera's poem has pushed itself and me to the limits of critical intervention. I dis-member what it would re-member. *Mea maxima culpa? Et tu...* (you) Brute! In my own view(ing) of 'Asimilao', the would-be empowered strikes back. In a reverse telescopy, the configuration both shows itself to and looks at its other, exploiting a simultaneity of neo-, post-, and intra-colonial optics, dialogics, and logistics. Calligrammatically – Calibanatically? – re-staged, the play, the die, is re-cast – 'I know how to curse. The red plague rid you/for learning me your language!' – and thus performs as a verbal/visual highlighter of politico-cultural relations. Through ear and eye, the threat of a re-colonizing assimilation is challenged in the very representation that identifies its dominant moves, its violating strategies.

'Primitive imperial accumulation', as formulated by Alberto Moreiras with respect to Marx and the pre-history of capital, 'holds the secret to a deconstitution of the *verum* – and hence also of what is false and has been set as such. This is another way of thinking the violence of empire' (Moreiras, 2000, 362). Such an accumulation would appropriate, and desires to oppress, the (ever un-Prospero/us) worker in the very act that drives a divorcing wedge between the body and its access both to its own production *and* to its self-representation. 'Asimilao' radically disavows the possibility of an outside/inside economy whilst drawing attention to the impossibility of self-definition other than via the tropes of the post-colonial. Insertion becomes inversion.

Inversion – deconstruction – of what? The ploy of a, whenever convenient, neo-colonizing assimilation of the other conforms to what Derrida has characterized as the ruse of a universalizing dominance: 'oriented, calculated, deliberate, voluntary, ordered movement: ordered most often by the *man* in charge. Not by a woman, for in general, and especially in wartime, it is *man* who decides on the heading, from the advanced point that he himself is, the prow, at the head of the ship or plane that he pilots' (Derrida, 1992, 14). *L'Autre cap*, Derrida's French title, less ambiguously than the English version, *The Other Heading*, foregrounds masculist promontory, protuberance, excrescence. The mode of resistance, the tropological man-to-man manoeuvre of 'Asimilao', however, is not to avoid violent scopophilia ('SEE') or 'deep' synecdoche ('Ass' *qua* 'ME'). Rather does it (en)tail a depiction and a projection of 'deeper' being, a defiantly intra-colonial identity construction. The point is emphasized, I suggest, by a comparison. Stuart Hall, in respect of post-colonial subjectivity, returned in a resonant radio interview to the notion of 'a hyphenated sense of belongingness' (Hall, 1999, radio interview). To regard the possibility of *assimilation* in traditional colonial terms, via such a mischievous equation as *Ass-SEE-ME* = *elation* (i.e. for the scopophilic *voyeur*), would be to license the outside to change the inside. Result? Victory to the libidinally dominant, and the abolition of otherness. Hall, however, reminded us that 'difference is here to stay'. And, pertinently, he continued: 'the only way we have of negotiating [...] is through the visual clues. Commonality defines us, otherwise racism will'. In this light, 'Asimilao', hands-on-hips, feet firmly on the ground, might be seen to negotiate obstinately, from a position of inner strength deriving from outer pressures. Painful input is converted into, inviolability is constructed on, the forceful output of a subject whose self-image takes (the form of) a stance, and whose voicing accentuates, albeit beLATEDly, a twice-LAOd resistance. The structuring of the discourse transfigures the repeatedly absorbed 'oh'... 'oh, oh' of colonial abuse into a diphthongized (i.e. both and neither) AO of post-colonial negotiation.

Performatively, as well as semantically, 'Asimilao' indeed proclaims untranslatability. Its voice mouths dissent, refuses to be 'assimilated', mocks shock through 'que', and spurns adoptive brother-hood(s). Playful inter-lingualism and *trompe l'oeil* flow from the text's head and shoulders through a predominantly Anglified upper body until it stands Hispanically on its own two feet. I have deliberately avoided the terms English and Spanish insofar as bilingualism is not the point: for 'if it is to be thought radically [...] being must be conceived of as presence or absence on the basis of play and not the other way round' (Derrida, 1981, 292). Playing in a no less theoretical spirit, but in an appropriately different 'popular' tone, the poem admits that 'we' include those who, in the past, have cosmetically masked the odour of being perceived as other. But, 'by the last count', then, long ago, 'as they say, it was pay-back time' – the U.S. was learning its Latin lesson: 'In the past decade, the Latino population has grown by 38% compared with the national growth rate of 9%. By 2005, Latinos [would] be the largest minority in the U.S.; by 2050, they will make up a quarter of the nation' (Campbell, 1999, 2). While it asks an empirical, even a statistical question, 'how can it be analyzed as american?' the text does not shy away from yet another cultural differentiality. For as strong as the dual language tensions are those 'black'/'prietos' – 'spanish'/'melao' (i.e. honey-coloured) dynamics which have combined to bring about a far-from synthetic, radical, closure-in-process. Transformations are triggered, but not completed, by change ('cambiaron'). The point made is that literary and theorizing performances function in negotiated complementarity. So, the poem recommends, recognize the performers, thank them: 'deles gracias' (as distinct from *Deo gratias*). Parodic blasphemy terminally serves as a *non serviam*. Look and listen, in the per-trans-formance of 'Asimilao', not for theological closure but for ideological exposure.

Ponderous cartographies:
Who took Guyana, Grenada, *out* of Latin America?

In a poetics of cultural and linguistic untranslatability, emphasis will fall again on the (im)possibility of semiotic categorizing, cataloguing, archiving, in a transatlantic locus of non-acculturation as threatening as any border performances staged within the art-lands of *homo americanus*. Now the addressee – *nosce te ipsum* – is that smug *homo academicus* on this, the other side of the Pond:

Listen Mr Oxford Don

Me not no Oxford don
Me a simple immigrant
From Clapham Common
I didn't graduate
I immigrate

But listen Mr Oxford don
I'm a man on de run
and a man on de run
is a dangerous one

I ent have no gun
I ent have no knife
but mugging de Queen's English
is the story of my life

I don't need no axe
To split/up yu syntax
I don't need no hammer
To mash/up yu grammar

I warning you Mr Oxford don
I'm a wanted man
and a wanted man
is a dangerous one

Dem accuse me of assault
on de Oxford dictionary imagine a concise peaceful man like
me dem want me serve time
for inciting rhyme to riot

but i tekking it quiet
down here in Clapham Common

I'm not a violent man Mr Oxford don
I only armed wit mih human breath
but human breath
is a dangerous weapon

So mek dem send one big word after me
I ent serving no jail sentence
I slashing suffix in self-defence
I bashing future wit present tense
and if necessary

I making de Queen's English accessory to my offence
(Agard, 1988, 5-6)

'Offence', a closing but never the final word – ever 'accessory' –
epitomizes the crisis of original and copy, ownership and appropriation.
As a virtual parody of deconstruction's by now classic procedures, it
situates only in order to dislocate all assumptions regarding primacy or
aetiology.

Strategically, I juxtapose with the text of Tato Laviera a poem by the
London-based Guyanese writer John Agard. His 'Listen Mr Oxford
Don' (1967) is an instance of the literary representation of metropolitan
minority identity, as post- and neo-colonialism interact with
globalization in generating spaces of tension between the local and the
transcultural. Traditions such as the oral and the performative,
repressed and overwritten by colonial history, undergo a rendering
visible (as distinct from a surrendering, invisible). Thus, invisibility and
orality are weapons taken up, rather than gestures passively re-
projected, by struggling subjects who turn to denunciatory effect the
very markers of the supposedly subaltern. Such performance poetry
affords me a further, deconstructive, comparison between literary
criticism and cultural studies. A long-standing resistance, on the part of
the proponents of *transculturation*, involves a radical, if problematic,
alternative to those policies of *acculturation* underlying all melting-pot
theories. The terms themselves indeed set interaction against authority
but become habitually locked into a repetitive binarism. No such
relation pertains in the refusal of border poetry to broach even a
putative trans-similation. The *frontera* text *mediante* stumbles at the
first term/turn, calculatedly refusing 'assimilation', let alone the

comfort of an unencumbered linguistic room of its own. It performs that play which is the disruption of presence *and* absence, precisely undoing its own locatability: for the place of an aporia is at the border 'or the approach of the other as such' (Derrida, 1993, 12).

The poem's confronting of the relationship between subjectivity and objectivity is self-indulgently multi-layered. A 'Me'/'me' re-doubled subject refuses the status of 'I', opting provocatively for the 'standard English' object pronoun, disjunctively emphatic as part of the unspoken (but doubly written) '[Listen to] Me/me'. The far from essential epithet of 'simple' is not delivered until a play with the double-bind negation of 'not no' has been exploited; firstly to distance the subject from place ('Oxford') and voice ('don') of authority; secondly, to put that 'Oxford don' in his place. The reminder of institutional power's trajectory (don < dom < dominus > dominance) is inscribed as inseparable from the institution's dependence on its (illusory) binary – Clapham – not only now the site of the 'immigrant' but also, epithetically, the distant habitat of the 'Common man'; the man or – belatedly – woman who underpins that English class-system which does allow graduation (though never *pro omnibus*), yet with controls no less stringent than those operating at immigration pressure-points from Heathrow to Guantánamo.

For translation specialists of a traditional bent, the voice of the poem says: 'Mr Oxford don' has inserted himself and his language, canonically, into the ever-to-be deconstructed locus of all standard-English enunciation. *I* therefore translate not (no!) an original text but (yes!) a hierarchical counterfeit of supposed *arch-écriture*, para-doxically pre-constructed by arch (that is, posing) orality. Accent, syntax, grammar, norms, canons… behold the unspoken elements of an apparently inexistent original which performs, nonetheless, according to the unwritten rules of 'good' behaviour, of manners, and of access to the Establishment. One can hardly begin to grasp the implications of cultural translation, therefore, unless the dismantling mechanisms of not only a post-structuralist but also, and inseparably, a post-colonial discourse are incorporated into the body of translation theory, semiology and, no less, cultural studies.

Key zones of the Agard poem might here be re-crossed with a view to showing how they operate in dialogue with the violated body-border lines of Laviera's *AmeRícan* 'Asimilao', with the aporetics of Derrida, and even more pertinently, with a poetics of cultural and linguistic untranslatability as posed by the Dutch-Aruba-born, Grenadian, London-based since 1983, Merle Collins. Her 'No Dialects Please' is a poem constructed, culturally speaking, on differences *within* no less discomfiting than Agard's, no more accommodating than Laviera's, mocking concentration on differences *between*. It is a strong instance of a literary text which might be said, again, to highlight in intensity the differences explored by such as Paul Gilroy's *There Ain't No Black in the Union Jack*, one of the most celebrated cultural studies titles of the period in question:

No Dialects Please

In this competition
dey was looking for poetry of worth
for a writin that could wrap up a feeling
an fling it back hard
with a captive power to choke de stars
so dey say,
'Send them to us
but NO DIALECTS PLEASE'
We're British!
Ay! Well ah laugh till me boushet near drop
Is not only dat ah tink
of de dialect of de Normans and de Saxons
dat combine an reformulate
to create a language-elect
is not only dat ah tink
how dis British education mus really be narrow
if it leave dem wid no knowledge
of what dey own history is about
is not only dat ah tink
bout de part of my story
dat come from Liverpool in a big dirty white ship
mark
AFRICAN SLAVES PLEASE!
We're the British!
But as if dat not enough pain
for a body to bear
ah tink bout de part on de plantations down dere
Wey dey so frighten o de power
in the deep spaces
behind our watching faces
dat dey shout
NO AFRICAN LANGUAGES PLEASE!
It's against the law!

Make me ha to go
an start up a language o me own
dat ah could share wid me people
Den when we start to shout
bout a culture o we own
a language o we own
a identity o we own
dem an de others dey leave to control us say
STOP THAT NONSENSE NOW
We're all British!
Every time we lif we foot to do we own ting
to fight we own fight
dey tell us how British we British
an ah wonder if dey remember
dat in Trinidad in the thirties
dey jail Butler
who dey say is their British citizen
an accuse him of
Hampering the war effort!
Then it was
FIGHT FOR YOUR COUNTRY, FOLKS!
You're British
Ay! Ay!
Ah wonder when it change to
NO DIALECTS PLEASE!
WE'RE British!
Huh!
To tink how still dey so dunce
an so frighten o we power
dat dey have to hide behind a language
that we could wrap roun we little finger
in addition to we own!
Heavens to mercy!
Dat is dunceness, oui!
Ah wonder where is de bright British?

(Collins, 1987, 86)

The crisp imperative of the poem's title proves to be but interrupted. It awaits implicit completion by a dominant metaphysics so present that a latent assumption can be deferred until an impersonal but authoritarian voice booms out. Announcers of so-called open competition blurt the unstatedly obvious: 'We're British!' (Don't you know). To anyone familiar with the cultural clichés of London theatre-going since the swingin' sixties, an echo of the famous comedy *No Sex Please, We're British* undercuts a historically constructed 'language-elect' in mocking memory of a national semi(er)osis non-erect; stereotype of a nation where only the upper lip was supposed to be stiff. Evocative of the days of black-and-white TV, the poem textualizes exclusivity-cum-exclusion. Clichéd meanings are inverted: what 'dey was lookin for' is virtually a pastiche of a traditional pedagogy's prescriptions for poetry. What they *get* turns 'hard', 'captive' and 'choke' into ciphers of age-old and colony-wide interdiction; is not (dear brute/us) in their 'stars' but in their selves, that they are treated – still – as underlings. Echoes less of Cassius than of two already cited post-colonial theorists resound. 'Commonality defines us, otherwise racism will' (Hall, 1999) is re-emphasised as an easily abused pairing: *you* may enter the competition... but ever as racially marked (cf. the pejoratively-termed 'influx' of the post-1948 *MV Empire Windrush* generation; *plus ça change*). 'Struggling subjects [...] turn to denunciatory effect the very markers of the supposedly subaltern' (Vieira, 2002, 178): *my* amusement is such 'ah laugh till me boushet near drop'. Out of the *patois* mouth of babes and sucklings pours proof of how the subaltern *does* speak, talk back, give lip; *will* enter not only 'this competition' but also that contest, that struggle, that conflict of an 'education' broader than mere 'British', more naughty than narrow, more laughing than law-breaking. Proprietary rights are easily turned into owners' wrongs: 'knowledge/of what dey own history is about' *reads* as part of a putative school-lesson's content; but may be *heard*, broken down, re-iterated, as an about-turn in routine assumptions of just who owns what when it comes to 'my' story. No small irony is the meta-textual dimension of a poem that has now entered the classroom, anthologized on the 'United' Kingdom's national curriculum of school pupils invited to see its dis/investment in slavers' CAPITAL/s, to hear its cultural difference, to observe its deferring to no master... nor to his discourse. The six capitalized phrases stand out and stand up (though *not* to attention), initially maintaining the polite veneer of persuasion, 'PLEASE'. The historic colonial project is no less explicitly conveyed by the first three. Their message is clear: 'make sure *we* can understand you speaking *our* language; don't get uppity but remember who *you* (still) are; and don't think that that Edward Said nonsense about curable monolingualism applies to *us*... but, just in case, remember, too, that your own/other languages don't count (and never have)'.

Only after the subject under construction is forced by 'the law' (not to cry Woolf but) to 'go/an start up a language o me own', room for manoeuvre that rapidly 'ah could share wid me people' and, soon, further disseminated 'when we start to shout/bout a culture o we own/a language o we own/a identity o we own', is skin-deep courtesy dropped: 'STOP THAT NONSENSE NOW'. Primitive accumulation of CAPITAL is nakedly reasserted. Again, it would appropriate, and desires to oppress, the subject, driving a divorcing wedge between the body and its access both to its own production and to its self-representation. The subject, however, proclaims both a particular history and a pertinent cultural memory.

As the poem closes, the educationally and culturally subaltern emerge, are denounced, as being those benighted dunces unaware that monolingualism is not a disease for empowered citizens. A cure is still needed only for those interlocutors on whom the British Empire's sun has long since set, leaving but an aporetic interrogation of them: 'ah wonder where is de bright British?'. Yet, *The Sun Also Rises*: 'London is the most linguistically diverse city on earth [with] 307 languages spoken by the conurbations' children. The first survey of modern London's languages showed that only two-thirds of its 850,000 schoolchildren speak English at home [...] The total of 307 clearly identified languages excludes hundreds more dialects and may well be an underestimate, given that several local authorities had no detailed records' (Charter, 2000, 18). Loca(l) authority... mad, but it makes one 'l' of a (cultural) difference.

To those British, 'bright' or other/wise, of Merle Collins's projection; to '[los que] no pudieron con el AO de la palabra principal' of Tato Laviera; to that *dom*/in/us all who, for John Agard, can only sing 'Police, police me'. To all who never wait for the other's next line... border-breaking poetry sings out: Listen! 'I don't want to sound complainin' but you know there's always pain in'... any cultural study unmediated by the potentially transgressive complexity of literary criticism, reductive of – or further policing – the subject under analysis.

At, and beyond, the limits of intra-colonizing control, of herded minds, of reconstituted true/false verities, the sting and the contamination of the *tse-tse* flies in the face of hygienic, much less immune, bodies such as text, context, literary, semiotic or cultural studies. In border performances, trans-terrritorial or trans-oceanic, as we have come to see, trans-textuality is a new wor(l)d... but it is readable, habitable; like *tse*xtuality.

Interventions. International Journal of Postcolonial Studies, in its inaugural number, threw up, out, and in, a century on from the triggering of many an agonizing, unresolved meditation, in the fields of Hispanic and Latin American Studies, on so-called loss, gain, disaster, liberation, ignominy, celebration, identities lost or re-gained, unresolvable binaries all, an invitation taken up by many a distinguished reactor to Robert Young's challenge regarding writing 'now valued as much for its depiction of representative minority experience as for its aesthetic qualities (1998/99, 7). In its second volume, of 2000, I could not but lend a voice to, even interjecting in, the explosive textuality of the ever-resonant cultural events cum transcribed performances of Guillermo-Gómez Peña and Coco Fusco. Furnished with a photograph and accompanying tag – '1992 "Two Undiscovered Amerindians Visit Spain". Coco Fusco and Gómez-Peña lived for three days in a golden cage placed at Columbus Plaza in Madrid as "Amerindians from the (fictional) island of Guatinaui". They were taken to the bath-room on leashes and hand-fed through the bars' (Gómez-Peña 1993, 136-37) – classrooms often cage-house rocked at innumerable re-stagings as their texts were opened up, each time to and with new and multiple co-voicings.

II. TRIALOGUE/S
At the poetry-frontier
with Guillermo Gómez-Peña and Coco Fusco

Magical wheeler dealerism

Performing? Not always. *Carrying out* negotiations is the more conventional terminology of the teleologically determined language of diplomacy. *Realpolitik* obliges. Treaties between nations – also inter-texts – may be signed, but they are never co-signed by tangential players in the game of cross-addressing border-texts.

The urgencies of frontier negotiations are rarely more arrestingly captured, ever further from secular clichéd patriotisms of popular song and repetitive utopic stagings, always challenging the reader/viewer to feel other than at ease let alone at 'Home on the Range', the desolate war-zones rather, of his *Warrior for Gringostroika* (1993), *The New World Border: Prophecies, Poems & Loqueras for the End of the Century* (1996) or *Dangerous Border Crossers* (2000), than by the Mexican-born, US-resident, Guillermo Gómez-Peña.

I had taken as tongue-in-cheek the fly-leaf end-page admonition in *The New World Border*:

> Warning: Guillermo Gómez-Peña's performances contain material and visual effects that some people may find offensive. (Disclaimer from a paranoid presenter, placed in the lobby of the theatre).

Until, that is, at a momentous Madrid 2002 *De Signis* conference 'Comunicación y Conflicto Intercultural. Fronteras y Traducciones', on the evening of my talk that gave rise to the title 'Triálogo/s con Guillermo Gómez-Peña y/en la poesía-frontera: ¿Es la traducción una (in)curable enfermedad (ir)repetible?' (McGuirk, 2004, 139).

José David Saldívar had generously enquired of me whether I had encountered any opposition from students when prescribing or teaching such material in the UK. 'They can't get enough of it' had been my ingenuous reaction... Not necessarily so was the gist of what he went on to recount from his own experience, prompting me to reflect on what I had albeit half-forgotten since covering Walter Mignolo's sabbatical leave and delivering undergraduate and graduate classes at the University of Michigan some thirteen years before. There where God is will god-fearing be; quite a distance from Freud's dictum on the *id* and the *ego*(d)...

Mea culpa – a maxim: 'We have really everything in common with America nowadays, except, of course, language'; in the gospel according to Saint Oscar, a 'truth' stumbled upon by Sigmund's near contemporary perhaps a century prior to travelling theory's relatively recent discovery of the ever-uneven passage.

In any classroom where context competes so powerfully with text that the con trick of fundamental preconception, belief in some transcendental signifier, precedes that suspension of even *dis*belief required in the open-minded approach to words rather than, *in principio* and in principle, to the Word and its *apud*. In this game of chance, and *pace* the Irish-Catholic parentage, my un-inherited ace – the -ism of sharp textual practice, close reading – would often (prolepsis?) be trumped by the strong-suit card carrier, however insignificant the member, of privileged clubs; for, in the academy, this was the era of encroaching 'Cultural Studies'... often, *sans texte*.

I have not forgotten that Lucrecia Escudero Chauvel-inspired *De Signis* encounter nor that resonant conversation; not least, because Walter had already asked me whether I was still teaching Latin American literary texts and, then, disconcerted, I was confronted by the question that became an opening epigraph to the published version of my meditation: 'In England, are you seen as black or white?'... My unqualified thanks, now as then, to Ramón Grosfoguel.

*

Late in 1939, aged 24, William Joseph left his native Newry, crossing the Irish Sea to the north of England to join the 'war effort'; employment at the Royal Ordnance Factory at Risley, near Warrington, Lancashire. Gertrude, a local girl, in 1940, just eighteen, was 'detailed' – commandeered (to say no could have meant gaol) – to do essential work there in munitions; soon, and fortunately, in the stencilling of bombs section. William's job was more basic; the Risley-specializing filling of explosives into the various casings, then primed, to produce the finished munitions. William and Gertrude did not meet in that period. He shared 'digs' with a fellow Ulsterman Jack Galbraith, the Protestant friend who would enter the nearby tobacconist's, with their respective ration cards, to buy cigarettes for them both. 'No Catholics' read the sign in the window.

A little Warrington schoolboy, at five, knew and proudly pronounced the word tri-nitro-toluene; he could have quoted the 'TNT poisoning' description of the former munitions workers, and the stories of the nicknamed 'Canary Girls' and the male fillers whose skin had been stained yellow by toxic chemicals and their causing of a potentially fatal condition amongst such workers. But he liked big words... At eight, far away, three weeks aboard ship in those days, in Singapore, and by now a pupil at the Royal Naval School, Sembawang, he rather delighted in responding insolently to the oh-so-English question 'So, is your father from Northern Ireland or from the South?'. He would repeat the resistance to the re-colonizing gesture he had already witnessed so often and could hear in his father's lilting brogue: 'Sure, now, when I was born there was no such separation. Partition – and the border – came seven years later'. William McGuirk and Gertrude McKay had met in 1942... They married in 1948.

Thus – perhaps the more I followed up, the more I got it – thank you, again, Ramón:

> When I came to New York everything was rationed [...] So my *mamá* sent me to get a ration card [...] I noticed the girl was writing down everything in a questionnaire. She asked my nationality and my cousin answered 'Puerto Rican', but she wrote down 'Negro'. My cousin protested, 'No, no, no, not Negro, Puerto Rican'. She gave him a look but she erased 'Negro' and wrote down 'Puerto Rican'. It was my first experience of that kind up here' [narrated by Soledad, as quoted by Lewis, 1966, 227]. (Grosfoguel, in Laó-Montes and Dávila, 2001, 106)

*

In approaching the divining lines of self-defining 'multi-media performance artist, social and cultural critic' (Gómez-Peña, 1996, 247), I choose to look firstly at extracts from his spectacular 'Border Brujo' [Frontera Wizard, if you insist] of 1988-89, from *Warrior for Gringostroika*, (1993, 75-95), and then at one of his celebrated co-performances with New York-born Cuban American Juliana Emilia Fusco Miyares, Coco Fusco.

Patently, Gómez-Peña's transcribed text is both accessible and yet challenging enough to confound traditional, or other, critical analyses. It also, flagrantly, defies translation, for the border linguist, itself a site of aporia. I would simply preface my engaging with his work by pointing to the type of psychoanalytical claim which it at once appropriates and pastiches. If, for Jacques Lacan, 'I am not wherever I am the plaything of my thought' (Lacan, 1966, 136), for Gómez Peña, the very conditions whereby post-colonial subjectivity can be thought also imply the undoing of even a notional national identity. The play's the thing *and* the thinker. Early in the show, a distinctive polemicist's voice intrudes:

V

[*Soundtrack: Supercombo*]
TIJUANA BARKER VOICE [*very fast*]:
welcome to the Casa de Cambio
foreign currency exchange
the Temple of Instant Transformation
the place where Tijuana y San Diego se entrepiernan
where the Third becomes the First
and the fist becomes the sphincter
here we produce every imaginable change
money exchange kasse
cambio genético verbal
cambio de dólar y de nombre
cambio de esposa y oficio
de poeta a profeta
de actor a pelotari
de narco a funcionario
de mal en peor
sin cover charge
here everything can take place
for a very reasonable fee
anything can change into something else
Mexicanos can become Chicanos
overnite
Chicanos become Hispanics
Anglo-Saxons become Sandinistas
[...]
& surfers turn into soldiers of fortune
here, fanatic Catholics become swingers
& evangelists go zen
at the snap of my fingers
for a very very modest amount
I can turn your pesos into dollars
your 'coke' into flour
your dreams into nightmares
your penis into a clitoris
you name it, Califa
if your name is Guillermo Gómez-Peña

I can turn it into Guermo Comes Penis
or Bill, 'the multimedia beaner'
or even better, Indocumentado #00281431
because here Spanish becomes English, ipso facto
& life becomes art with the same speed
that mambo becomes jazz
tostadas become pizza
machos become transvestitas
& brujos become performance artists
It's fun, it's fast
It's easy, it's worthwhile
you just gotta cross the border
[*He stands and performs a biblical gesture.*]
¡Lázaro gabacho wake up and cross!
crosss... cruzzzzz... crassss

Much later, a postmodern interlocutor:

XXII

[*Soundtrack: old instrumental blues*]
MACUARRO VOICE: [...]
I was literally born in the middle of a battle
I'm almost an aborigine you know
a Hollywood Indian, iajjuua!
me dicen el Papantla Flyer
de la Broadway, bien tumbado
'cause I love to show my balls to strangers
& to talk dirty to gringas feministas
too much Foucault & Baudrillard
& Fuentes & Subirats & Roger Bartra
& other writers you haven't even heard of
I could fulfil your expectations much better
if it wasn't for the fact that I wrote
this text on a Macintosh
& I couldn't even memorize it all
& I shot my rehearsals with a Sony-8
I would really fulfill your expectations
le bon sauvage du Mexique
l'enfant terrible de la frontière

(Gómez-Peña, 1993, 80, 88)

In her searching *English is Broken Here: Notes on Cultural Fusion in the Americas,* Coco Fusco addresses to Gómez-Peña questions pertinent to the issues I have raised in analysis of 'Traducción simultánea' and 'Asimilao'. For example, the possibility of outside/inside economies perhaps utopically disavowed by 'Asimilao' is raised, again, by Gómez-Peña's 'Border Brujo'. Self-locating Tijuana/Macuarro voicings differ, if only in fulfilment of '(y)our expectations'. In 'Nationalism and Latinos, North and South', CF asks:

> Who was asking them in the 1980s to take note that only whites cross the border with relative freedom, and that only Americans escape the repressive apparatus of the border patrol? Who was asking about the significance of the fact that all the border books and blockbuster shows were being done by whites? If Chicanos did, the postmodern Anglo *borderólogos* would just write them off as incorrigibly retro nationalists. (Fusco, 1995, 162)

GG-P answers:

> In the 1990s, we cannot speak of Latin America as a linguistic community, since it is clear that not all of us speak Spanish. There are British and Portuguese Latin Americas; there are Latin Americas outside Latin America, those being the Chicano world in the South West and the Caribbean world of New York. This linguistic community begins to come apart when we cross the border. In the North, different Latinos have different degrees of closeness to the Spanish language. Even though some speak clumsily, or in a syntactically deformed manner, they don't stop being Latinos. This is not yet understood in Mexico. It is also reflected in the absolute lack of communication between Chicano writers, whose work is mostly in English and Spanish, and Mexican writers, who are more interested in dialogue with other Latin Americans and with Europeans. They see our literature as a minor art, picturesque in the best of cases. (Gómez-Peña in Fusco, 1995, 163)

In a compelling polemic with Gómez-Peña, as well as taking him to task on problems of identity, gender politics and the abuse of centre-margin categories by Latin American intellectuals 'for the most part *criollos* and male' (165), Fusco extends and further contextualizes his argument:

Capitalist, post-industrial society defines itself by its lack of emotion and ritual. 'Exotic' art from the Third World provokes a series of primordial emotions for that society. That art is associated with kitsch. The apolitical appropriation of popular culture by Neo-Mexicans is perfect for gringos: it offers them sentimental iconography, which they so desperately need to fill their spiritual void. On the other hand, Chicano art represents another kind of 'primitivism', a more irritating, cruder, and vulgar kind. It is more threatening, and full of political significance that questions the hegemony of Anglo-culture. It also reminds middle-class Mexicans that our roots are not in Paris or New York; on the contrary, they are in this land, and are its fruit, that is why, with few exceptions, there is little amicability between neo-Mexicans and Chicanos. (Fusco, 1995, 167-8)

In commenting on the international reaction to 'two major events that [had] radically altered [her] understanding of the perceptions and misperceptions of *Two Undiscovered Amerindians*' – when she and Gómez-Peña posed at museums as newly discovered Amerindians from an overlooked island – Fusco writes that 'One pertains to the Latin American reception of the work [...] The other to the video documentary of the performances, *The Couple in the Cage*' (60):

We received an invitation to take the cage performance to Buenos Aires [...] Our piece seemed to serve as an ice-breaker in an extremely elitist cultural milieu, drawing street vendors, poor children and others [...] often to the dismay of the institution's regular patrons. Scores of mestizos and indigenous immigrants to the city from Bolivia, Peru and Argentina's northern regions watched us evening after evening with extraordinary sadness in their eyes. Meanwhile, dozens of Argentine intellectuals sat sipping coffee in the bar behind us, often pretending to ignore the scene unfolding before them. The many psychologists and anthropologists who attended were divided as to whether such a piece was too disturbing for the Argentine public, traumatized by the military dictatorship [...] Only a handful of people we met reminded us that Argentina had conducted its own highly successful extermination campaign against its indigenous populations around the same time that Americans had conquered the West. (61-62)

'AMÉN' or '(OMEN)'? Goodbye to all that, again; including a resigned so-be-it to any illusion of pan-Latin Americanism; or presage of an urgent necessity, this time, for 'traducción simultánea Latino Americano-Latino Americano'? Or both, Susana...?

'Border Brujo' makes no bones – shaman's or otherwise – about the need to threaten hegemonies, be they those of 'Anglo-culture' or any illusory vestige of Latin Americanness. Set against such a performance as that of Gómez-Peña, any such project, or projection, is rendered as irrelevant as the passive-cum-comic expectations of the poem's implied interlocutors. The audience is aggressively challenged and, at once, enticed: 'it's fun, it's fast/it's easy, it's worthwhile/you just gotta cross the border'. While the biblical gesture which the 'brujo' stands and performs is designed to mime Moses, there is no longer a rod, let alone a promised land; only a $-wad, and a promised wand. For this border magician operates not only post-colonially but also post-theologically, post-teleologically. The 'Temple' is now that of 'Instant Trans-formation', a banal flattening, a pastiche, of previous communing via transubstantiation. Dead Lazarus is, inseparably, the Southerner beckoned north and the Northerner beckoned south. Thus, 'cross' is made to perform as a classic sign of erasure; respond to its metaphysical presence, be scandalized by its self-besmirching absence from a site of no fixed addressee, of no one, true, 'crosss, cruzzzzz, crassss'. Borderness cruises crassly across every imaginable trans-action: its shuttle effects are ever transgressive, shifting from fiscal to fisting, from religious to racial, from linguistic to libidinal, from martial to musical... at least in the (Mexican) voice of the tauntingly and self-flauntingly aggressive Tijuana barker. Trafficking in the other direction comes the (US-) 'born in the middle of a battle' Papantla Flyer, ensuring that there can be no, however new, hegemony of border discourse. The shock of the old ('Indocumentado'?) Tijuana dealer (no papers? no identity!) confronts the shock of the new (the techno-logical?) Macuarro, each potentially 'fulfilling expectations', but never arriving... 'Macintosh' or 'Sony' notwithstanding, or permitting.

Inscribed on the baggage-labels of either the 'multimedia beaner' one or the 'almost an aborigine' other are ciphers of '40s ('blues'), '50s ('Hollywood Indian'), '60s ('surfers'), '70s ('swingers'), '80s ('evangelists go[ne] zen'), or '90s ('coke') dealings, not excluding modishly excessive intellectual trends. A magic border-dialogue moves from *Paris, Texas*-tainted 'gringas feministas', through an ill-assorted two-piece suite 'Foucault & Baudrillard', to the very Roger Bartra who wrote the 'Introduction' to *Warrior for Gringostroika*:

The border is an anathema to the ambiguity of people like
Guillermo Gómez-Peña [...] Latin America does not end at the
US border; rather, Latino culture has penetrated the anglo(*sic*)-
world. In the United States, the 'Hispanic' sector of society, of
the economy, of politics, and of culture is enormous and
exercises considerable influence. Mexican nationalism has
traditionally refused to recognize this, since the Mexicanization
of life in the United States is more likely to be seen as the
Americanization of the Mexicans [...] This cultural process has
been defined by Guillermo Gómez-Peña as the borderization of
the world [...] As an anthropologist, I cannot conceive of a
border territory between cultures where processes of
transculturation do not occur. Any intent to impede this is, in
the best of cases, utopian [...] Life on the border, far from being
a danger, could be the starting point of the *gringostroika* that
has been called for since the fall of the Berlin Wall [...] That is
the territory of an immense cohort of vagabonds or permanent
exiles to which Guillermo Gómez-Peña belongs. (Bartra in
Gómez-Peña, 1993, 11-12)

As an anthropologist, certainly not, merely as some fellow travelling
through the by-ways of literary-critical analyses as they have
meandered into the back waters of swamping preoccupations with
what is to be read as distinct from *how* to read it, I cannot but collude,
be complicit, with whatever discipline lends itself *instrumentally*, for
that is my key, to open up that can of words called text. The less
literature itself is read, taught, *pace* Walter, the more the institutional
discourses of criticism and, encroachingly, academe, will purport to
appropriate, as discoveries or revelations, those perceptions assumed to
derive – in eras prior to the un/clothed empire of *homo academicus* –
from unapologetically and illimitably performative texts. The frontier
that I cross, and from where I write, is at the interface of an 'Old
Country' of literary semiotics and the strongly sign-posted 'New
Territories' of the dis-united states of Cultural Studies. Transgressive
only if you wish...

Of(f) limit(ation)s

Whilst supposedly post- first/second/third worlds are hesitantly or
violently still confronting borders, the tic-infested discourses of the
campus-locked patrollers are already converting their struggles into

'borderization'. Frontier nouns are demonstrably less abstract, however:

> U.S. Border Patrol officials discovered a group of 14 dead Mexican migrants in Arizona's desert [...] Agents found another 16 corpses from Mexico, but this time spread out across Arizona's scorched expanse. While a Border Patrol spokesman called the deaths 'an aberration' [...] migrant deaths along the U.S.-Mexico boundary [...] demonstrate the opposite: such deaths have become a way of life in the border region [...] They also gave rise to a renewed effort by the governments of the United States and Mexico to ensure 'border safety' [...] Such numbers and the human suffering they embody demonstrate that there is nothing surprising about the deaths. Instead, the fatalities are the inevitable outcome of a lethal political charade – one in which the federal government provides ever greater amounts of boundary enforcement resources in full knowledge that they will not significantly reduce overall levels of unauthorized immigration, but will have increasingly deadly consequences for migrants [...] As a result, countless migrants are still successfully beating the enforcement web. But many more than before are also dying. (Nevins, 2002, 1)

Amidst such unchanging brutalities, the imperative of experimental, performative, 'border' but – perish the term –, never *borderóloga*, literature is to challenge the very notion of ever 'beating the enforcement web', or of escaping the protracted violence that by no means ends at, or with, the crossing over.

A 'state of conflict', whether or not officially declared, will habitually find expression as powerful as any open warfare or clandestine policy of control. For all the distance and difference between identifiable regional political conflicts in the USA *versus* Latin America dialogics of unequal power-blocks, and that shuttle-space of Latino writing from which I take my examples, the performative construct still derives from persistent colonial insistencies and resistances:

Freefalling toward a Borderless Future

Performed live, voice filtered by delay effect; with a live simultaneous translation into French, Gringoñol, or Esperant. Soundbed: A mix of Indian drums, Gregorian chants, and occasional police sirens.

...per ipsum ecu nipsum, eti nipsum
et T.Video Patri Omni-impotente
per omnia saecula saeculeros
I see
I see
I see a whole generation
freefalling toward a borderless future
incredible mixtures beyond science fiction:
cholo-punks, pachuco krishnas,
Irish concheros, butoh rappers, cyber-Aztecs,
Gringofarians, Hopi rockers, y demás...
I see them all
wandering around
a continent without a name
the forgotten paisanos
howling corridos in Fresno & Amarillo
the Mixteco pilgrims
heading North toward British Columbia
the Australian surfers
waiting for the big wave at Valparaiso
the polyglot Papagos
waiting for the sign to return
the Salvadorans coming North (to forget)
the New Yorkers going South (to remember)
the stubborn Europeans in search of the last island
                    -Zumpango, Cozumel, Martinique
I see them all
wandering around
a continent without a name
el TJ transvestite
translating Nuyorican versos in Univisión
the howling L.A. junkie
bashing NAFTA with a bullhorn
El Warrior for Gringostroika
scolding the First World on MTV
AIDS warriors reminding us all
of the true priorities in life
Lacandonian shamans
exorcising multinationals at dawn
yuppie tribes paralysed by guilt & fear
grunge rockeros on the edge of a cliff
all passing through Califas

en route to other selves
& other geographies
(*I speak in tongues*)
standing on the map of my political desires
I toast to a borderless future
(*I raise my glass of wine toward the moon*)
with...
our Alaskan hair
our Canadian head
our U.S. torso
our Mexican genitalia
our Central American cojones
our Caribbean sperm
our South American legs
our Patagonian feet
our Antarctic nails
jumping borders at ease
jumping borders with pleasure
amen, hey man

(Gómez-Peña, 1985; revised in 1995; 1996; 1-3)

A classic/al case of polysemy here performs an archetypal positive-cum-negative carnivalizing. Mockery by inversion updates the reader on the Latin sub- (or pre-) text of *Latino*. For Mass-ending (*Ite, missa est*) read mass sending-up of the (un-)completable (droopy) project of omnipotent patriarchy. In the era of 'T. Video', I see, I see and, again, I see you, but only via my deferred panopticon of sempiternal erotic longing. *Mea culpa, mea culpa, mea maxima culpa* is now but a shadow *Confiteor*, a long-lost totalizing guilt replicated in scopophilic trebled stare at a future of 'incredible mixtures'. In this literary pre-figuration – or is it a proleptic defiguring? – of the hybridity theories of, say, Néstor García Canclini, the self-styled *performero* Guillermo Gómez-Peña stages a corrective to any theorist of cultural studies, Latin American or other who, in order to think movement, has to suppose some prior stasis. To suggest that hybridity was not always already there would be to re-perform that very reductionism which made the thinking of hybridity difficult (or censored) in the aetiologically unsound 'first' place. Colony? An early performance, of 1985, prefaced a border poetics that he was to develop across a decade or more in an internationally acclaimed series of 'prophecies, poems and *loqueras* for the end of the century', subtitle of his *The New World Border*. Hallucinations of no new world, but rather of one 'free falling towards a

46

borderless future', bode inseparably the *Credo* of an anomalist and utopianist trip wherein cultural memory will play tricks on the ear and the here, the eye and the I.

Compass-points flee centrifugally from national identity markers. Culture and language lapse into polyglot parroting of a futile nostalgia for semiosis – a 'waiting for the sign to return' – amidst a neo-Babelic investment in 'the true priorities'. And what are they? Shamanic manics performing behind the 'Lacandonian' mask of disoriented non-being in a virtual acting-out of the post-psychoanalytical nightmare-cum-'political desire': *You* are not [*my erasure*] wherever *you* are the plaything of *my* thought. The poem thus dramatizes a heady millennial lunacy: 'I toast' therefore I am... incomplete; 'with...' (-out you/all). A putative wandering consciousness, 'en route to other selves', would re-embody an Alaskan to Antarctic kin-graft, despairing in-corporation of (albeit hemispheric) plenitude. 'Other geographies' are revealed as dystopia. For 'a borderless future' is soon discovered to have been visited already by the ever-un-exorcised 'multinationals' who, long since, have trampled all national borders, leaving as imprints but the bullish index of their stock exchange futures.

'Political desires' will point ever to re-configurations of a *body politic*. The monstrous semiotic mapping of *homo americanus*, spawned by the hippy-Frankenstein magus of the poem's finger-snapping interlocutor, cannot escape a sinister cultural loading in its North-South, head-to-toe, re-anatomizing. For the (macho) body still has balls; giving rise to impregnating threats in the projected 'jumping [of] borders'. In the reader's mind's *I*, little doubt is left as to where the post-ease pleasure will come from. Whether I/you agree ('amen') or not... be persuaded ('hey man'). Gómez-Peña, self-styled 'nomadic Mexican artist/writer [...] a border Sisyphus', offers retrospectively his manifesto of *mis*-translatability:

> Since I don't believe in the existence of *linguas francas*, my choice not to translate (or to purposely mistranslate) the sections in Spanglish, Gringoñol, bad French and indigenous languages is part of an aesthetic and a political strategy. I hope that this is apparent to the reader who, at times, will feel partially 'excluded' from the work; but after all, partial exclusion is a quintessential contemporary experience, que no? The 'Glossary of Borderisms' appended at the end of the book contains some conceptual clues that might help when travelling across my performance continent. (Gómez-Peña, 1996, i-ii)

His personae perform ever *intra-*, ever dialogically, address-less but addressing:

> I just don't know what to think of your country
> [...]
> dearísima M,
> this nameless country of yours
> deleted my original identity
> and replaced it with a brand-new hybrid self:
> *el homo fronterizus (1955-?)*
> I just don't know what to think of your country
> for the moment
> I'm taking a trip back to Mexico
> Bruja, my tongue and muscles need some serious rest
>
> Signed: el resident alien
>   in search of a new residence
>   ¡la tuya!

(Gómez-Peña, 1996, 48)

The *homo fronterizus* affects many voices, many guises, but habitually projects a self that is embroiled in violence (as victim) and sex (as avenger). Whether locating the intertextual voice in (dusty) Springfield or (evangelist) Arlington, this poetry enters the streets and riskily penetrates the gringo anatomy even unto its spare rib... but at a price:

> I could only fight back in my poetry
>
> it was the spring of '87 in the city of Arlington
> I tried to explain to you in my very broken English
> that Texas had once been a Mexican ranch
> & that truth was not a 'gringo-bashing ideology'
> but you had seen too many Stallone films
> and felt obliged to let me have it, que no?
> so you tried to beat the Meskin out of me
> of course, since you were a foot taller & 85 lbs. heavier
> & not that skilled in cross-cultural diplomacy
> I could only fight back in my poetry
> in fact, I'm fighting back right now
> you claimed you hated my accent and my arrogance
> but the real reason you despised me
> was that your wife was just about to leave you

& hit the road to sexy Mexico
to escape the Texan nightmare, your inflexible arms,
your smelly feet & psychotic eyes
so Mexico became the source of all your fears
the red light district where gringos are poisoned by
       midget whores
the mountain of trash where kids make
holes to sleep in
the bus that keeps breaking down on your way to
       some generic jungle
the gentle mariachi who touched your wife like you
       never did
you saw all these images in my eyes before you broke
       my ribs
& I could only fight back in my poetry

P.S. #1 I don't harbour any resentments but I sure
hope one of these days you learn to read &
write

P.S. # 2 See, I told you culero, I win most fights in
the streets of my poetry

P.S. # 3 I heard you joined the militia movement
     last month... I must say that you are
     consistent in misplacing your anger, man
           (Gómez-Peña, 1996, 58-59)

From 'The Birth of Border Brujo' (1988) to 'The Last Migration: A Spanglish Opera (in progress)' (1993), Gómez-Peña glories in opportune opposition to world-wide quincentennial spotlights. Dysjunctions confront frontiers national and linguistic; collision courses of and on geographies, gender and genre are cultivated by a *frontera* wizard of osmosis-cum-gnosis, to-and-fro shuffler of third-term binary-breakers:

Des-Encuentro de 3 Mun-2

(This conceptual poem in Spanglish was proposed as the text for an anti-Columbus 'intercontinental tourist poster' at the Universidad de la Rábida in Spain.)

México en Aztlán
Califas en Spa-ña
Ex-paña en Mé-xico
Triángulo de las Ver-mudas/triangle
Palos buenos pa'los malos
Calógicamente hablando digo
El Viejo Mundo
se imagina pus-moderno
El Nuevo, se reinventa
en la contigüidad
contínuo, sin-tínuo sin ti no
te
tenepantla tinemi tajoditzin
untranslatable sablazo
against the New World Order
trans-afloat
the Great Atlantic border
border fronteraabordo y desembarco.
Asss I wasssaying last night
De Palo en Palo hasta el Caribe
taíno non plus ultra fornicare
de Veracrúz a Tenochtitlán
de Mexicou Cida a Tijuana-Nirvana
de Lost Angeles a San Antonio
and güey beyond
de Manhattan a Madrid
& then to Sevilla & back again
to Palos
two palitos can make one child
o one poema en su defecto
so I defect. caput
mañana retorno a Califas.

(Gómez-Peña, 1996, 179-80)

The locus (never the location) of such performance textuality is the shuttle space (not the place) of (un)translatability. Reader, I challenge you to translate. But would it be from Spanish to English or from English to Spanish?

Stop press

May 2002. I hear reports of the founding of the world's first *cátedra* of Spanglish; – in Chi/cago? Or was that shit/cargo? No. Yet rumour does turn out to be fact, and still in 'my kind of town'; that locus of enunciation called *paranomasia*. The University in question is Amherst (*Ah must* say Am[h]erst, without that tell-tale, oh-so-English, 'h'... lest, *mea maxima*, word-play take the total 'p'). Pertinently, in its coverage of this news, *El País* repeats, for cultural studies, a cheap paradigm (parrot-dime?); and reports, for semiology, a challenging if somewhat peremptory reaction:

> El polémico filólogo mexicano [...] Ilan Stavans, convencido de que 'la pureza de la lengua es una abstracción' y de que 'sólo las lenguas muertas no cambian', ha comenzado la primera traducción de *El Quijote* al 'spanglish' [que] puede empezar así: 'In un placete de la Mancha of which nombre no quiero remembrearme...'. Stavans sostiene que utilizan este dialecto, salpicado de anglicismos y de palabras adaptadas en forma *sui generis* directamente del inglés, más de 25 millones de personas a ambos lados de la frontera entre México y Estados Unidos [...] 'Somos testigos y partícipes de la creación de una nueva cultura que es una realidad y no puede ser ninguneada'. [Le] gusta soñar con el 'spanglish' convertido en un idioma muy imaginativo y alegre, 'algo parecido al jazz', algo con lo que no está de acuerdo el Director de la Real Academia Española (RAE), Víctor García de la Concha. [Él] señaló: 'De lo que estoy absolutamente seguro es de que eso que se llama "spanglish" no es una lengua'. A su juicio, 'afirmar que lo es, lingüísticamente, es una falsedad'. Para [él] es un típico caso de lengua en contacto. 'Lo que se está produciendo es la alternancia de códigos, que consiste en que un hispano que no domina el inglés está utilizando un esquema sintáctico del español con palabras inglesas'. (*El País*, 6/7/2002)

> [The polemical Mexican philologist [...] Ilan Stavans, convinced that 'the purity of the language is an abstraction' and that 'only dead languages don't change', has begun the first translation of *El Quijote* into 'spanglish', [which] can open thus: 'In un placete de la Mancha of which nombre no quiero remembrearme...'. Stavans maintains that using this dialect, sprinkled with Anglicisms and words adapted, in *sui generis* form, directly

from English, are more than 25 million individuals on both sides of the frontier between Mexico and the United States [...] 'We are witnesses to and participants in the creation of a new culture that is a reality, and cannot be annulled'. [He] likes to dream of 'spanglish' converted into a very imaginative and joyful language, 'something like jazz', something not agreed with by the Director of the Real Academia Española (RAE), Víctor García de la Concha. [He] pointed out: 'What I am absolutely sure of is that what is called "spanglish" is not a language'. In his judgement, 'to affirm that it is, linguistically, is false'. For [him] it is a typical case of language in contact. 'What is being produced is the alternating of codes, which consists of someone Hispanic who does not command English using a syntactic schema of Spanish with English words'.]

What *is* being, and has been, produced – demonstrably, in the case of Guillermo Gómez-Peña – is not only a semiological code-switching but also a culturally radical goad-itching. His scabrous but no less mordant performance poetics point to a very considerable command of that social semiosis out of which arise both a recognizable *literature* and a theoretically problematic *(un)translatability*; making (for) a distinctive room of their own. *Déjà* Woo...?

Calculatedly (mis)appropriating the terms of 'Des-Encuentro de 3 Mun-2', I choose to read the press report as dangerously characterizing – caricaturing – differing institutional viewpoints as but polarized dis- (or *dos*) encounters. Does *El País* not also speak for Spain, with a condescending nod towards a 'third' world perceived as interfering linguistically and culturally in the hierarchy of an Establishment dialogue *à deux*? If so, such a two-term tension will always and easily be deconstructed by the ever-lurking other of a third term, a *différance*, within; but that's another story – *otro cuento de 3 Mun-2...*

Whereas I have claimed that literature highlights the differences that cultural studies explore, the poem 'Des-Encuentro de 3 Mun-2' would take us, epistemologically, even further. Literature *is* the culture ever at and beyond the frontier of all studies. But Gómez-Peña already and always knows as much. If your model were to be, for instance, psychoanalysis, he would have a couch-confrontation for/with you, too:

XXX: El Hamlet Fronterizo

TWO VOICES:
me ama/no me ama
me caso/no me caso

me canso/no me canso
chicano o mexicano
que soy o me imagino
regreso o continúo
me mato/no me mato
en México/en Califas
to write or to perform
in English or in Spanish...
I forgive you,
I crave you
ansiosamente tuyo
de nadie más
frontera mediante...
te espero, mi loca, te sigo esperando...
you are it, tu sangre, tus cicatrices...
(Gómez-Peña, 1996: 230-31)

'Country matters' as little (or as much) for the *Performero* as for the Bard. Just think. Schizo-poetics. Or feel yuh self. No blur in the mind? Have *you* ever been picked up by the (border) fuzz? It hurts... splits you up, brings tears to your *I/s*.

To be or not to be... outrageous? Fortune forever slings the critic against the 'frontera mediante' of poetry and poetic analysis. From border performance to Nuyorican calligram, I shall now stretch appropriation beyond the limit of necessary (un)translatability. On display will be another body politic, posing; re-posing the challenge for a no-longer capitalizable semiotics. How is the sign, constructed not on the (im)possibility but rather on the (un)necessity of interlingual translation to be (uncomfortably) accommodated *within* the other('s) culture?

Goodbye, Columbus?

While having directed the committed reader to other spectacular performance texts such as the 'prophecies, poems and loqueras for the end of the century', sub-title of *New World Border* (1996), I conclude my consideration of intra/post-colonial productions by focussing on a short extract from *Radio Pirata: Colón* [Columbus] *Go Home* (1992). In this transcript of a live National Public Radio Broadcast, Coco Fusco and Guillermo Gómez-Peña perform, inimitably, together (193-95). In the spirit and tone of the political staging of this chapter, and further blurring outside/inside, critical/performative borderlines, I choose, provisionally, and dialogically, again, to intervene. My particular interventions, transcriptions of a third voice (2nd MALE on the right), might be read horizontally, vertically, differently, indifferently, or not at all. I shall never know. 'But [...] it is precisely through this kind of cross-examination that one still hangs onto it. Western [identity] walks a tightrope' (Levinas, 1989, 263):

FEMALE:	2nd MALE:
Dream about the future of your America	Whose?
Euro America	Yes, I am implicated
Your own America	but not there
Su América	*Pseudo*
Suya	*but still yours*
Sudamérica	*Geography*
Suda y sangra	*History*
Latinoamérica despierta	*identity politics*
Hispanoamérica dormida	*travelling cliché*
Iberoamérica borracha querida	*pissed or sour?*
bórrame del mapa	*Violent cartographies*
(Sound of crying then in erotic voice)	*('oh'... 'oh, oh', again?)*
Adonde estoy	*Temporary residence*
Adonde estamos	*à deux?*
Estamos Unidos en América	*Country matters?*
Estar dos unidos	*It takes two*
Estar dos sumidos	*to submit*
el uno en el otro	*to marrying cliché*
Norte	*'Death*
Sur	*And*
Este	*The*
Oeste	*Compass'*
Europa	*con*
Asia	*tin*
Africa	*gent*
América	*incontinent*
Where Chingadas are we?	¿Dónde the fuck estamos?
[...]	[...]
CF: Europe owns no other continent	So who put the Latin in Latin America?
GG-P: Eurown discovery,	Or invention?
CF: not continent	Sub-mission?
GG-P: disco-	(Az)teca
CF: very strange	just defamiliarized (like Inca)
GG-P: co-	It still takes two
CF: *descubrimiento,*	*for intervention*
GG-P: *descubro*	*Me, too,*
CF: *miento*	*who doesn't?*
GG-P: I lie to you	traduttore
CF: we don't lie together	traditore

GG-P: in the end
CF: we never lie together
GG-P: *vecinos abismales*
CF: still undiscovered
 to one another
GG-P: not quite *carnales* yet
CF: not quite connecting
GG-P: you are here
 against my will
CF: I am here
 against yours
GG-P: we are damned
 to repeat
CF: *la conquista liberación*
 del Nuevo Mundo
CF: This is Coco Fusco and
 Guillermo Gómez-Peña,
speaking to the territory of arteamérica.
Buenas Noches.

Teleology?
False consciousness?
'The place of aporia is at the border'
[that, I'll disclose,
 was Jacques D.]
Are we all still deferring?
not yet ready for *différance?*
I link therefore I am
But if I'm intruding at this point,
there's presumably no room
 for a third party
Yet hell is others (3 terms, at least)
So, if I withdraw
who will supplement
 the post/colonial binary?
This is Bernard McGuirk's
 in(ter)vention
It's too late to translate.
What's the time difference?

(Fusco, 1995, 193-5)

Identity politics of the high era of cultural studies – misread – have too often misled. Confusions of bathwater and baby have been known to prompt over-zealous cleansers to throw out close reading as an unhealthy rearing practice. Sullied -isms turned schisms; and, soon, the acolyte body politic, laid empirically bare, reeked sovereign, if ill-scoured, tyrannies: 'Out, damned spotter of tropes'... Faithful travellers – ill-disguised their circumspection regarding all textual analysis performed whether in private or in public – would frequently find voice in a predictable first question(er). 'What is your *locus* of enunciation?'.

Cognizant of the commonplace but wary of the clichéd lure, whereby – inseparably from the time and timing – the *place* of one's tightrope walk might subsume or pre-empt(y) the *space* of its performance, I might thus have opted for a showing rather than a telling; via the rhetorical riposte: 'What is my *focus* of translation?'.

Instance, an engaging with act as action, art as agency, pen as sword, here, at the hand of Haroldo de Campos; in translating, transacting, transgressing, in his parlance, *d'après* Walter Benjamin, 'transluciferating', through my transjection of his poetry's commemoration of the murder of nineteen landless *sem terra* in the 1996 massacre of Eldorado dos Carajás.

As, I surmise, a deferred effect of having complemented – via a neologism – what de Campos was subsequently to term the *'ludus* linguístico' of a translational strategy of amplification, and of having engaged through a parallel poetics with the starkest exposure of criminal acts, two decades on I received a long-deferred invitation: 'to establish a dialogue with and among scholars working on the intersections between translation studies and memory studies as they are presently configured and might be envisioned in the future'; to write, in 2017, for *Translation: a transdisciplinary journal*. Transposing, I accepted; for the personal has never been other than the political – *Il n'y a pas de hors discipline*...

À suivre. On trans(at)l(antic)ation.

III. TRANS-MEMORIES OF HEAVEN AND HELL
Haroldo de Campos and 'the angel on the left of history'

In 'Committing Translation or the Task of the Trans(at)l(antic)ator', the preface to my translations of the ineradicably political memories and cultural expressions of ideological indignation of the MST (Movement of the Landless Rural Workers in Brazil) in *Landless Voices in Song and Poetry. The Movimento dos Sem Terra of Brazil* (2007), I addressed and now return to the challenges posed in translating memory, memories, as the retrieval, reconstruction, inscription, and leaving of traces and their effects of a markedly memorializing act; in and for a Brazil confronting its own secular inequalities and injustices, alerted to that sovereign state's and that nation's continuing struggle to emerge from the cliché-ridden inscription on its national flag, the ever-ironic 'Ordem e Progresso'. Under whose orders and for the progress of whom was national memory to be re-inscribed, translated, indeed transferred from the hegemonies of a very recent twenty-year military regime and its transitional legacies in the period of re-building a democracy from 1984?

Further, I recalled the advice of Umberto Eco as I reflected on the experience of having worked, together with the Brazilian critic and translation theorist, Else Vieira, in preparation of *Haroldo de Campos in Conversation* (2009), the volume that arose, *in memoriam*, not least from the numerous meetings that, as editors, we held between 1999 and 2002 with Haroldo and his wife Carmen Arruda Campos in the hospitality of their Library of Babel home:[1]

I frequently feel irritated when I read essays on the theory of translation that, even though brilliant and perceptive, do not provide enough examples. I think translation scholars should have had at least one of the following experiences during their life: translating, checking and editing translations, or being translated and working in close co-operation with their translators [...] Between the purely theoretical argument that, since languages are differently structured, translation is

---

[1] This volume contains renderings in English of the following Haroldo de Campos essays touching variously on his theories of translation: 'On Translation as Creation and Criticism'; 'Constructivism in Brazil: Concretism and Neo-Concretism. A Personal Post Scriptum'; 'On Mephistofaustic Transluciferation'; 'On Homerotherapy: Translating *The Iliad*'; 'The Ex-centric Viewpoint: Tradition, Transcreation, Transculturation'.

impossible, and the commonsensical acknowledgement that people, after all, do translate and understand each other, it seems to me that the idea of translation as a process of negotiation (between author and text, between author and readers, as well as between the structure of two languages and the encyclopaedias of two cultures) is the only one that matches experience. (Eco, 2003, 36)

In such 'a process of negotiation', in that multiple 'in-betweenness', here evoked by Eco but previously the subject of an indispensable meditation on a specifically Latin American project, the 'entre-lugar' of Silviano Santiago, 'between sacrifice and play, between prison and transgression, between submission to the code and aggression, between obedience and rebellion' (Santiago, 1978, 11), and as translator of the poems and songs of the *Movimento dos Sem Terra*, I soon confronted commitment, in various of its encyclopaedic forms.

What had they done to my song?

The preceding decades had witnessed the revitalizing of popular music as a vehicle for political activisms in Brazil. One obvious source had been the *música sertaneja* of land-deprived migrant workers, driven towards the cities and taking with them their country music, be it traditional or, more recently, influenced by the commercial brands of the southern cultures of the United States. No less influential had been the *pagode* movement's samba-esque registering of the violent tensions of poverty in hardly couched critiques of repressive regimes, military or otherwise. The performances echoed, consciously or subliminally, the prosodies – high and low – of Brazilian Portuguese and the broadsheet and *cordel* strains of popular imaginaries from across and beyond the nation. For Brazil has never ceased to explore and express its sensitivity to the ideological power of the protest song; not least, and latterly, against 'the imagined and projected versions of what is to come' peddled, for many of its displaced, un-represented and unlikely-to-be-remembered victims, by the invasive myth-makers of a nation awarded the Trojan horses of a World Cup and an Olympic Games.

At the time of committing to undertake the translations of unabashedly radical texts, it was the centenary of the birth of the celebrated Chilean poet Pablo Neruda. Inspiration of politically committed poetry and song for not a continent but a world, he had been long ago described by Federico García Lorca as being closer to blood than to ink. It was on such a note – often indissociable from tears or from wine – that the anguish and euphoria, the despair and hope that suffuse the texts I translated were approached and embraced. My locus of trans-creation was, and is, unavoidably and unapologetically, Anglophone; it is also, though tempered, European. As a critic and translator of, primarily, literatures in Portuguese, Spanish, French and Italian, I exploited the availability of translation alternatives from those traditions as well as from any Brazil-specific contexts that informed the choices made. *Pace* Umberto Eco, I often wrote as both *Mouse* and *Rat*, chewing or munching in a further in-betweenness or the negotiated hybridity that I had experienced in tussling with Haroldo de Campos himself.[2] For part of our 'translating, checking and editing translations, or being translated and working in close co-operation' had been the daunting enterprise of re-visiting 'o anjo esquerdo da história'; beginning with the resonantly intertextual reference to Walter Benjamin's 'angel of history. His face [...] turned towards the past' (Benjamin, 1999, 249), broached at once in the title of this long de Campos poem. Written to commemorate the victims of the notorious massacre in 1996 of nineteen protesting members of the *Movimento dos Sem Terra* at El Dorado dos Carajás in the State of Pará, and originally rendered into English by Haroldo himself as 'the left-winged angel of history'. Engagement with the calculatedly syntagmatic discontinuity and attendant staccato rhythms of the Brazilian Portuguese text also had to take into account a context of commitment and contributions, to and in the Movement, of such distinguished Brazilian artists as Chico Buarque, Caetano Veloso, Gilberto Gil, Milton Nascimento, Frei Betto, and many others, including Haroldo de Campos himself, and thus re-address previous tasks of the other – cultural inseparably from linguistic – translator(s).

The Latin American protest-song explosions of the late 1950s, 1960s and 1970s, of which Robert Pring-Mill reminded us in, in *'Gracias a la vida' The Power and Poetry of Song* (1990) had hardly left Brazil unaffected by the echoes, influences, hybridities and inter-texts of contemporary trans-culturations. He listed civil rights, the peace movement and the anti-Vietnam war demonstrations in the USA; Italian Cantocronache; the Greece of Theodorakis; the Catalan Nova Cançó; the Portuguese Nova Canção; Irish songs of 'the troubles'; and Asian and African instances from the Philippines, East Timor and

---

[2] See the facsimile of de Campos's scribbled distinction between chewing and munching with reference to my translation of 'quoheletic poem 2: in praise of the termite' (reproduced in this volume, 96-97).

Mongolia, to Mozambique and Angola. Not least of the intertexts of Brazilian protest song and poetry were the Cuban, Argentine and Chilean expressions that sprinkled the *MST* artists with inspirations taken from the archives of the Fidel Castro, Che Guevara and the *nueva canción* traditions. If any one element of Pring-Mill's seminal analysis can be said to have informed the texts of the *MST*, it is this evocation: 'Asked about his own songs (in 1973), the Uruguayan Daniel Vigliette said firmly that they were as much *de propuesta* as *de protesta*: designed not merely to protest but to propose – in other words not merely to "tear down fences" (quite literally so in Viglietti's own anti-*latifundista* "A desalambrar!") but also "to build bridges" and to be constructive'. Pring-Mill identified three functions of such texts: 'response to an immediate environment'; 'instrument of political and social change'; communicating a 'horizon of expectations' and 'presuppositions'. Yet he was quick to add a vital rider on cultural difference: 'the whole rhetoric of such poems and songs is very different from ours, partly because Spanish [and here read Portuguese] handles issues more violently – more dramatically and emotionally – than English (sometimes in ways which we may find indecorous)' (Pring-Mill, 1990, 10-14). He continued:

> The messages of individual Latin American songs function within the framework of belief they foster and reinforce, in that extremely different social context. In countries where illiteracy is as high as it is in most of Latin America, where censorship and repression are so often at work, and where the official media are so rarely to be trusted, the message-bearing function of *poesía de compromiso* – sung or unsung – has an importance which it is not easy for a more literate academic audience to appreciate. Its messages perform a varied series of useful social functions [...] all of which are doubly important in the context of predominantly oral cultures. Thus they serve both to report and to record events (interpreting them, naturally enough, from specific points of view, which will strike all those who disagree with them as prejudiced); they praise, or lament, heroes and denounce tyrants; they protest against abuses and propound solutions (whether these are viable or not); and they teach many kinds of practical lessons, which their listeners are encouraged to put into practice. (77)

Pring-Mill, a decade or so on, would hardly have been surprised not to have the last word. He might also have smiled at the risky certainty, in respect not only of rhetoric but also of politics, of Perry Anderson, as a heady mixture of denunciation and the recuperation of misappropriated national memories promised to turn to propounded solution in the form of a first left-wing figure, Luiz Inácio Lula da Silva, democratically elected in 2002, on the crest of the *MST* wave of popular protest: 'the symbolism of a former shoe-shine boy and street vendor achieving supreme power in the most unequal major society on earth speaks for itself [...] A climate of popular expectation surrounds Lula that no President of the New Republic has ever enjoyed at the outset of his mandate. Hope of relief from the misery of the last years will not vanish overnight'. (Anderson, 2002, 21)

Get thee behind me Satan, I want to resist...

The risk of failing to render the textual wrath of a poem written in the indignation of 1996 protest amidst the 2002 days of heady triumphalist expectation – with popular memory of tyranny and criminality and a consciousness of the threat of impunity all too readily fading – seemed but one looming contention. The task of the trans(at)l(antic)ator therefore involved not abandoning but suspending certain spontaneous choices of literal translation in favour of inter- and trans-action. The challenges were: differ, defer, never with indifference, always without deference; address not only issues dear to the *MST*, primordial in Brazil, but also the transactions, with and in the Movement, of so many poets and song-writers and now, perhaps even more challengingly, but with a Brazilian inflected counter-theory to the rescue, of de Campos himself, from his essay on 'On Mephistofaustic Transluciferation':

> Translation, like philosophy, has no Muse [...] says Walter Benjamin ('Die Aufgabe des Uebersetzers'). And yet, if it has no Muse, it could be said to have an Angel [...] Translation has an angelical function, that of bearer, messenger [...] It is even, for the original [...] a messianic point or, in lay terms of modern theory of signs, – semiotic place of convergence of intentionality [...] Benjamin inverts the relation of servitude which, as a rule, affects ingenuous conceptions of translation as a tribute to fidelity. Fidelity (so-called translation literal to meaning, or, simply, inverted, servile, translation) [...] Therefore, in the Benjaminian perspective [...] the original is what in a certain way serves the translation, at the moment when it unburdens it from the task of transporting the unessential content of the message [...] and permits it to

dedicate itself to an other enterprise of fidelity [...] the 'fidelity to reproduction of form' [...] It is oriented by the rebellious slogan of *non serviam*, of non-submission to a presence which is exterior to it, to a content which remains intrinsically unessential to it [...] a satanic enterprise. The 'cursed' counterpart of the angelical nature of translation is *Hubris*, the semiological sin of Satan, *il trapassar del segno* (*Paradiso* XXXVI, 117), the transgression of sign limits [...] A translator of poetry is a choreographer of the inner dance of languages... (de Campos, 2009, 233-36)

How many angels?

On the head of opin... ionated Manicheans be it, however, whether scholastic or materialist, to limit the inspirers of Brazilian or any other translators to but two angels: the good, the bad. And the ugly configuration of Haroldo's predecessor poet Drummond de Andrade's 'anjo torto' ('crooked angel'), in 'Poema de sete faces' ('Poem of seven faces'), as long ago as 1930, should have alerted subsequent and would-be theorists to both the revelations and the dangers of going transcendental in 'the retrieval, reconstruction, and inscription' of remembering, as surely as the Shakespearean 'seven' it echoes had led to 'mere oblivion/Sans teeth, sans eyes, sans taste, sans everything'.[3] The figure of the post-modern angel, always and already fallen, was also one too easily overlooked, left behind (Drummond's *'gauche* na vida'/'*gauche* in life'?), in the long march of historical materialism... often the most dogmatic of 'the imagined and projected versions of what is to come' on the part of de Campos's Marxisant Brazilian detractors, as will be revealed in and after a reading of the poem; and of its guest.[4] For into the space of neglect – of suppressed memory – de

---

[3] The caution of such philosophers as Richard Rorty in respect of the temptation to go transcendental in the memorializing of historical events had long ago been poeticized by Drummond de Andrade and, inherited, by Haroldo de Campos, not least in echo of William Shakespeare's Jaques in *As You Like It*, Act II scene VII, on: 'Last scene of all, that ends this strange eventful history'.

[4] In 'Constructivism in Brazil: Concretism and Neo-Concretism. A Personal Post Scriptum', de Campos offers his riposte to Roberto Schwarz, as emblematic propagator of the attacks levied against the concretists and de Campos's notion of a post-utopical poetry. The next chapter, 'Laughin' again he's awake: Haroldo de Campos *à l'oreille de l'autre celte*', addresses the dialectics of the political legacy of radical poetry.

Campos had injected 'o anjo esquerdo da história'; for him, 'the left-winged angel of history' ('the angel on the left of history' in my *trans*jection, my inherently 'transformative' but necessarily subsequent swerve, my own anxious *clinamen*).

o anjo esquerdo da história	the angel on the left of history
os sem-terra afinal	the landless at last
estão assentados na	are settled in
pleniposse da terra:	full possession of the land:
de sem-terra passaram a	from landless to
com-terra: ei-los	landed: here they're
enterrados	interred
desterrados de seu sopro	their life's breath
de vida	unearthly
aterrados	earthed
terrorizados	terrified
terra que à terra	earth which onto earth
torna	returns
pleniposseiros terra-	land-holders pleni-
tenentes de uma	potentiary of a (single
vala (bala) comum:	bullet) common grave:
pelo avesso afinal	outside in at last
entranhados no	holed deep into
lato ventre do	the broad-bellied
latifúndio	acres of the *latifundio*-
que de im-	land once barren
produtivo re-	so sudden-
velou-se assim u-	ly shown to be most f-
bérrimo: gerando pingue	ecund: udder-spawning profit
messe de	crop of
sangue vermelhoso	reddening blood
lavradores sem	un-laboured
lavra ei-	labour: here they're
los: afinal con-	larvaed at
vertidos em larvas	last
em mortuá-	on mortal
rios despojos:	remains
ataúdes lavrados	coffins laboured
na escassa madeira	from the scanty timber
(matéria)	(timbre)
de si mesmos: a bala assassina	of themselves: the assassin bullet
atocaiou-os	stalks them

mortiassentados
sitibundos
decúbito-abatidos pre-
destinatários de uma
agra (magra)
re(dis)(forme) forma
– fome – a-
grária: ei-
los gregária
comunidade de meeiros
do nada:
enver-
gonhada a-
goniada
avexada
– envergoncorroída de
imo-abrasivo re-
morso -
a pátria
(como ufanar-se da?)
apátrida
pranteia os seus des-
possuídos párias –
pátria parricida:
que talvez só afinal a
espada flamejante
do anjo torto da his-
tória cha-
mejando a contravento e
afogueando os
agrossicários sócios desse
fúnebre sodalício onde a
morte-marechala comanda uma
torva milícia de janízaros-ja-
gunços:
somente o anjo esquerdo
da história escovada a
contrapelo com sua
multigirante espada po-
derá (quem dera!) um dia
convocar do ror
nebuloso dos dias vin-
douros o dia

thirst-squatting
death-settlers
decumbents cut down pre-
destined for a
meagre (earth) acre a-
grarian
– famine –
re (de)(formed) form
here they are: gregarious
commune share-cropping
nothingness:
shame-
faced in
agony
vexed
– shamecorroded by
inmost abrasive re-
morse-
landless
('how shall we extol thee?')
homeland
laments its dis-
possessed pariahs –
parricide *patria*
for maybe only at last the
fiery sword
of the crooked angel of history flam-
ing against the wind and
burning the
agrokilltural cronies of that
sombre sodality where
field-marshal death commands a
grim militia of janissary-gun-
men:
only the angel on the left
of a history groomed against
the grain shall manage with its
multiswirling sword
(if only!) one day to
convoke from the nebulous
mass of days to
come the at last

afinal sobreveniente do	overriding day of the
justo	just
ajuste de	adjustment of
contas	accounts

(Haroldo de Campos, 1996; translation © Bernard McGuirk, 2020)

The task of transacting – trans/dancing – with Haroldo de Campos's poetry was made the more challenging by his Mephistofaustic promptings. In the essay on transluciferation, he had willingly re-engaged with both Marx and Nietzsche in a reminder that translation in particular and writing in general always perform the act of transcreation, a refutation of original (aetiology) and target (teleology), not only linguistically but also culturally and, let it be stressed, ideologically. Self-consciously, he had echoed Marx's precursor complaint against the censuring of his style. Self-mockingly, he had appropriated Nietzsche's plea for the necessarily sublime 'maldade' – the 'evil' – of mischievous content *and* form.

Radical content radical form radical translation

Countless Brazilian artists had reacted, in creative political interventions, to the obscenity of the murderous repressions perpetrated against the *Movimento dos Sem-Terra* (*Movement of the Landless Rural Workers*) – as did de Campos, here, to the massacre of Eldorado dos Carajás. Cyclical repetitions of organized violence, the option *against* the poor – in cynical inversion of the '*for* the poor' slogan of Liberation Theology – had triggered the indignation *and* the artistry of such as Frei Betto's 'Receita para matar um sem-terra' ['Recipe for Killing the Landless'], Sebastião Salgado's photography, in *Terra*, and Chico Buarque's 'Levantados do chão' ['Raised from the ground']. These contemporary artists, however, no less than their predecessors Graciliano Ramos, João Cabral de Melo Neto or Glauber Rocha, will not be remembered for their indignation alone. Each – and differently – had had to make another option, broadly definable as the style of mischief-making that is the prerogative of any radical art. Style also functions as a sharecropping, a participating in the intertextuality available to the individual artist; or, in de Campos's formulation, Karl Marx's 'property of form', inseparable from his 'individual spirituality'. Such an option, being *for* the poor, should never *be* poor. Even to think as much would be either to neglect the need for creativity or to misread it. To confuse, say, Graciliano Ramos's calculatedly daring minimalism, in *Vidas secas* [*Barren Lives*], of 1938, with some unmediated response to the prescriptive exclusions of the Soviet Writers' Congress of 1934. To ignore João Cabral de Melo Neto's career-long engagement with the materiality of words or with what Francis Ponge called *le parti pris des choses*. To undersell, perversely, the difficulty of his own challenge: 'É difícil defender/só com palavras a vida' ('It's hard to defend/only with words life') (*Morte e vida severina* [*Death and Life of Severino*]), of 1956. To imagine a *tabula rasa* (inter-cine-text-less) Glauber Rocha deprived, in the 1960s, of a dialogical relationship with Italian neo-realism. To conceive that, in postmodernity, the compassions of Sebastião Salgado did not reflect, and reflect on, Don McCullin's 1970s photography of the oppressed. To fail to hear in Chico Buarque's song the 1990s echo of José Saramago's 'Do chão pode levantar-se um livro, como uma espiga de trigo ou uma flor brava. Ou uma ave. Ou uma bandeira' ('From the ground a book can rise, like an ear of wheat or a wild flower. Or a bird. Or a banner'). But there is neither need nor time for doubt. The urgent indivisibility of radical content from radical form is better demonstrated by critical artistry than by artless criticism.

An unapologetic option for the inseparably transcendental *and* material underpins the very title of 'o anjo esquerdo da história'. Whether God is dead or not (and whether such a dominant metaphysics of absence might be Marxian or Nietzschean in inspiration), the conspiracies of history are still played out amidst the configurations of narrative. Which is not to see history *as* narrative (i.e. only as troped) – for that would be to de-radicalize both history's powers and any reading of it. In *Le monolinguisme de l'autre* (1996), Derrida elaborated on the 'call for an outside'. In 'o anjo...', de Campos called upon a figure, that of the avenging angel, which inhabits, simultaneously, both the inside and the outside of 'a história'. He even staked out for it a particular location, the place of enunciation for a nuncio to a nation, for a committed messenger. Yet the call is not voiced until after that necessary delay which enables the poem to re-visit, to re-inhabit, to re-live the arduous struggle for a hearing, paradoxically, on behalf of a voice – that of poetry – no less excluded, traditionally, than the referents of its echoing anger. Thus, by way of (not) analysing the poem, I prefer to comment on aspects of my own transjection of it.

Cheek to cheek... and the ear of the other

Cast at me as a throw of the dice, the poem impelled me to reject paraphrase. Haphazardly, I projected it, rather, only as re-castable. For the game was too serious to stop at a single appropriation. The ear of this other, too, had its particularity, its 'properties of form', its 'individual spirituality'. An Irish specificity of a past inherited, part-interred (ex-*patria*), in an England pre- , pro- , and post-Thatcher, suffused and infused my option for an irony which filtered distorted echoes of another, unofficial, 'national' anthem: 'Land of Hope and Glory'. 'How shall we extol Thee?' who were born not of, but only *on*, Thee. Here I played with another geo-politics, one of parallel clichés, *terra firma*, 'broad acres', 'field-marshals' of a homeland *unheimlich* and – sublime 'maldade' – of the *Mal*-vinas, with their no less sombre soldiery.[5]

That the translation must speak for, and of, itself is but part of the point. In language, for Bakhtin, the word was always half someone else's... whether spoken or written. Had de Campos not taken but half of Mallarmé's angelism, appropriating poetry's power of memory but adding to it a specifically Brazilian infernal vision ('quem dera!'), that of Canudos, and of Antônio Conselheiro? A post-Blake m(isc)arriage wherein the legacy of revolutionary mysticism assailed, as forcefully as does dialectical materialism, the hell-on-earth of landless utopians yet to glimpse a Brazilian heaven of agrarian reform? Such a politico-poetics could not presume to deprive those *sem terra* of the configurations, including the martyrs, saints and avenging angels, of their local narratives, small or grand... *sem céu*? Heaven-less? Who knows? Who would impose? If their collective history had certainly been groomed against the grain (where every day was – is? – a last day), at least the poem leaves its protagonists 'lying still' with their theology and with its (dis-)placements.[6]

Haroldo de Campos was no angel, least of all in his own poetic practice. He was unstintingly confident, certainly enough to lampoon critical and ideological rigidities and excesses. Acutely alert to the fact that Brazilian neo-Hegelians, no less than their counterparts elsewhere, in their determination to confront the brutality of much of Latin American society, had fallen precisely into the lure of a discourse too mimetic of brute reality, too mirroring ever to achieve a cutting edge, de

---

[5] 'Land of Hope and Glory' operates as a much-appropriated English national hymn. It has been adopted as the official anthem and is sung at the annual conferences of the Conservative Party.

[6] The reference is to the 1902 foundational memorializing of the Canudos war of 1896-1897 in the seminal text of Euclides da Cunha, *Os Sertões*, in which the rebellion and massacre of the *sertanejo* inhabitants of the Brazilian interior, in the State of Bahia, prefigure the plight, a century on, of the *sem terra* of El Dorado dos Carajás.

Campos convoked the figure of poetry itself. He knew that poetry is a master teaser, a baiter of stiff contemporary realists or the limp lamp-bearers of reflection theories past and present. The inter- and intra-cultural transluciferations of his textual performances had allowed for the inter-action of Brazilians speaking and listening to Brazilians being listened and spoken to; in turn, they inspired that other, the present trans(at)l(antic)ator whose sign/ature shuttles to and fro, ever seeking to perform intra-, but never faithful, ever faith-less, illusorily face-less, scorn-fully masking source, mourn-fully eschewing target, settling (lawlessly), for an ever extra-trans-mission of occupations, pre-occupations, needs, urgencies.

Stormy (whether you like it or not...)

Whence, for Haroldo de Campos, the 'anjo esquerdo da história'? In his unapologetic rejection of 'unacceptable cognitive models' the challenge is consistent, not least when addressing the angel as an appropriated icon of the left, inherited from Walter Benjamin's seminal formulation:

> This is how one pictures the angel of history. His face is turned toward the past. Where we perceive a chain of events, he sees one single catastrophe that keeps piling wreckage and hurls it in front of his feet. The angel would like to stay, awaken the dead, and make whole what has been smashed. But a storm is blowing in from Paradise; it has got caught in his wings with such violence that the angel can no longer close them. The storm irresistibly propels him into the future to which his back is turned, while the pile of debris before him grows skyward. This storm is what we call progress. (Benjamin, 1999, 249)

His reconfiguration, in poetry, of the readily packaged but not so smoothly imported 'anjo', regarded by Vieira as a de Campos 'mutation' in the poet's resistance to allowing Benjamin's 'Angelus Novus' cum 'angel of history' to be unproblematically appropriated as emblematic of a Brazilian historical materialism, must also be seen as an instrument of Haroldo's staunch debunking of those theorists who would unquestioningly identify their ideological stance with 'the storm of progress'.[7] Most notoriously, Roberto Schwarz, 'sociologizing critic,

---

[7] See the sections 'Protean Angels: Shifting Spectres of Walter Benjamin' and 'Crooked Angels, Satanic Angels: From Determinism to the Recovery of

of vocational incompatibility with the new in poetry' (de Campos, in McGuirk and Vieira, 2009, 197):

> The basic scheme is as follows: a tiny élite devotes itself to copying Old World culture [...] As a result, literature and politics occupy an exotic position, and we become incapable of *creating things of our own that spring from the depths of our life and history* [...] But why not reverse the argument? Why should the imitative character of our life not stem from forms of inequality so brutal that they lack the minimal reciprocity [...] without which modern society can only appear artificial and 'imported'? (Schwarz, 1992, 85-89)

Far from resembling 'devoted copying', such Haroldo de Campos performances as I deal with here, whether in his criticism or in his poetry, are, to use his own formulation, 'textos de ruptura' ('rupture texts'). In *Panorama de Finnegans Wake* (1962), the de Campos brothers, Augusto and Haroldo, had already embarked – for a hybrid genre of transl-*iter*-ation – on the journey of strenuous excursions demanded, by the modern artist *par excellence*, Stéphane Mallarmé.[8] As has been seen in respect of 'o anjo esquerdo da história', any 'angelism' inherited from Mallarmé is supplemented by the daemonic; is traced (as even Roberto Schwarz might admit) by the diabolic. The recuperative moves of the poem play with 'fallen' transcendentalism and that corrective shift which – for Haroldo de Campos, no less than for any Marxist – tugs 'a história' ('history' *and* the 'story' of history) always to the Left. *Not* 'going transcendental', but refusing to forget that particular -*ism* (without being '-ista'). *Not* appropriating an already unbalanced Brazilian history (which ever was and still is on the Right).

Revolutionary Possibility' in 'Weaving Histories and Cultural Memories. The (Inter)National Materialisms of "o anjo esquerdo da história"' (in McGuirk and Vieira, 2009, 170-75).

[8] 'The double effect required to allow Mallarmé's gaps their full disjunctive and destructive power, yet at the same time remain attentive to the multitude of invisible currents which pass back and forth between the separated segments, will strike many readers as inexcusably arduous and unrewarding [...] such moments are of the essence in Mallarmé [...] the type of modern artist [...] intent on breaking up ready-made *Gestalten* and smooth surface textures in order to compel his audience to look elsewhere for artistic coherence, to venture beneath the surface into the difficult, undifferentiated world of unconscious process, to interrupt the easy flow of horizontal perception with strenuous excursions into multi-level, all at once verticality' (Bowie, 1978, 8-16).

Rather engaging with it and in it through concrete performances; destabilizing the dubious claim that we judge our own time by its politicians, the past by its artists. Searching for poetry's re-admission to a *Res Pública Brasileira* in which the artist (in academic freedom, *pace* Roberto *et al*) might also stage the still-to-be-negotiated identities of the nation. Writ(h)ing, in agon, so that sub-alterity (*sic*) might no longer be a leper's bell to be hung, by the dark forces of any 'sociologizing' thought-police, about the neck of Brazil's excluded artists.

Are Haroldo de Campos's 'o anjo esquerdo da história' and my transjection of it – as not abandoned or to be forgotten, mutilatedly only 'left winged' and but formerly 'of history', but rather ever active, whole, uncut, as 'the angel on the left of history' – merely a further negotiated staging? Or are they both just a plea for the performative poet-critic to be heard as also improvising *politically* against, in counterpoint to, 'unacceptable cognitive models' of a Brazil in construction... though sorely lacking in deconstruction?

Trans memoriam

To Jacques Derrida's 'there is always something sexual at stake in the resistance to deconstruction' (1984, 12), this particular re-reader – and re-hearer – of Haroldo de Campos would add: '*and* cultural, *and* ideological'. But isn't that where the guest translator came in, invited, between 1999 and 2002, by and with Haroldo and Carmen, and with Else, into the hospitality of the Babelic home of Brazil and Brazilian letters? Unheimlich? Years on, I am still questioning the possibility of speaking or hearing 'do exterior', 'from abroad'; but, now, it is because I have journeyed, listened, learned, read, and may even write, re-*iter*-ate, that intra- has a history which includes extra-; that *il n'y a pas de hors-contexte*.

At, and beyond, the limits of the languages and the antics of nations – not least in transatlantications – aporetic threshold performances, differences between some 'outside' and some 'in', are never abolished but are ever open to be re-undermined, not merely inverted but politically re-subverted. The task, the discourse, is to perform that approach to translation theory to which it attempts to give (further) voice. Subsequent to the medium chosen by Haroldo de Campos to deliver a poetic rebuke to the perpetrators of the 1996 massacre at El Dorado dos Carajás, will there have been, will there be, a creative intervention that, similarly or comparably, addresses and challenges the contemporary social upheavals and political manifestations of the opposition to a contemporary Brazil that projects as heaven-sent the staging of a World Cup and an Olympic Games in the best of all possible wor(l)ds?

Panglossian (in)articulators of latter-day (un)saintly, neo-con, *bolsa*-narrow-minded values will ever propagate prosaic nostalgia for their order, their progress, that of re-appropriated nationalism, illiberalism and the military dictatorships of yesteryear. Their discourse has been pre-voiced, with markedly different inflections: '*We*, the land-holders pleni-potentiary, come from the broad-bellied acres of the *latifundio*, spawning profit and promising the re-newed order of our bullets; for *we* are come again, born-again, death-settlers all'. The riposte – *déjà et toujours écrit* – is already penned: '*You* are ever the possessed pariahs of the parricide *patria*; *you* are the agrokilltural cronies, that same old sombre sodality, overseers, as your field-marshal death commands its grim militia of janissary gun-men; *you* are the angels of death on the Right, forever theologizing your neo-fundamental(ist) adjustment of accounts'.

A diabolic *fait accompli;* or do post-Haroldo undoings – the transluciferations of successor artists – loom...? The task of the present trans(at)l(antic)ator is to await texts from writers who, also, will have undertaken such 'imagined and projected versions of what is to come'. Then, in a necessarily matching performative meditation, will it be conceivable to 'update'. *Ite, missa est.* The sacrifice (of the masses) in the interim will have found but formulaic, liturgical, expressions of their material – street, stadium, factory, *favela*, commune, congress – protests, however real, however righteous; whether or not arising from the left of history. Chronicles of a dearth foretold; testimony to a lack of devilishly challenging artistic engagement? The avenging angel of *poeisis* awaits; translations will follow.

There are occasions when a personal statement, especially of gratitude, will give context to the development of one's choices and, inseparably, one's critical discourse, one's style; for the one finds, and uncovers, the other. In asking 'Is there a Latin American text in this class?', I acknowledge the generous invitations to ask the prior, foreshortened, question 'Is there a text in this class?', in Latin America and, specifically, in Brazil, extended to me throughout the nineteen-nineties and beyond. And so began a journey, magnanimously hosted, across the regions and the decades, in subsequent teaching or lecture tours, often in the inspirational company of the most insightful of comparative Americanists, David Murray, in Minas Gerais, Rio de Janeiro, São Paulo, Salvador de Bahia, by such forbearing sponsors as Else Vieira, Eneida Maria de Souza, Solange Ribeiro, Heloisa Buarque de Hollanda, Marina Heck, Leyla Perrone-Moisés, and the power behind many a throne, Silviano Santiago himself, engineer of my 1995 UFRJ Rockefeller Foundation Visiting Fellowhip. Many of these distinguished thinkers were hosted, in reciprocation, in the UK and elsewhere in Europe; notably in Vieira's enterprising introduction, successively, of Frei Betto and Haroldo de Campos into the circle of ensuing international co-operations.

Saddening echoes of the prophet's voice, ever crying in the wilderness of intra-colonial criminal collusion with international economic exploitation, resound two decades on in an open letter:

> Esse genocídio não resulta da indiferença do governo Bolsonaro. É intencional. Bolsonaro se compraz da morte alheia... trato o presidente por BolsoNero – enquanto Roma arde em chamas, ele toca lira e faz propaganda da cloroquina, remédio sem nenhuma eficácia científica contra o novo coronavírus. Porém, seus fabricantes são aliados políticos do presidente... Agradeço seu solidário interesse em divulgar esta carta. Só a pressão vinda do exterior será capaz de deter o genocídio. (Frei Betto, 16/7/2020)

> [This genocide results not from the indifference of the Bolsonaro government. It is intentional. Bolsonaro rejoices in the death of others... I call the president by the name of BolsoNero – while Rome goes up in flames, he fiddles and indulges in propaganda for chloroquine, a remedy with no scientific effectiveness against the new coronavirus. Yet, its manufacturers are his political allies... I thank you for the solidarity of your interest in making this letter public. Outside pressure alone will put a stop to the genocide.]

Landless Voices; lifeless voices? In vain does the indignant theologian of liberation plead? An ear of some other will have been always and already there, albeit elsewhere... or everywhere. *D'après* Georges Bataille, 'a kind of rupture – in anguish – leaves us at the limit of tears: then we lose ourselves, we forget ourselves and communicate with the ungraspable beyond'. Yet the outside is never the beyond in the text; in the literary trope of re-naming, in drawing on echoes of inquisitorial memory and legend, via 'BolsoNero'; ever in those inverted commas wherein any outside-inside difference will be abolished; in *différance*. Bataille again: 'If we didn't know how to dramatize, we would not be able to get out of ourselves' (Bataille, 2014, 18). All the world's *that* stage...

IV. LAUGHIN' AGAIN HE'S AWAKE...
A Modest Proposal *à l'oreille de l'autre celte*

> I have been assured by a very knowing American of my acquaintance in London, that a young healthy child well nursed is at a year old a most delicious, nourishing, and wholesome food, whether stewed, roasted, baked, or boiled; and I make no doubt that it will equally serve in a fricassée or a ragout.
>
> Jonathan Swift (1729)

Frei Betto – Carlos Alberto Libânio Christo – takes up the weapon of poetry, to Swiftian denunciatory effect, and in a revised 'modest proposal' – with mordant irony against those who, in brutal disregard for alternative and characteristically subaltern *cuisines*, would abolish all threatening differences between any outside and inside. Cooking pots, as iron cast as the shackles of any enslaving ideology, too often serve to melt down differences for oppressive regimes of national construction or ominous reconstruction. Thereby, they can also raise the temperature of deconstructive ingredients to be added to the mix of contemporary political recipes, as in the blistering counter to cyclical intra-colonialism performed by the noted liberation theologian in what is perceived and projected as the dis-united states of Brazil:

Receita para matar um sem-terra	Recipe for killing the landless
Tome um agricultor	Take a rural worker
Desplantado de sua terra,	Unplanted from his land,
Desfolhe-o de seus direitos,	Strip the leaves of his rights,
Misture-o à poeira da estrada	Mix him up with road dust
E deixe-o secar ao sol.	And lay him in the sun to dry.
Deposite-o, em seguida,	Drop him, in an instant,
No fundo do descaso público.	In the common pit of discard.
Adicione a injúria da baderna.	Stir in the slur of riot.
Derrame o pote de horror ao pobre	Spill the pot of horror on the poor
Até obter a consistência do terror.	'Til the mix is thick with terror.
Acrescente uma dose de mau presságio	Add a dash of ill-omen
E salpique, com a mão do ágio,	And sprinkle, speculating,
Denunciosas fatias de pedágio.	Threatening strips of toll-charge.
Deixe repousar no silêncio	Leave to set in silence
A ganância grileira,	*Grileiro*-grabber land-greed,
As áreas devolutas,	Lands left fallow,
A saga assassina	Assassin saga
De quem semeia guerras	Of war-sowers
Para amealhar terras.	Land-hoarders.

Ferva a mentira	Boil down the lies
No caldeirão oficial	In official cauldrons
Até adquirir densidade	'Til density's settled
Em rede nacional.	In a national network.
Sirva à repressão	Serve up repression
Impunemente	With impunity
Na bandeja do latifúndio.	On the latifundium's estately tray.
(Frei Betto, 2002, revised	(© Translation Bernard McGuirk, 2020)
and translated 2007, 77-78)	

On undertaking translations of the ineradicably revolutionary texts conveying the interwoven memories and cultural expressions of indignation of the MST (Movement of the Landless Rural Workers in Brazil) in *Landless Voices in Song and Poetry by The Movimento dos Sem Terra of Brazil* (2007), I had addressed multiple and varied discourses of resistance, as raised in the previous chapter, characteristically as much *de propuesta* as *de protesta*: modest or emphatically otherwise. Instance Christo's fulminating twenty-first century Brazilian updating pastiche of Dean Swift's *A Modest Proposal for Preventing the Children of Poor People from Being a Burthen to Their Parents or Country, and for Making them Beneficial to the Publick.*

This dialogical cleric-to-cleric pitched performance, as staged in culinary echo of the Irish Anglican satirist by the *Mineiro* Dominican, himself incarcerated, for four years from 1969, under the prevailing military dictatorship, more than swiftly, and with no hint of modest circumlocution, as the recipe's title propounds, turns invisibility and orality against the arch-*écriture* of the implicit cum exploited 'Law of the Land'. The poem flags proposal as protest; it targets those legislators, from within and beyond the law, who would further impose on struggling subjects the will of a nation's singular devotion to a homogeneous slogan of capital 'Order and Progress'. No 'melting pot' text is this; rather a crucible in which the unfinished colonial project re-heats the left-overs of the left-out. The yet-to-be finished-off, land-less, roof-less, food-less, clothes-less, school-less occupiers of borders *within* are to be again and ever deemed, thus situated, *without*; not nation-less but without rights, civil let alone voiced, unless re-heard as recusant angels of the death of a nation's oppression. Unless, through the echoing intervention of an inheritor crusading satirist, they be offered the voice of protest through poetry, through song, vehicles too of international awareness and consciousness-raising.

Frei Betto's defiance is a challenge, no less, to the discipline of his would-be translator. Any transactor with the poems and songs of the *Movimento dos Sem Terra* soon confronts commitment of and to an

74

ideologically multi-layered and unyieldingly heteroglossic complexity. Thus, in seeking to explore a subaltern space of *différance* wherein artists also explore and express a contestatory sensitivity to the ideological power of protest poetry and song, the translator faces a no-less daunting task than that of capturing the cultural linguistic particularity of even the most experimental poetic expression. However free the interpretative role of the words and figures of speech deployed, in my rendering into English, a certain rhetorical discipline will have guided my decision making... Quintilian.

Reduplication amplifies the appeal to pity for the *sem-terra* and, in discursive terms, persuades the hearer while inflicting a however-glancing blow on the opposition, the land-hoarding *grileiro*-grabbers whose echoing original epithet, in Brazilian, is retained, deliberately, in the supplementing hyphenation. War-not-seed sowers of unabated master-lies, inheritors of ever self-pleasuring if never-to-be satisfied, insatiable, *coronelismo*... The age-old, single-handed, dispensers of cyclical injustice, land-whoring border-keepers of the great estates, stand erect and omnipotent in their spawning abuse of the dispossessed. In starkest contrast with their displaced and impoverished *sem-terra* opposition; the often *sem* teeth, *sem* taste – for what have they to eat, let alone cook? – *sem* everything (*pace* the Bard). As you like it, we shall – obscene Juvenal delinquency, not *politesse*, *oblige* – continue. *Synonymy* duplicates here not by repetition of the same word but, in replacement of one seemingly objective step-by-step instruction, by alternative yet unchanging exhortations to criminality; in effect, a cumulative outrage in the reader is delivered... 'on the latifundium's estately tray'. *Reciprocal Change* has been teasingly deployed and, just as swiftly, inverted: 'Live to eat' those who would but 'Eat to live'. *Elimination* thereby follows as the enumeration of the ways in which the recipe might be accomplished is discarded after the last-supper-anticipating closing imperative. 'Sirve'... insists – ironic paronomasia – on the irrefutability of the poem's alternative theology cum ideology. *You* may dish out the orders but *I*... *Non serviam*.

Serendipity... windfall; landfall

Since, in May 1982, with a transatlantic ten-day indulgence passage, as the sole passenger and, indeed, only non-Brazilian, aboard the Fortaleza-crewed Vitória-bound Lloyd Brasileiro 12,000 tonnes container vessel *SS Itaimbé*, – and shades, I felt, of 'El fantasma del buque de carga', but that has been another story – diverted from my planned lecture-visit to the University of Buenos Aires by the outbreak of the Malvinas-Falklands conflict, I had been to Brazil almost every year. Such visits were made in the context of the contractual terms of my newly established UK-based research-and-teaching post in Latin American literature. Not until 1992, at the invitation of the then President of the Associação Brasileira de Literatura Comparada (ABRALIC), Silviano Santiago, with whose pioneering writing I was familiar but whom I had not met personally, was a whole new world opened up to me. For the Niterói event, we were to address issues provoked by the topic *Limites*: 'na produção teórica e analítica [da] interdisciplinaridade [e da] intertextualidade'. Key orienting terms, therefore, of the then and, it is to be trusted, the now. 'De volta à sutura: o discurso patriarcal e a *Ova completa* de Susana Thénon' was my contribution... Back to the future, too, it would seem, as I re-write. Reactions were generous, cordial, and, questioningly, happily... mixed. White, European, male, I might know what I was doing, but what did I *think* I was doing? And in what, whose, contexts? Was this *inter-* or, still, despite the pitch, some however veiled inner, monological, discourse. I might claim to know where I was speaking from, but what did I know of whom I was speaking to...?

So what is all this about? Nostalgia? Far from it, for early in the maelstrom, of an ensuing lecture tour of Minas Gerais, in Ouro Preto... Solange Ribeiro had said, 'I want you to meet Haroldo'. Life changed again; but, enough. Back, at last, to *l'oreille de l'autre*...

Grief Encounter

Haroldo de Campos had come to my attention in the 1970s, when I knew of him exclusively as a poet. For so long as I was confined to reading at a safe cultural distance, the encounter was unproblematic, prompting intellectual stimulation and a delight in his myriad concretist experimentations. Here was an exceptional artist, a multi-lingual architect of polyphonic access from territories familiar to zones uncharted. This poetry spoke to me of Mallarmé, of Apollinaire, of Pound, of Vallejo, of Paz, of e e cummings but, above all, of itself. It was Brazil-derived yet it confronted aesthetic and political frontiers beyond mere cartography. In the practice of de Campos – and in my first negotiations with it – not only national-linguistic but also genre and disciplinary boundaries were being crossed. Though a narrow I was reading broadly and, falsely, I presumed, *hors-contexte*, all felt strangely *heimlich*. Most familiar of all, and consonant with the poetic

76

practices and performances of the poets with whom I was already comparing de Campos, was the radical inseparability of formal experimentalism and cultural subversiveness.

Not before the early-to-mid 1980s was I to have, *in situ*, my first (brief) encounter with divers Brazilian receptions of the writing, the resonance and the role of the different Haroldos now discovered to me. For here too was a polemical figure... and so I was confronted by a dialectics in which his name was appropriated and polarized as that of hero or villain, of inspiration or infamy. At first, it was difficult for me ideologically to question such polarities; in my 'thirdness', in my search for another other – un-besmirched by such crude political labellings – to rush in where even Engels might have feared to tread would have been foolhardy. Yet the already passing age of high poststructuralism – and my own involvement in it – should have forewarned me of that *tout est toujours déjà dit* problematic whereby the *jamais vu* of first encounter blinds one to familiar griefs.

Customs and ex(er)cise

Smuggling 'continental' theories through the tariff-barriers of common-sense Anglo-Saxon critical practices was an activity in which I had already been indulging for some time. I even knew escape-routes from the long-familiar tensions of Nietzsche-Marx binaries but, here, in Brazil, I was flummoxed. Alert as I might have been to the seductions and to the dangers of travelling theories, it took me much longer than I had anticipated to negotiate respectfully – and from that location ascribed to me as being 'do exterior' ['an outsider'] – a site of acceptable in-between-ness. Piecemeal, I ingested reactions to my own critical interventions which, in one and the same session, might include 'radical demais' ('too radical') and 'pára, pára essa ironia' ('stop, stop that irony'). Was I too far to the Left, or was I a Right-thinking purveyor of undecidability, weighed down with an excess baggage of literariness? Possibly both... but the message was clear-cut: 'cuidado!' ('take care!'); or 'watch out!'. Pedagogically speaking, I was receiving my first Brazilian lessons on the pervasive need to recognize and to respect, to rehearse and, not seldom, to recycle a national nostrum, a placebo, of 'cordialidade' ['cordiality']. And so, as well as to listen and to learn, I continued to read.

Irony of ironies

Looking back, as I attempt to situate the texts and the sects associated with the phenomenology of 'Haroldo de Campos' (and ever chary of the philosophical ruse of handy reductionisms), it seems a pity that I had not encountered much earlier a neglected archive dating from 1895:

> Essa graça não admite a ironia. A ironia, como o 'humour', mais ainda talvez que ele, é estranha à índole brasileira. Uma e outro são entre nós produtos de cultura, resultados de imitação que em certos individuos, por disposições especiais de temperamento, podem ter sido assimilados perfeitamente, completamente, mas que são em todo o caso raros e exóticos.

> [That grace [charm] does not admit irony. Irony, like 'humour', perhaps even more than that, is alien to the Brazilian nature. Amongst us, irony and humour are products of culture, the results of imitation which in certain individuals, through special dispositions of temperament, may have been assimilated perfectly, completely, but are in any case rare and exotic]. (Veríssimo, 1976, 67)

'Oh! The horror!'. Had I but realized that the use of irony would be still, a century later, enough to blunt one's elsewhere most incisive literary cut and thrust one's critical voice into some art of darkness. If I was to emerge without premature dismissal, or worse, to a fatal echo – 'Mister cuts ∴ he dead' – then I would have to trade with the other side of that coinage minted as *cordialidade*, namely, *fofoca*. (To *gossip*, presently, I shall return; for which culture does not deal in its own, particular, version of that currency?). Meanwhile, I should have to choose what (will) to excise, and what (still) to exercise, in a peculiarly Brazilian customs-house of academic literary criticism, namely, a politically correct superstructure and a base of institutional sniping, wherein schools of thought or – in university rivalries – *linhas de pesquisa* often led to ill-disguised enmities. Walter Moser has encapsulated the issue with admirable tact:

> [We] can observe a persistent dichotomy in the Brazilian milieu of literary studies between formalists and semioticians on the one hand and representatives of a socio-historical approach to literature on the other. Haroldo's identification with the formalists is directly linked to his experimental workings in

language, although it would be wrong to affirm that they make him an a-historical author and thinker, alien to social concerns. (Moser, 1998, 149)

To P (perform) **or not to P... C** (conform)

... *that* is the gesture. Whether 'tis nobler in the mind to excise the native hue of resolution, sicklied o'er with the pale cast of thought? or to take arms against a C of troubling 'correctness'? To exercise, still, the slings and arrows of outrageous dialogics or, by opposing word-plays, end them? Perchance to sleep? Thus conscience does make cowards of us all. And lose the name of action in the undiscovered country by heeding 'Soft you now!'

Dream on! For to hear one's voice and one's (own) otherness in addressing 'the ear of the other that signs' (Derrida 1988: 51) is no less an institutional than an ideological imperative. The alternatives, in what was, what is, and whatsoever shall be 'a theatrical infraction of the laws of genre and academicism' (26), then for Nietzsche but now for me, were the desperate predictabilities of having to listen to *Made in Brazil* theories-cum-clichés. Within the laws of my own generic academicism, and in an era of burgeoning alertness to discourses of post-coloniality, I had already perceived that to identify and criticize differences *between* cultures was more readily shareable – because more obviously amenable – than to seek and analyse differences operating *within* cultures. So, reticently, I would mask my concerns by framing them in, say, the Derridan terms I knew to have been long since adopted by Brazilian academe.

Silviano Santiago's *Glossário de Derrida*, had been a striking, if then as yet unheralded, instance of a perspicacious intervention in an institutionalized *fofoca*-speak by no means exclusive to Brazil:

> quem abre *La Dissémination* desiste muitas vezes de sua leitura na terceira ou quarta página. Tal problema vinha dando o tom e sendo o lugar-comun dos comentários de corredor e de esquina sobre a obra de Derrida.

> [people who open *La Dissémination* often stop reading at the third or fourth page. It is that problem which gave rise to the tone and became the commonplace of corridor and corner commentaries on the work of Derrida]. (Santiago, 1976, 5)

Slyly, Silviano had slipped his hand into the glove of *fofoca* in order to lay it bare in the corridors of non-power, the corner shops, of busy-body academe.

To my question 'What is the difference between difference and *différance?*' two consistent resistances were erected. Did I not know that, in respect of the former, the nation had, since 1500, preferred to swallow rather than confront difference? Had I not further grasped that the anthropophagic law had been reinforced emblematically, in the first modernism of the 1920s, by the dazzling seductiveness of a Brazilian primitivism? If I was not convinced by the manifesto prescriptions of Oswald de Andrade's landmark *Manifesto Antropófago,* least of all by his pseudo-Trinity of proto-salvation, 'Magia. Antropofagia. A transformação permanente do Tabu em totem/magic' ['Magic. Anthro-pophagy. The permanent transformation of Taboo into totem/magic'] (Oswald de Andrade, 2), then I should sate my *littérateur*'s curiosity by respecting the (curricular) centrality of Mário de Andrade's *Macunaíma.* There all would be rendered trans/parent. Any reservations I might have regarding the implausibility of an (official) acculturation policy of *whitening* by gradual assimilation of the non-European other would be readily countered – and prefigured – by Mário's celebrated 'pooling' of the experiences of his eponymous protagonist and two of his brothers. From a local heart of darkness would emerge one, two, three primitives, in turn to pass through the font of initiation into urban modernity: Macunaíma to be whitened, Jiguê to be (less) whitened, Maanape to be (least) whitened – by (first, second, third) degrees. Was I being asked to read a foundational narrative or to re-narrate a foundational reading? In fact, an overt if tacit governmental and societal complicity in keeping racial differences off the agenda of political debate would not be so strikingly articulated for me until Heloisa Buarque de Hollanda's meditation on the 1988 black-consciousness slogan of: 'Não deixa sua cor passar em branco' ['Don't let your colour slip into whiteness']. An (un)conscious echo of *Macunaíma?* An (up)dated ironizing of the tacit project of 'deixe seu corpo passar em branco' ['let your body slip into whiteness'] of countless Brazilian evolutionists? To indulge a post-Darwinian language-game – re-Joycing of a Browne[1] de Campos hue – is just too tempting; 'a man-ape' 'jig' [on the] 'uê' to [Mac] unanimity.

I had glimpsed the blankness of modernism's black-and-white experimentalism before, in the superficial and short-lived effects of, for example, appropriations of the masks of primitivism ('Christs of

---

[1] Haroldo Eurico Browne de Campos: the family name, richly, *dis*covers his Irish heritage.

another creed another guise/The lowly Christs of dim expectancies/ Adieu, Adieu/Sun corpseless head') in a failed-'cos-self-deluding European avant-garde.[2] Its protagonists had also indulged ethnocentric illusion: they did not and could not assimilate the primitive – only some available, commodified, representations of it. Theirs was thus self-deluding appropriation, too; appropriation of a projected self. The mask had operated not as an objective correlative, rather as correlative objectivization.

So could I now bear to hear again uncritical dinnings on Oswald's distant drum, banal yet pervasive misprisions of his 'Tupi or not Tupi?', that is my question, without succumbing to – this time – scurrility? No. Prior to heeding any invitation to ponder cultural difference, the ear of this other would simply prick up to a more pressing urge... translatable only by an early escape (down) to the men's room. Tupi? *That* was a question of urgency; any excuse to escape from the uncomfortable lecture-theatre of ostensibly Left-*versus*-Right homilies, nobler in the mind than on an outraged body, uncomfortably seated amidst the factions and – it was apparent – the lurking P C of much local academic discourse. That *was* the question... and, now, 'it is to this ear that I myself will feign to address myself [...], as promised, about your and my academic freedom' (Derrida, 1988: 33). Whilst alert to Gayatri Spivak's defence of the strategic essentialism of the colonized as a move to break (with) the structures and stratagems of further colonizings – 'I think it is absolutely on target [...] to stand against the discourses of essentialism, [but] *strategically* we cannot' (Spivak, 1984-5, 184) – I could not help thinking of her plea as a subtle echo of Derrida's 'We *must begin wherever we are* [...] *wherever we are*: in a text where we think we are' (Derrida, 1976, 162). Substitute 'context' for 'text' and, hey presto, behold the con-trick of cultural studies' claim to have (dis)placed post-structuralism.

Zones libres?

In another context, I have considered how Mary Louise Pratt's proposals for a 'linguistics of contact' are acutely relevant to the

---

[2] Samuel Beckett's rendering of the final lines of Apollinaire's 'Zone' (1912): 'Ils sont des Christ d'une autre forme et d'une autre croyance/Ce sont les Christ inférieurs des obscures espérances/Adieu Adieu/Soleil cou coupé'. For further analysis of this self-delusion see my 'Machinations: Shock of the Old, Fear of the New – Apollinaire and Alberti', in Giles, 1993, 52-86.

ideologico-critical polemics in Brazil and to Latin America in general.[3] I am prompted again to juxtapose with her salutary attack on that linguistic community which constantly presents itself as a 'nation'; adult, monolingual, mono-dialogic, de Campos's response to the coruscating assault on Concretism and its proponents levied by the prominent Brazilian Marxist critic Roberto Schwarz; indeed, to rehearse both argument and counter-argument since they will be shown to contextualize my analysis of the de Campos poem that I shall revisit in the light of the claims made regarding the rhetorical effectiveness of Frei Betto's declamatory recipe, namely, Haroldo's 'Ode (explícita) em defesa da poesia' ['(Explicit) Ode in defence of poetry'].

In 'Marco histórico', of 1985 (reproduced in John Gledson's translation as 'A Historic Landmark', in *Misplaced Ideas*, in 1992), the notions of Augusto and Haroldo de Campos had been subjected to a damning examination. Schwarz referred first to Augusto's poem 'Póstudo' and then to an article by Haroldo on post-utopical poetry:

> Others, and that includes me, will see the poem as the *n*th example of a key trick played by the concretists, always concerned to organise Brazilian and world literature so that it culminates in them, a tendency which sets up a confusion between theory and self-advertisement as well as being provincial nonsense [...] Behind the globalized form of the real, from which contradictions, differences, and other marks of concrete reality are missing, maybe there is an element of indifference. (Schwarz, 1992, 191-5)

Gledson himself, in a perceptive contextualizing of Schwarz's polemic *apparently* with the Concretist de Campos brothers, adds a telling afterthought (my italics) – to which it will be necessary, presently, to pay particular and attentive heed:

> It would be easy to see Roberto Schwarz as a pessimist. He certainly is unwilling to ignore the brute facts of mass poverty and exploitation which have plagued Brazil's past and continue to plague its present. One can feel his anger at those who try to argue, with singularly contorted logic and deafness to the calls of common sense, that things are better because they are worse: because Brazilians have always imitated, but are now told there

---

[3] In McGuirk, 1997, 5-6, and, in an updating retrospective, in '*Pas*: locating inequality. Post-, trans-, intra-', in McGuirk, 2018, 17-32.

is no reason to think that imitations are inferior to the things they copy, they are suddenly in the vanguard. *The fact that the theory used to 'prove' this is that of a French philosopher (Derrida) only sharpens the irony.* (Gledson in Schwarz, 1992, xix)

The (supposed) 'sleight of hand' whereby, 'suddenly, the periphery becomes the centre' will never, according to Gledson, convince an 'enlightened materialist' such as Schwarz that 'differential nationalism' transferred 'to our tropical latitudes' (in Haroldo de Campos's words) can be anything other than a dangerous and irresponsible 'slipperiness'. Not only of signifiers, but also of that 'rarified realm of absolute desires' where all that 'is left is the abstract gesticulations of the desire to transform, wrapped up in attractive lettering' (Schwarz 1992, 195).

For de Campos, the 'straight-line logophonies' of Brazilian nationalism might be said to operate similarly to the calling-card and sales-pitch of that 'mono-lingual, mono-dialogical community' attacked by Pratt. Each is constructed by a familiarly contested Utopianism, pulled hither or thither without, however, daring to admit dystopic non-homogeneities. I need hardly reiterate, in support of my opening claims, that the 'watered-down' social interaction of 'cordialidade' operates no less forcefully, as one of the dominant hypotheses raised by de Campos, than the more publicly and nationally flagged 'entified substances' of the conventional, the official, 'order and progress'.

Though as yet confined to brackets (barracks?), the 'disruptions and infractions, the margins, the "monstrous"' still characterize, for de Campos, crucially 'differential' discursive activities. They thus follow that double trajectory, that toing-and-froing, that shuttle, of a practice which settles on no one word, much less a binary pair, preferring – opting – to perform in the space of *trans-*. *Trans-* is the ever mobile 'third term' of such a theory. Thus, *trans*ference, *trans*lation, *trans*culturation (all familiar starting points within the discipline of linguistics) act only as initial points of reference. Disconcertingly close both to Baruch Spinoza's notion of *becoming* and to Gilles Deleuze's phenomenon of *double capture* and, I now suggest, to Derrida's *oto(bio)graphies*, the impact of de Campos's claims has been perhaps most observable, as was suggested in the previous chapter, in the field of post-modern translation theory. However, it is important to stress that, within Latin America, debates comparable to the polemics stoked elsewhere by critics such as Edward Said, Gayatri Spivak and Homi Bhabha have been both as heated and as relevant to cultural and literary theories as they have been to linguistics.

With a difference in respect of a further and not necessarily modest proposal; not *do exterior*, not confinable to any *interior*, Haroldo de Campos's texts might serve more broadly and for generations to come as *de rigueur* reading for classroom, or otherwise, students or readers of Latin American literature... Take the trouble – much as Silviano had pleaded in 1976 in respect of Derrida and *La Dissémination* – to tackle the arduous but rewarding task of (re-) reading that rare, exemplary, intellectually and politically engaged and engaging critic who practises what his writings teach, inseparably, whether in their presumed creative or critical forms.

One nation in/versions

In the context of literary criticism, Haroldo de Campos has intervened on countless fronts in the undoing of the monologisms of many a nationalizing project. A telling case in point is his double visitation to José de Alencar's so-called foundational fiction of the Brazilian 'myth of origins', first in '*Iracema*: une archéologie d'avant-garde' (1986) and, later in '*Iracema*: A Vanguard Archaeography' (1993). The shift from -*ology* to -*ography* is not accidental. It is as if the critic, in the interval, becomes suddenly self-aware, hearing through the ear of the other *logos* a call to (re-) write, to inscribe on his prior performance, the sign of further unsettlings:

> Selecting fabular chronotopes with folkloric roots, *Iracema* goes back to the pre-history of the *epos*. It is articulated as a 'myth of origins', structurally exposed in terms of the symbolic tale of adventures and variegated with idyllic-pastoral moments. Referring to this phase of Alencar's production, in which *Iracema*, in my opinion, is the only truly exponential text, Brito Broca has spoken of 'true pastorals in which there is much of a fairytale nature'. In this sense, it is a 'monological' work (close to 'epic monologism'), elaborated in a serio-aesthetic fashion (the 'carnivalization' of this paradigm occurs in *Macunaíma*, where the fable is disguised as a farce, taking on a 'parodic mode'). Still, on the plane of the signifier – a plane which, from the operational perspective of its 'poetic function', should be understood in a broad sense, involving both its 'form of expression' and its 'form of content' – the text of the Alencarian 'legend' is sliced through by polyphony, in the Bakhtinian sense of the word. The intervention of language 'in a savage state', presented as a programme for a critical awareness

84

of Brazilian poetic practice, breaks with the statutes of 'epic monologism'. It also reveals a moment of the 'romanticization of the *epos'* via language in the sense of the re-education of the Brazilian poet through an apprenticeship of the 'state of nature' via Tupinized writing. This is the moment of 'experimental provocation' (Bakhtin) in *Iracema*, which re-projects it in the future, rescuing it from the secrets of 'epic distanciation' where Alencar had inscribed it with an augural stroke, fascinated by the recovery of the 'historical infancy' of the Brazilian (a theme capable of provoking 'an eternal instigation', as Marx himself recognizes referring to those 'normal children' the Greeks must have been). In this sense, Alencar acts like a translator aspiring to radicality. (de Campos, 1993, 14-15)

He further claims that 'with *Iracema*, everything occurs in reverse [...] *Iracema* radicalizes and subverts *Atala* [...] Alencar intuitively comes close to an idea of translation as a "making strange" of the vernacular, which implies exposing the translator's language to the violent impulse coming from the foreign language [...] In the historiographic "fiction" of Brazilian Indianist Romanticism, one might say that Alencar's Tupi represented, like an imaginative scriptural "counterfeiting", the "Ossianic Poem" that was lacking, by indicting, as a "strange-making" (extravagant or *extra*-vagus) "supplement", the erasure of the "origin" promoted by the repressiveness of colonial culture...' (de Campos, 1993, 17-18).

To my ear, the shift from an *archaeology* of, say, Bakhtinian chronotopes and polyphonies – already radical in any counter-reading to putative constructions of Brazil as one nation – to an *archaeography*, *à la* Derrida, is implicit in the original French version. By indulging, unapologetically, the supplementary relation of writing to voicing, de Campos confirmed his reluctance to (de)limit fiction either to Lukácsian or even to Bakhtinian models of the novel, to either 'the form of mature virility' or to 'experimental provocation' respectively. In a tell-tale metaphor, his claim that 'Alencar's most consequential aesthetic contribution was elsewhere on the chess board of the literary field' (12) constituted a tactical re-framing of the political moves available to Brazilians still coming to terms with the 'repressiveness' of *intra-* as well as of *post*-colonial culture. Inescapable base and superstructure relationships were supplemented, further mediated, but neither diminished nor relegated, in the range of *plays* available in the staging of negotiated identities. And, in these moves, de Campos joined other important exploiters of the structural turn in re-reading the

Brazilian cultural mosaic.

At this juncture, a strategic juxtaposition of critical discourses can be invoked. Let the ear be lent to another voice, that of Phyllis Peres, speaking, and writing, of 'Subaltern spaces in Brazil':

> Carnival was undoubtedly privileged by the Estado Novo as one of the spaces that best expressed negotiated Brazilian identity [...] If the black bodies [...] could not be harnessed by the élite [...] they could be paraded once again as *pieces* [my italics] in the yearly celebration of miscegenated Brazilian identity. Ironically, this staging of negotiated identity is, indeed, inversion, but not that, as argued [by Rowe and Schelling], of social hierarchies in Brazil. Carnival's so-called space of liberation is, in fact, an attempt to reclaim and parade black bodies through contemporary market places that offer up the (utopian) ideal of a carnivalized Brazil. This does not mean, however, that subalterns are silenced or silent [...] nor [...] that they are condemned to suffer history rather than make it. What it does mean is that Brazilian subalterns are speaking in carnivals and unmaskings, just as they have always done. (Peres, 1994, 119)

Where de Campos and Peres, to my hearing, addressed similar strategic possibilities was indicated in the latter's summarizing claim: 'where hegemony would deny any discrete groups of subalterns their histories, history will not be denied, only misread' (Peres, 115). The 'translator[s] aspiring to radicality', in de Campos's phrase, but no less as executed in his own practice, would also *only* be misread (however perversely). (T)He(y) would not be denied. Nor should I be denied that analysis of a hegemonic *antropofagia* which would radically translate the scandalous absence that lay – lies – at the nub of the whitening project it at once masks as it masquerades. *Dicta*ts (whether *duras* or *moles*) could permit the import, may even voice approval, of *trans*lated (and *multi*-national) inversion theses, safely packaged (for re-export). Paradoxically, at the same time as a growing, trans-national, economic elite was allowed to play a(c)t such inversions with impunity, any hint at intellectual elitism could too readily be branded supra-national and, as a consequence, lacking in that solidarity which, locally, from Left or Right, often paraded itself, utopically, as 'we'. Whilst the *content* of would-be social inversions might have been recognized, if seldom tolerated, that radical *form* of rereading – a rereading which must be allowed to operate from outside as well as from inside any text –

namely, *irony*, was broadly condemned as the gravest *mis*reading of the (one) body politic. For language was less easily controlled than social action. 'Radical demais' is often accompanied by 'humanamente impossível' ('humanly impossible'), another cliché drawn from suppositions of oneness, of unity, of a common restriction on the possibility of, and for, change. Such a plea (for conformity, for complacency, for sympathy, for inaction or, guess what, for cordiality?) addressed *a* human nature; suppressed difference(s); would not hear *différance*.

The impact of the theories and the resonance of the literary practices of such as the de Campos brothers have certainly been recognized but have also been challenged, famously, indeed necessarily, by the searching critique of Schwarz, the insistently utopian terms of which ought now, also and ever, be re-assessed.

Gaol-breaks

Are we again to be bolted into a this time Brazilian version of rusting if no less constricting Nietzsche *versus* Marx shackles? Not inescapably. Particularly, and *pace* Schwarz, literary criticism need not passively accept assumptions based stubbornly on reflectionist theories, circumscribed by shibboleths of original and copy. Despite – and it must be admitted because of the insistent international pervasiveness of – such institutionalists as those that would police academe, criticism might well have to recognise its position in the side-lines of literary activity, but it can never be content with – indeed, must struggle against – marginality, or its complacent conversion into an ivory-tower comfort.

Authoritarianism regarding what ought to be purveyed in or out of the classroom has always been and shall ever be, condescendingly, with us. But why should poststructuralism and, in particular, Derrida have been so threatening to the Left, and to such a committed reader of Brazilian literature as Roberto Schwarz? Given a fair re-reading; judge for yourself:

> A commonplace idea suggests that the copy is secondary with regard to the original, depends upon it, is worth less, and so on. Such a view attaches a negative sign to the totality of cultural forces in Latin America and is at the root of the intellectual malaise that we are discussing. Now, contemporary French philosophers such as Foucault and Derrida have made it their

speciality to show that such hierarchies have no basis. Why should the prior be worth more than the posterior, the model more than the imitation, the central more than the peripheral, the economic infrastructure more than cultural life, and so forth? According to the French philosophers [...] it would be more accurate and unbiased to think in terms of an infinite sequence of transformations, with no beginning or end, no first or last, no worse or better. One can easily appreciate how this would enhance the self-esteem and relieve the anxiety of the underdeveloped world, which is seen as tributary to the central countries. We would pass from being a backward to an advanced part of the world, from a deviation to a paradigm, from inferior to superior lands (although the analysis set out to suppress just such superiority). All this because countries which live in the humiliation of having to imitate are more willing than the metropolitan countries to give up the illusion of an original source, even though the theory originated there and not here. Above all, the problem of mirror-culture would no longer be ours alone, and instead of setting our sights on the Europeanization or Americanization of Latin America we would, in a certain sense, be participating in the Latin Americanization of the central cultures. (Schwarz, 1992, 6)

Schwarz is as reasoning as he is forthright. He, unsurprisingly, requires the intellectual to hang onto cause and effect as unmediated, non-differential, relations. Alas, his misreading of the butt of his complaints is a common one; as the most notorious of those butts was quick to rebut. No shrinking violator of neo-Hegelian paradigms – notoriously anti-modernist, anti-poetry – and by no means backward in forwarding the least *implicit* of deviations from any slavish mirror-culture, in *Educação dos cinco sentidos* (1979-1984), de Campos had dangled the following provocation:

Ode (explícita) em defesa da poesia no dia de são Lukács

os apparatchiki te detestam
poesia
prima pobre
(veja-se a conversa de benjamin
com brecht sobre lukács gabor
kurella
numa tarde de julho
em svendborg)

Ode (explicit) in defence of poetry on the day of St. Lukács

the apparatcheeks detest you
poetry
poor cousin
(viz the conversation of benjamin
with brecht about lukács gabor
kurella
on a july evening
in svendborg)

poesia
fêmea contraditória
te detestam
multifária
mais putifária que a mulher de
putifar
mais ofélia
que hímen de donzela
na ante-sala da loucura de hamlet

poetry
contradictory female
they detest you
multifarious
more putipharious than the woman of
putifar
more ofelia
than maidenhead
in the ante-room of hamlet's madness

poesia
que desvia da norma
e não se encarna na história
divisionária rebelionária visionária
velada/revelada
fazendo strip-tease para teus
próprios (duchamp)
celibatários
violência organizada contra a língua
(a míngua)
cotidiana

poetry
which deviates from the norm
and is not incarnated in history
divisionary rebellionary visionary
veiled/unveiled
doing strip-tease for your own
(duchamp)
bachelors
organized violence against everyday
(lack)
language

os apparátchiki te detestam
poesia
porque tua propriedade é a forma
(como diria marx)
e porque não distingues
o dançarino da danca
nem dás a césar o que é de césar
   não lhe dás a mínima (catulo):
sais com um poema pornô quando
ele pede um hino

the apparatcheeks detest you
poetry
because you property is form
(as marx would say)
and because you don't distinguish
the dancer from the dance
nor render onto caesar what is caesar's
   not even the minimum (catullus):
you come out with a porno poem
when he asks for an anthem

serás a hetaera esmeralda
de thomas mann
a dragonária agônica
de asas de sífilis
?
ou um fiapo de sol no olho selenita
de celan
?
ana akhmátova te viu
passeando no jardim
e te jogou nos ombros
feito um renard
de prata mortuária

will you be the emerald mistress
of thomas mann
the agonic dragonfly
of syphilis wings
?
or a glint of sun in the eye
selenite of celan
?
ana akhmatova saw you
strolling in the garden
and threw you over her shoulders
made you into a mortuary
silver fox-fur

walter benjamin
que esperava o messias
saindo por um minúsculo
arco da história no
próximo minuto

walter benjamin
who awaited the messiah
coming out through a minuscule
arch of history in
the very next minute

certamente te conheceu
anunciada por seu angelus novus
milimetricamente inscrita num
grão de trigo
no museu de cluny

adorno te exigiu
negativa e dialética
hermética prospéctica emética
recalcitrante

dizem que estás à direita
mas marx (le jeune)
leitor de homero dante goethe
enamorado da gretchen do fausto
sabia que teu lugar é à esquerda
o louco lugar alienado
do coração

e até mesmo lênin
que tinha um rosto parecido com
verlaine
e que no entanto (pauvre lélian)
censurou lunatchárski
por ter publicado mais de mil
cópias
do poema '150.000.000' de
maiakóvski
papel demais para um poema
futurista!
mesmo lênin sabia
que o idealismo inteligente está
mais perto
do materialismo
que o materialismo
do materialismo
desinteligente

poesia
te detestam
materialista idealista ista
vão te negar pão e água
(para os inimigos: porrada!)
és a inimiga
poesia

só que um dervixe ornitóloga
khlébnikov
presidente do globo terrestre
morreu de fome em santalov
num travesseiro de manuscritos
encantado pelo riso
faquirizante dos teus olhos

certainly knew you
announced by his angelus novus
millimetrically inscribed in a
grain of wheat
in the museum of cluny

adorno demanded you
negative and dialectic
hermetic prospectic emetic
recalcitrant

they say that you're on the right
but marx (le jeune)
reader of homer dante goethe
enamoured of faust's gretchen
knew that your place is on the left
the mad alienated place
of the heart

and even lenin himself
who had a face like
verlaine
and who meanwhile (poor lelian)
censored lunatcharski
for publishing more than 1,000
copies
of mayakovski's poem
'150.000.000'
too much paper for a
futurist poem!
even lenin knew
that intelligent idealism is
closer to
materialism
than the materialism
of dis-intelligent
materialism

poetry
they detest you
materialist idealist ist
they'll deny you bread and water
(for enemies: a beating!)
you are the enemy
poetry

only that a dervish ornithologist
khlebnikov
president of the terrestrial globe
died of hunger in santalov
on a pillow of manuscripts
enchanted by the fakirizing
laughter of your eyes

e jákobson roman
(amor/roma)
octogenário
plusquesexappealgenário
acaricia com delícia
tuas metáforas e metonímias
enquanto abres de gozo
as alas de crisoprásio de tuas
paronomásias

e ele ri do embaraço
austero dos savants

e agora mesmo aqui mesmo
neste monte
alegre das perdizes
dois irmãos siamesmos e um oleiro
de nuvens pignatari
(que hoje se assina signatari)
te amam furiosamente
na garçonnière noigrandres
há mais de trinta anos
que te amam
e o resultado é esse
poesia
já o sabes
a zorra na geléia
geral
e todo o mundo querendo
tricapitar
há mais de trinta anos
esses trigênios vocalistas
   que idéia é essa de querer plantar
ideogramas no nosso quintal
(sem nenhum laranjal   oswald)?
e (mário) desmanchar
a comidinha das crianças?

poesia pois é
poesia

te detestam
lumpenproletária
voluptuária
vigária
elitista piranha do lixo

porque não tens mensagem
e teu conteúdo é tua forma
e porque és feita de palavras
e não sabes contar nenhuma estória

e por isso és poesia

and jakobson roman
(amor/roma)
octogenarian
morethansexappealgenarian
caresses with delight
your metaphors and metonymies
while you open in pleasure
the chrysoprasian of your
paronomasias

and he laughs at the austere
embarrassment of the savants

and even now even here
on this hill
joyful of partridges
twin samese brothers and a
pottery of pignatari clouds
(today signed signatari)
love you furiously
in the noigrandes garçonnière
they've been loving you
for more than thirty years
and the result is that
poetry
you already know
the mess in the mass
morass
and everyone wanting to
tricapitate
more than thirty years ago
those trigenial vocalists
   what an idea wanting to plant
ideograms in our garden
(with no orange-grove   oswald)?
and (mario) wiping up
the little meal of the children?

so poetry is
poetry

they detest you
lumpenproletarian
voluptuarian
vicarian
elitist scavenge-tip piranha

as you have no message
and your content is your form
and as you're made of words
and can't tell any stories

and therefore you are poetry

como cage dizia	as cage used to say
ou como	or as
há pouco	a while ago
augusto	the august
o augusto:	augusto:
que a flor flore	let the flower flower
o colibri colibrisa	the colibri colibreezes
e a poesia poesia	and poetry poesies

(de Campos, 1997, 94-98)   (© Translation Bernard McGuirk, 2020)

Poiesis will continue to highlight the differences and the often irreconcilable ideological discourses of both the material referenced and all would-be refereeing materialists; as *they* write and *it* is written, as it 'poesies' and, yes, poses... performs.

I must reiterate, in the context of any such as a Schwarz versus de Campos polemics, but two oppositions; the one, relatively distant, as we were reminded by Raymond Williams, 'from a Marxist: Brecht against Lukács and his Moscow colleagues in the 1930s':

> They are, to put it bluntly, enemies of production. Production makes them uncomfortable. You never know where you are with production; production is unforeseeable. You never know what is going to come out. And they themselves don't want to produce. They want to play the *apparatchik* and exercise control over other people. Every one of their criticisms contains a threat. (Williams, 1977, 199)

The other counter, again from Left to Left, is Terry Eagleton's half-a-century later, and near-contemporary rejection of Perry Anderson's 'seriously one-sided approach to his topic', his 'summary treatment of Derrida', in the latter's *In the Tracks of Historical Materialism*.

> Language, as Anderson interprets Derrida's view of it, is a 'system of floating signifiers pure and simple, with no determinable relation to any extra-linguistic referents at all' (Anderson, 1984, 6). This is indeed the ridiculous case touted by many of Derrida's less canny acolytes on both sides of the Atlantic [...] Derrida has insisted [...] that deconstruction is a political rather than textual operation – that it is by touching solid structures, 'material' institutions, and not merely discourses or significant representations, that deconstruction distinguishes itself from analysis or 'criticism' [...] Anderson's polemic quite fails to distinguish between 'left' and 'right'

92

deconstruction – between those for whom the theory merely offers an opportunity for hermetic textualism and self-indulgent word-play, and those who have discerned in it [...] political possibilities. (Eagleton 1985, 5)

For Lukács, for Anderson, read Schwarz... and travellers since.

The coincidence of critico-ideological invectives operating, at play, between Eagleton's polemics and de Campos's poetics is as striking as it is characteristic of two notoriously ironizing *provocateurs*. The one has engaged, Wildely, with *Saint Oscar*;4 the other has disengaged, luke(ash)warmly, from Saint Gyorgy. Whether in his explicit ode's staunch debunking of *identifying* (with) and *deifying* an icon of the Left, or in his unapologetic rejection of 'unacceptable cognitive models' such as 'the supercilious alternative given by *over*altern First-World critic Fredric Jameson to *sub*altern writers of the underdeveloped peripheric World, [when referring to] João Guimarães Rosa's *Grande Sertão: Veredas*, as that curious Brazilian *high literary* variant of the western', the challenge is consistent:

> What I definitely cannot accept is the act of imposing a 'normative paradigm' upon Third-World writers and their literatures, as a 'cognitive model' apt to rescue them from the dangers of super-developed cultural Post-Modernism [...] [T]he

---

4 See Terry Eagleton's 'Foreword' to his play *Saint Oscar*: 'I first thought of writing about Oscar Wilde when I discovered that hardly any of the Oxford students who asked to study him with me realized that he was Irish [...] English students of literature would know of course that Yeats and Joyce were Irish, and probably – thinking of those tasty babies of *A Modest Proposal* – Jonathan Swift [...] British cultural imperialism has long annexed these gifted offshore islanders to its own literary canon [...] [H]ow astonishingly Wilde's work prefigures the insights of contemporary cultural theory [...] Language as self-referential, truth as a convenient fiction, the human subject as contradictory and 'deconstructed', criticism as a form of 'creative' writing, the body and its pleasures pitted against a pharisaical ideology: in these and several other ways, Oscar Wilde looms up for us [...] as the Irish Roland Barthes [...] [as] socialist proto-deconstructionist [...] The colonial subject, pitched into a permanent crisis of identity, will not be over-impressed by the solid, well-rounded characters of classical literary realism, but will feel itself fluid, diffuse, provisional; and the same sense of provisionality will apply to social forms and conventions, breeding an ironic awareness of their fictive, ungrounded nature [...] Wilde hailed from the city Joyce spelt as "Doublin"' (Eagleton, 1989, vii-xii).

93

author of *The Political Unconscious* ignores the Brazilian Portuguese language and has built a fake, oversimplified image of the complex Faustian, metaphysical struggle between God and the Devil embedded in the deep structure of Rosa's masterpiece [...] By suppressing most of the fascinating invention of language and by watering-down the corresponding semantic density, the main distinctive features of Rosa's prose, that version converts *Grande sertão* into a trivial 'banana Western'. The Anglophone master-discourse of the *over*-altern 'salvationist' critic works as a rhetorical by-product of unconscious Imperialism, by effacing the *sub*-altern 'minor' languages and by underrating their creative verbal power. 'Outmoded realism' – I would like to outline it – is not a fit standard for [...] Guimarães Rosa, with his multifaceted *Grande sertão* and his gift for word-playing, [and who] has been compared to Joyce, [...] being utterly distinct from [...] 'First World' counterparts, since [...] profoundly anchored in [his] own literary and linguistic tradition, and persistent in [his] singular way of decrying (or rather defrauding) the universal code, by deviating from its resulting European products. (de Campos, 2009, 244-45)

With S(i)ame(se) brother Augusto,[5] Haroldo (Browne) – as shall we – hears in Guimarães Rosa, indissociably, echoes of that 'hermetic textualism and self-indulgent word-play, and in it [the] discerned political possibilities' dispensed in his own explicit 'defesa da poesia'. As he writes, and as he re-reads Joyce anti-teleologically, *à l'oreille de l'autre celte* (for Bernard's no saint either), *la fin* (laughin'?), again, is awake. The selfsiam ears re-listen non-aetiologically to Stéphane. Forever joined (at the waste?), 'l'alphabet des astres'-cum-'l'alphabet désastres' implodes, inseparably constellettered, transcendental and fragmentary. Yet, still and forever, ostensibly, (out) there. Big bang cock-up...? Or Brazilian *bofetada*, slapping (down) a bare-faced (apparat)cheek.

The avenging angel of *poeisis* did wait; translation, be it for Betto or versed, sometimes prosed, for Haroldo, did follow. Translation – modest proposal – has also performed; as interventionist literary criticism, always, putatively, *à l'oreille de l'autre* self... self in the other, the other in the self-same word.

---

5 See Augusto de Campos, 'Haroldo S(i)ame(se) brother', in McGuirk and Vieira, 2009, 301-03.

Post(trans)scriptum

From beyond the grave, Haroldo de Campos objects to whomsoever transjects. When last I sat with him, in August 2002, Carmen, his wife, taking advantage of a momentary pause in his inexhaustible conversational energy, called me to look at the destruction of one of his most precious books, by worms. Within seconds, he was bidding me to transfer ('transverme'?) my attention to: 'poema qohelético 2: elogio da térmita'. Our last correspondence, characteristically, tugs the other's trans-story hither and thither. Were our worm(s) to be singular or plural? Does one chew more silently than one munches? And do (English) weevils justify the onomatopoeic supplement of 'sheer'? *D'outre tombe*, the memory strikes back, refusing closure, refuting completion, repugning the perfection appropriated by that monological translator *par excellence*, that intolerable mono-theos projected into a singular transparency by a Greco-Roman empire of the (non-)senses, that total metaphysics of presence, God. Devilishly, Haroldo's pride (re-)transluciferates: (my) Creation is insufficient; to cast our nets – *por co-troiar* – as fishers of *meaning*, prompts contestation; implies a (further) Fall. *Lucifero gratias.* And what of (mis)[mass]translation? Post-transcreation, intra-transluciferation, it has (not sufficed) been sacrificed. Ite, [...] est.

95

poema qohelético 2 : elogio da térmita

os cupins se apoderaram da biblioteca
ouço o seu áfono rumor
o canto zero das térmitas
os homens desertaram a biblioteca
palavras transformadas em papel
os cupins ocupam o lugar dos homens
gulosos de papel   peritos em celulose
o orgulho dos homens se abate   madeira roída

tudo é vão

a lepra dos cupins corrói o papel   os livros
o gorgulho mina o orgulho
assim ficaremos   cadáveres verminosos

escrevo este elogio da térmita

*Ao Bernard,
caro e admirado amigo
e "expert" em ludus
linguístico,
com o abraço do
S Paulo
21.08.2003*

38

96

FROM: HAROLDO DE CAMPOS   FAX (55+11) 3862 1954
TO: Prof Bernard McGuirk   FAX (00-115)
The University of Nottingham   951 5894 or 5999
Faculty of Arts / Dept of Spanic and
Latin American Studies.

in praise of termites

1 woodworm owns the bookshelves now
i hear its noiseless hum
termite canto zero
men have quit the library
words transformed to paper
woodworm takes the place of man
for paper greedy   in cellulose well-versed
men's pride droops   gnawed wood

all is void

2 leper woodworm munches paper   books
3 weevils worm their way through pride   — sheer
so shall we abide   a vermin-ridden corpse

of termites do I pen this praise

Handwritten annotations (right margin):

Dúvidas

1 — "woodworm" ou "woodworms" ? (sing.) (plur)

chew(s)

2 — munches : "chew noisily" (não concorda com a linha 2 "noiseless hum")

3 — through sheer pride (TALVEZ fique melhor c/ sheer)

weevils

(c) translation by Bernard McGuirk of "elogio da térmita" by Haroldo de Campos

Dear Haroldo
   My first nibble at your text...

   Yours ever

      Bernard

Meu caro Bernard: Excellent! My compliments!
Acima, algumas poucas observações / sugestões.
      Best regards! Um abraço, grato, de
         SPaulo,   Haroldo
            19/09/2000

97

Susan Sontag's at-the-core 1960s' plea for an erotics in preference to a hermeneutics of reading informs, still, too few and too little of classroom experiences; albeit arising from reluctance on a so-called 'teaching' side or on that of its imagined 'learning' other. A thread of letting the text speak and be spoken to has informed not a practice but practices plural, ever changing, and in multilogues with, culturally and, urgently, shifting preoccupations, nay, demands on both sides of some imagined (hardly communitarian) lectern. An opening gambit has for years been to state nothing; to cast a die (live, please...) in reading together a t/sexuality. Come-on:

> el struss
> uno de los grandes males
> que afectan a la womanidad
> antes se llamaba stress
> y antes strass
> o Strauss
> es como un vals trastabillado
> por la mujer sin sombra
> no hay drama
> está borracha
> borracha la puerca
>
> el struss (39)

[struss/one of the great evils/affecting womanity/before it was called stress/ and before strass/or Strauss/it's like a tripping waltz/for the woman without shadow/there's no drama/she's drunk/drunk the sow/struss]

The replacement of analysis, textual and psycho-therapeutic, is one of the devices constantly exploited by Susana Thénon. In her poetry, song and dance figure and, usually, disfigure, triggering a series of dislocations of fixed or fixable meaning, of meta-textual presence, of the power of any interdictory original law-giver; the path to Strauss is paved with good inventions, a stressful, strassful, strussful trajectory. Untranslatable... that's what you are, untranslatable... from near or far; it's incredible that someone so untranslatable as you thinks that I'm untranslatable, too. But, might the cultivated bi-lingual humour throw up (on) 'grandes males' as overbearing males? Overdue, coming out, breaking free, from the intra-colony of machismo, and defying translatability, a mordant alternative libidinal economy rises up to challenge domineering male and indeed female canonicities. Therein and thereby an erotics of writing unsettles the readings of would-be hermeneuts. Might poems of such as Thénon and Perlongher be re-heard as voicings repressed, crying in that in-between wilderness of cyclical dictatorship never abashed to speak its – and only its – name?

98

V. IN AND OUT OF THE CLASS *ET ALII; ET ALIBI...*
Disrupting masculist metaphysics:
Susana Thénon and Néstor Perlongher

Quis custodiet ipsos custodies?

Who and where are the others? Who would consign them, under guard, to an elsewhere? May their voices still be heard? Might they be included again, resounding, post-exclusion? Eventually, the question: Who is watching the watcher, the agent of removal of the ostracized, of those summarily dispatched, often amputated, indeed, from a body politic appropriated by perpetrators little concerned to go through even the motions of custodial sentencing?

The 'powers that be' have ever been; they operate as constructed, governing, yes, yet in and with that always to be deconstructed framing discourse of governmentality that, sooner or later, renders them 'were'. For regime change will also ever operate, will be the however deferred agenda; *malgré* the Ozymandias 'King of King' clones and echoes of a thousand and one authorities and authoritarians and their 'Look on my works ye Mighty and despair'. Opposing 'works', of might-less voices raised in the contesting, the refuting, of historic presumptions, will also have been written, their texts produced, under pressure, in exile, whether extra-, or intra- ; for isolation, marginalization, banishment – repressions and repressors all – would erect excluding frontiers as barriers of convenience; 'safe', from within, for custodians alone.

Demagogues recent as demi-gods of yore: in an Argentina of 26 August 1982, for Borges, 'próceres de bronce [...] en un tiempo que no podemos entender' ['forebears in bronze [...] in a time we cannot understand']; *d'àpres* Shelley, a statue in monumental stone, of which 'nothing beside remains' but 'two vast and trunkless legs', to be re-discovered only under the sands of time.[6] The written text, *sin pedestal*, might yet serve – despair not – as levelling inscription to be 'stamped on these lifeless things', boding ill for the 'shattered visage' of 'frown, And wrinkled lip, and sneer of cold command' of fallen dictators ever before, contemptibly during and even after *los juicios* of their eventual criminal trials. The *déjà et toujours écrit* will have augured well for the irrefutable pre-judgement verdicts proffered by corrosive protest poetry that, as we shall now see, will have anticipated their downfall. Their

---

[6] Borges, Jorge Luis. 'Juan López y John Ward', *Clarín*, 26 August 1982; Borges, Jorge Luis. 'Juan López and John Ward', *The Times*, 18 September 1982; Shelley, Percy Bysshe. 'Ozymandias', London, *The Examiner*, 11 January 1818.

names...? If you struggled over Ozymandias, imagine who will recall by buried nomenclature the uniform, regime-dated, Juan Carlos Onganía (1966-70), Marcelo Levingston (1970-71), Alejandro Lanusse (1971-77), Jorge Videla (1976-81), Roberto Viola (1981), Leopoldo Galtieri (1981-82), Reynaldo Bignone (1982-83) or their troupe of clones without number; when the common pit of epitaph will, faded, have read, *de iure*, 'State terrorist'?

©Horatius

In September 1982, *Humor* (89, 19) published a cartoon by Horatius. It depicts, inseparably, a Defeat and Victory Parade; in a single frame, and at a glance. Or in a gaze. Seven pale blue and white sash-draped and medal-heavy high-ranking military officers file past a placard that reads: 'Gran Desfile Presidentes De Facto' ['Grand Procession (of) De Facto Presidents']. Facially, they are all too recognizable as leaders of the various *juntas* who had carried out the (far from *de iure*) 'functions' of Head of State. As they march, from the Right, in high goose-step but in low dudgeon, the attendant populace that throngs the road-sides directs its collective gaze from left to right, no doubt in expectation of more uniformed authoritarians to follow their likes. But the last of the top brass, Bignone, already out of kilter in wearing carpet slippers rather than be-spurred jackboots, uses his arms and hands in another proleptic unfolding of regimented discipline. He points to his feet with the left hand while raising the right to cup his mouth in a gesture of obsequious farewell: 'iEpa! ¿Qué están mirando? Yo soy el último' ['Hey! What are you looking at? Me, I'm the last']. A glance at his headwear reveals that the peak of his cap bears only the fading resemblance to the penguin-figure that, in varying degrees of prominence, sits atop the 'frowning' expressions of each of his predecessors.

As in many an embryonic undoing of despotic power, it is the once authority-bearing figure in the cartoon that triggers the awareness of – and for – a different gaze. Beatriz Sarlo, was to take up the challenge implied, for both the people as a whole and for a new generation of thinkers who would have to see differently, but never with indifference:

> They were disposed to theorize the need for organizations of iron, panopticons from the control tower of which all could be seen and things be decided upon. There were intellectual leaders who were suspicious of intellectuals in general because they were showing themselves to be prepared to abandon specific perspectives according to the historic task that knowledge, and the power of knowledge, had placed in their hands. They believed then that social change is something that very few can direct and to which, through argumentation, education and force, the ones being directed must yield themselves up. (Sarlo, 1994, 174)

The caricatural will draw habitually on the stereotype of recognizability but will be the more effective, as an agent of potential change, when it details what is different. Similarity draws attention; difference calls to attention.

The process – *el proceso de reorganización nacional* – of repression and, specifically, the unyielding power of resistance in literature to any such circumlocutory nostrum prompts me to return to case studies opened and more extensively pursued elsewhere. The two instances, to differing degrees, addressed the literatures of war, the discourses of conflict and post-conflict, and what I referred to as 'word games [that] disrupt masculist metaphysics, narrow erotics and linear temporality, not least in the title of the collection *Ova completa*' (McGuirk, 1997, 229; 2018, 238). I choose to revisit, with particular insistence, poems of Susana Thénon and Néstor Perlongher, juxtaposed here for the first time, and with a view to casting them into dialogue, or into trialogues with any others, or an @ther... The one will be voiced from an inside out, the other from an outside in; abolishing such difference but re-asserting, in the act, *différance*.

Thénon's reaction, to both the particular Malvinas moment and its aftermath of the early 'eighties and the general *proceso* effects of Argentina's Dirty War from the mid-'seventies, inscribes conflict into the very fabric of her text. Her poetics is a confrontation with a politics of the now: it demands that an ear be alert, also, to periods and rhythms past, or very recent, in order to pursue, find, reveal and accuse the guilty. Such poetry, certainly confronting what Paul Fussell, in his *Killing in Verse and Prose* (1990), termed 'actual and terrible moral challenges', as cited by Simon Featherstone in his own reminder of the urgent 'closeness of writing to often appalling personal experience' (1995, 1-2), indulges voicings that will be not final but phonal: loud; screaming out for justice; baying against impunity:

> PUNTO FONAL
> (TANGO CON VECTOR CRÍTICO)
>
> 'la picana en el ropero
> todavía está colgada
> nadie en ella amputa nada
> ni hace sus voltios vibrar'
>
> ¡ESO ES DECLAMACIÓN!
> (Thénon, 1987, 47)
>
> [PHONAL POINT (TANGO WITH CRITICAL SLANT)/'the prod in the wardrobe/is still hanging there/no one amputates anything on it/or makes its volts vibrate'/THAT IS DECLAMATION!]

President Raúl Alfonsín's later notorious first law, a guillotine to prevent military personnel 'acting under orders' from having to face due legal processes, was designated, on 23 February 1987, *Punto Final*. Amen? Full Stop? Are the instruments of torture, and the memories of torturers, to be hidden away, in the Argentine psyche, as easily as the sadly dormant guitar of the popular tango, 'Mi Noche Triste'?[7]

la guitarra en el ropero	the guitar in the wardrobe
todavía está colgada	is still hanging there
nadie en ella canta nada	no one sings anything on it
ni hace sus cuerdas vibrar	or makes its strings vibrate

[7] From Pascual Contursi's 'Mi Noche Triste' of 1915. Carlos Gardel first sang it in 1917.

The play 'final'/'fonal' occurs at the intersection of politics and of art, and of the direct ideological and intertextual echo of tango with an unquestioningly conservative and unquestioning society, all-too-readily sucked back into a sentimental but violent solitude of yesteryear and the story of its sad night of the soul.

Thénon's poetry foregrounds a heightened awareness of the dangers inherent in any writing, or any reading, too dependent on the ludics of language. *Ova completa* plays with the impossibility of plenitude in the very moment that it echoes *Obra completa/Complete works*. The feminist eggs of *Ova* are broken, of necessity, in order to make yet another *hommelette* of self-contained and satisfied man.[8] She is ever prepared to subvert her own practice in order to achieve an effect that is politically the more subversive.[9]

Gabriela Nouzeilles and Graciela Montaldo, in a chapter on 'State Violence', in *The Argentina Reader: History, Culture, Politics*, look back judiciously, and with no reduced incredulity, twenty years after the Malvinas conflict, at the climate against which Thénon's poetry had railed:

> The persecution of political dissidents – which began at least two years before the coup – was institutionalized and expanded to create a systematic killing machine. Scholars have found no easy explanation for the degree of cruelty and indifference to human life shown by the military and its supporters [...] During the eight years of the dictatorship, thousands of people mysteriously 'disappeared' at the hands of death squads, which, acting with total impunity, kidnapped union leaders, writers, journalists, students, and political activists. Cultural life was meticulously screened by a censorship committee, and all universities and unions came under government control. Efforts to maintain a repressive security state were complicated by an economic model that generated unemployment, corruption, and inflation [...] The art and literature produced under the dictatorship bear the scars of political brutality. Although some artists openly denounced state violence, others cloaked their opposition in hidden messages of muffled despair

---

[8] 'Exposing what is mortal and unsure/To all that fortune, death and danger dare/Even for an egg-shell', *pace* Hamlet.

[9] Cf: 'Women writers are similarly excluded from a canon predicated upon 'major writers' whose moral and literary development is dependent upon the pressure of war experience on literary sensibility' (Featherstone, 1993, 20).

[...] In 1982, after six devastating years of dictatorship, the poet Néstor Perlongher catalogued in 'Corpses' what remained of a society that had become utterly suffused with death. Just as art provided the tools for protest, it also created a locus of resistance. (Nouzeilles and Montaldo, 2002, 395-96)

William Rowe's meticulous rendering into English of Perlongher's harrowing long poem 'Cadáveres', written in 1981, during a journey from Buenos Aires to São Paulo, is reproduced in full in *The Argentina Reader* (457). Rowe's own tellingly chosen fragment and his brief commentary on it will suffice to echo the point made in respect of Thénon's inseparable subversions of content and form in the delivery of political effect:

En eso que empuja	In the thing that pushes
lo que se atraganta,	that sticks in the throat,
En eso que traga	In what swallows
lo que emputarra.	what prostitutes.
En eso que amputa	In what amputates
lo que empala.	what impales.
En eso que iputa!	In what whores
Hay cadáveres.	There are corpses.

Perlongher's (1949-92) major poem, 'Cadáveres' [Corpses], explores the interstices of the language, its smallest everyday gestures, as the place where the corpses – the disappeared – of recent Argentinian history can be located [...] The poem enters areas of the language where there is no clear meaning, where nothing is being expressed, but where there is complicity with the violent facts; for that purpose, Perlongher recombines sounds, tones and the different historical and social layers of Argentine Spanish, always moving towards the outside of the uttered, to the web of unacknowledged social violences that infiltrate it. He preferred the term 'neobarroso' (neomuddy) to neobarroco, since it was closer to the actual muddy waters of the River Plate. (Rowe, in King, 2004, 165)

When it comes to changing the frame, indeed to declamation, few have confronted that other notorious instrument of torture, homophobia, with the polemical poetic power of Perlongher. His is an overtly critical slant on the repressive consequences of a homophobic Argentina for the psyche both of individual victims or scapegoats and of the nation. Expressed in three short essays, it can be summarized thus:[10]

> El solo hecho de que guapos adolescentes, en la flor de edad, sean sacrificados [...] en nombre de unos insalubres islotes, es una razón de sobra para denunciar este triste sainete. (Perlongher, 1997, 179)

> [The mere fact that handsome adolescents, in the flower of their youth, may be sacrificed [...] in the name of certain insalubrious islands is reason enough to denounce this sad farce.]

The profound critiques of the manner in which the nation had sought to constitute, project and protect itself within 'safe' borders are addressed by Benjamin Bollig, who encapsulates the attack that Perlongher carries to the repressive demarcators of the national territory as follows:

> Perlongher can be seen [...] in the early 1980s proposing an alternative approach to territory – soldiers as lovers, mobile communities based on desire, porous borders – not only to the *proceso* dictatorship but also the left-wing opposition to the dictatorship. [His] writing focuses on desire and the social. [He] uses the concept of nationality to discuss communities united by specific interests, in this case desire, and the social organisations that challenge or oppose them. Furthermore, he uses the concept of territory to present and discuss the places or sites where such a community, perhaps only briefly or as a possibility, may find its very marginalised space. These sites, once acknowledged or recognised in Perlongher's poems, can question the rules for the construction of the nation-state that

---

[10] 'Todo el poder a Lady Di: Militarismo y anticolonialismo en la cuestión de las Malvinas' (1982); 'La ilusión de unas islas' (1983); and 'El deseo de unas islas' (1985). ['All power to Lady Di: Militarism and Anticolonialism in the Malvinas Question' (1982); 'The Illusion of Certain Islands' (1983); and 'The Desire for Certain Islands' (1985)].

combat the development of new forms of political communities. (Bollig, 2008, 57)[11]

In an emblematic poem 'Las tías'/'Aunts' (1985), Perlongher takes up a stance and a point of view that differs from a looking in and looking at the homo-erotics and the homophobia of Argentine society; he looks both back and from within a discourse. This framing of conflict occurs at the frontiers of war and sexuality:

Las tías

y esa mitología de tías solteronas que intercambian los peines grasientos del sobrino en la guerra en la frontera tías que peinan tías que sin objeto ni destino babas como lamé laxas se oxidan y así 'flotan' flotan así, como esos peines que las tías de los muchachos en las guerras limpian desengrasan, depilan sin objeto en los escapularios ese pubis enrollado de un niño que murió en la frontera, con el quepis torcido; y en las fotos las muecas de los niños en el pozo de la frontera entre las balas de la guerra y la mustia mirada de las tías en los peines engrasados y tiesos así las babas que las tías desovan sobre el peine del muchacho que parte hacia la guerra y retoca su jopo y ellas piensan que ese peine engrasado por los pelos del pubis de ese muchacho muerto por las balas de un amor fronterizo guarda incluso los pelos de las manos del muchacho que muerto en la frontera de esa guerra amorosa se tocaba ese jopo; y que los pelos, sucios, de ese muchacho, como un pubis caracoleante en los escapularios, recogidos del baño por la rauda partera, cogidos del bidet, en el momento en que ellos, solitarios, que recuerdan sus tías que murieron en los campos cruzados de la guerra, se retocan los jopos; y las tías que mueren con el peine

---

[11] Bollig adds, in his seminal analysis of the writings of Perlongher: 'In 1981, after the publication of *Austria-Hungría* and another of Perlongher's many arrests, this time accompanied by a beating from the Mendoza police, Perlongher went into exile in São Paulo [...] I use the term "exile" with caution. Perlongher's exit from Argentina was entirely voluntary; he returned on several occasions even before the fall of the military. However, Perlongher's life in Argentina, both as a gay man and as a socialist, had been made impossible and untenable by the activities of the police and military in the country [...] The criticism that Perlongher received for his critique of Argentine intellectuals from exile is recounted by Patiño (2003)' (Bollig, 2008, 58).

del muchacho que fue muerto en las garras del vicio fronterizo
entre los dientes muerden degustan desdentadas la gomina de
los pelos del peine de los chicos que parten a la muerte en la
frontera, el vello despeinado (Perlongher, 1997, 82)

Aunts

and that mythology of maiden aunts who interchange the
grease-laden combs of the nephew in the war at the frontier
aunts who comb aunts who without object or destiny dribbles
lax like lamé grow rusty and thus 'float' float thus, like those
combs that the aunts of the boys in the wars clean take the
grease out of, pluck without object on the scapularies that
coiled pubis of a boy that died at the frontier, with his kepi
askew; and in the photos the grimaces of the boys in the pit of
the frontier between the bullets of the war and the musty gaze
of the aunts on the greased and stiff combs thus the dribbles
that the aunts lay like eggs on the comb of the boy who heads
off for the war and again touches his forelock and they think
that that comb greased by the pubic hairs of that boy killed by
the bullets of a border love even holds the hairs from the hands
of the boy who dead at the frontier of that loving war touched
that forelock; and that the hairs, dirty, of that boy, like a pubis
curling on the scapularies, gathered from the bath by the
rushing midwife, taken from the bidet, in the very moment that
they, solitary, that their aunts remember that they died in the
fields crossed by the war, adjust their forelocks; and the aunts
who die with the comb of the boy who was killed in the claws of
the border vice between the teeth bite taste toothless the lotion
of the hairs of the comb of the boys who set off for death at the
border, fuzz unkempt. (Translation © Bernard McGuirk, 2007)

The opening words, rendered without an initial capital, suggest a
continuum, an intervention into an already existing mythology,
rendered pejorative by the dismissive demonstrative 'ese'/'that' but
echoing, putatively, the 'mitologías' of the most internationally known
precursor text touching upon the 'islas demasiado famosas' [islands too
famous] of the 1982 South Atlantic conflict, untitled but commonly
referred to as 'el poema de los dos Juanes' [the poem of the two Johns].
Whereas Jorge Luis Borges had flirted with going transcendental,
Perlongher at once goes down; in register, linguistic and social, and in
getting quickly to the point.

Like any other mythology, the particular repository of 'Las tías' is there to be exposed, to be penetrated, to have the elements of its social construction identified, isolated, analyzed.[12] And the vehicle of this prose poem in such a process is an unusual confrontation of the elegiac and the abject. The form and the rhythms of a funeral dirge combine with a shuttle treatment of doubled abjection wherein the frontier is both the site of death of young men in war and the locus of lingering attachment to vivid memory of older homosexuals left behind in another border zone.

Perlongher's lyricizing of the 'place of aporia [...] at the border [...] the threshold line, or the approach of the other as such' brings his writing into communion with Derrida's seminal meditations on mourning. For 'Las tías' says, too, that 'there is no singular memory'; that 'Ego=ghost'; that '"I am" would mean that "I am haunted"'; that 'wherever there is Ego, *es spukt*, "it spooks"' (Derrida, 1994, 133). The spectres of war of the poem are the *revenants* of an in-betweeness that dare not speak its name amidst the trumpeted grand narrative of intensively male-processed nationalism. The text whispers its ambivalences in numerous word-plays that an Argentine reader might miss if not attuned to the jargon of a proscribed and perforce closeted world of 'floating' shadows; of *tías* 'without object or destiny'. Deprived of any straight-line logophony of their own, in a society of predominantly monological attachment to a project of war, the 'aunts' seek to avoid the literal labelling of their *ego* through repeated if futile attempts to return to where *id* was. If there is abjection in the act of return, it is characterized not by self-pity but by a transference onto objects spooked and spooking: grease-laden combs, a scapulary, and curled pubic hair, the war photographs that capture the image and the grimace of boys dying at a frontier of the battle but also in the pit of an *entre-lugar*, a no-man's land, of 'balas' or bullets and the 'mustia mirada' or 'faded gaze' that fixes on the twisted cap of the legendarily depicted 'sleeper in the valley' or 'mummy's little boy' inherited through the genre of war poetry. Echoes of Rimbaud and Pessoa perhaps, but with a difference; for 'dormeur' and 'menino' read 'sobrino', the loaded circumlocution of 'nephew' used by the older man when introducing the

---

[12] Cf. 'Paul Fussell argues forcefully for war poetry to be read as a richly mythologizing and fantasy-driven culture of sexuality, pastoral landscapes, superstition and rhetorical invention [a] movement [...] towards myth, towards a revival of the cultic, the mystical, the sacrificial, the prophetic, the sacramental, and the universally significant. In short, towards fiction' (Featherstone, 1995, 21).

young soldier-companion in, but not to, a society prepared to pitch boys into trenches if into no other, risky, conflictual, or unsettling position. Especially not the 'amor fronterizo' which, when the poem ends, will have been so strongly re-classified as the 'vicio fronterizo' as to bring down, too, the *tías* who clutch but the combs of the dead boys. 'Frontier' has operated as a transferred epithet in a dual conflict; the Malvinas moment and the claws of an unrelenting anguish, the private struggle of the 'campos cruzados' – 'crossed' but also cross-over 'fields' of battle, zones of lost contact.

A deadly game of solitaire is played out on multiple fronts. Indignities of trench or of bidet are transformed into an unsentimental but affectionate intimacy of a fate shared. Again, Perlongher's is a rare case of poetry into which conflict has entered in the very construction, rather than the mere representation, of war. Internal transformations, such as 'un amor fronterizo guarda incluso los pelos de las manos del muchacho' ['a border love even holds the hairs from the hands of the boy'], allow memory to re-trigger and perform arousal – always respectfully, tenderly, as 'en la frontera de esa guerra amorosa se tocaba ese jopo' ['at the frontier of that loving war touched that forelock']. Turning on the play of meaning on the word *jopo*, the forelock, or quiff, or bang, of the hair of the young man's head, in common parlance, another memory is roused. For, as in the slang of a Teddy-boy cum Elvis-era equivalent of the D.A., the duck's-arse hairdo, the term evokes, too, the naked buttocks of the young lover lost. Twice iterated, *jopo* might re-echo – to ears open to pick up the call – the *argot* expressions 'alborotar o explotar el jopo' which plays on and with the multiple connotations of the verbs to excite or to work, to exploit or to explode. Exploding genres, exploding gender roles... The play on 'pe[i]ne' and 'balas' requires no such elucidation; for, or by, circumspect critics literary or/and cultural. So come on, coxcombs. You make the balls, I'll fire them.

The shifting point of view, the gaze and the recollection of both the *tías* and the *sobrino*, interchanged, and intermingled, operate in a pro-lepsis-analepsis relation of intensifying effect. The 'vello', the soft hair, the down, of youth, and of affective memory, remains 'despeinado', uncombed, at the poem's end. The force of such a radical intervention finds no Borges-echoing 'arbitrary division' in the multivalent conflict. All is left unkempt, dishevelled, loose, undone... and, still, forever, in contrast with the panopticon order of things, seductive. Rising to whatever challenge, left over or behind, the poetry of 'Las tías' may be viewed as an equivalent to Susana Thénon's intellectual but no less visceral play; as Néstor Perlongher's *desova incompleta*.

If Thénon's poetry performs counter to the restoration of any one, originary, Edenic place via a temporal trajectory which stresses disjunction rather than the conjunctions of a 'historically' linear time, hers is a poetics, too, which revels in the fragmentation of Babel. In language, otherness and dispersion, far from producing nostalgia or anguish, are exploited and celebrated; even, if but occasionally, by receptive critics, too. Linda R. Boone has written engagingly of a direct parody of a Neruda love-poem, 'Barcarola', namely, Arsenio Cué's 'Si tú te llamaras Babel y no Beba Martínez', in Cabrera Infante's *Tres Tristes Tigres*: 'In order to satisfy Arsenio's requirements for the perfect woman, Beba must become precisely what she is not: Babel, fluent in witty language of literary wordplay'. Unlike that of Thénon's poetry, however, Arsenio's language 'is identified as an anti-language [...] aimed not toward communication but sheer playfulness' (Boone, 1990, 33-35). In Cabrera Infante's ingenious *mise en abyme*, the construction of an idealized transformation of Beba into Babel, yet another projection of male readership, is suggestively *culbuté* by being inserted in the (Anglo-Portuguese) b*anal*ity of *Arsenio Cué*'s name. Thénon's play, too, is both on and with, is both pun and fun, pleasurable steps within the choreography of difference:

AND SO ARE YOU

hay sacarina
la bandada de albatros
o yo qué sé
digo de albatros
dólares
*de albatros*dólares
nunca vi un pájaro pishar eso no quiere decir nada
los canadienses pishan aunque vos no los veas
y los peces
los peces pishan mar
vos sos poeta ¿no?
o Sappho made in Shitland
poetisa
¿no ves que es mujer?
vamos mujer
si no puedes tú con Dios hablar
¿para qué preguntarle si yo alguna vez?
te lo digo personalmente
en efecto
alguna que otra vez te he dejado de adorar

pero el inglés es más práctico
te ingeniás en todas partes
verbigracia en las pudendas
do it   don't
y aunque pronuncies mal
igual te entienden
do it don't
o te expresás por señas
vieras cómo te arreglás
cómo aprendés a *do it*
cómo *don't* te acostumbrás
cómo hacés *do* lo que querés
it cómo
don't

                    (13-14)

[there is saccharine/*the flock of albatross/or what do I know/I say of albatross*/dollars/of *albatross*dollars/*I never saw a bird pish that means nothing/Canadians pish although you don't see them/and fish/fish pish sea*/you're a poet, aren't you?/*Or Sappho made in Shitland*/poetess/can't you see she's a woman?/*let's go woman/if you can't speak with God/why ask him if I sometimes?/I'm telling you personally/in fact/some time or another I have stopped loving you*/but English is more practical/you show ingenuity everywhere/*for instance in the pudenda/do it don't*/and although you pronounce badly/they probably understand you/*do it don't*/or you express yourself by signs/you should see how you get by/how you learn to *do it*/how *don't* you get the habit/how you make *do* what you like/*it* how/*don't*]

Dialogics operate strongly in the title 'And So Are You', anticipating the question 'vos sos poeta ¿no?' The poet attempting self-definition depends heavily on the reader/interlocutor... and vice-versa. The saccharine-sweet legacy of the post-Baudelairian image of a *poète par définition* of 'L'Albatros' ('prince des nuées [...] exilé sur le sol'), is at once evoked and derided by Thénon's 'de albatros/o yo qué sé'. Intrusively, 'dólares' thrusts writing forward as profession rather than as confession; 'Le Confiteor de l'artiste', for Thénon, involves an economy of art, '*albatros*dólares', a rejection of *l'art pour l'art* purity, illustrated by the four-line bi-lingual play on 'pishar'. The grossness of tactic renders 'for the birds' too facile a definition of poet:

vos sos poeta ¿no?
o Sappho made in Shitland
poetisa
¿no ves que es mujer?

The interplay of 'pish' and 'shit' besmirches the ready-made label ineptly attached to the 'poetisa'-inheritor of Sappho. Poet-ess thus becomes the unacceptable term; rejected as forcefully as was the reified 'esa mujer' and, again, in a pastiche of popular art, subverting a famous *bolero*:

¡Ay! mujer, si tú puedes con Dios hablar
Pregúntale si yo alguna vez
Te he dejado de adorar.

[Oh! woman, if you can speak with God/Ask him if I ever/stopped adoring you]

The 'undoing' of the inherited bolero-perception of woman – a creature who needs to corroborate male declarations of love by reference to nonpareil masculine Authority, the Great-Man-in-the-Sky – says simply: 'Who needs all that? I'm telling you *"en efecto"*, here and now, watch this space, hear this voice. And while we're at it, I have on occasion stopped loving you!'. The sudden shift sideways, to the apparently lateral thought, in the categorizing and pervasively interdictory domineering English broached by the poem's title, of the *'do it don't'*, is subtly relevant. For woman as capricious creature of whim, of 'now I love you, now I don't', is not only portrayable in the saccharine poetry of the *bolero* line, where her yes/no is dressed up. Undressed, too, she may playfully change her mind – *'verbigracia en las pudendas'* (eloquent sextuality?); and across language-barriers, regardless of pronunciation, even by sign-language. The final lines of the poem are a bonanza of vertiginous word-play, of pun as fun: 'te arreglás' – 'get by'; 'have your period'; 'get made up'; and so on. All is a chaotic learning process of 'aprendés', 'acustumbrás', *'do'*, *'don't'*, *'it'*, 'como', 'lo que querés'... desire, what you will, or will not (have done to you) ... *'don't'*.

The heteroglossic and transcultural, as pseudo-intellectual commerce, are not by any means automatically liberating. One of the things 'done' to poets, even 'women' poets, is to be anthologized. This particular version of having a label hung round the neck is hilariously broached by Thénon:

LA ANTOLOGÍA

¿tú eres
la gran poietisa
Susana Etcétera?
mucho gusto
me llamo Petrona Smith-Jones
soy profesora adjunta
de la Universidad de Paughkeepsie
que queda un poquipsi al sur de Vancouver
y estoy en Argentina becada
por la Putifar Comissión
para hacer una antología
de escritoras en vías de desarrollo
desarrolladas y también menopáusicas
aunque es cosa sabida que sea como fuere
todas las que escribieron y escribirán en Argentina
ya pertenecen a la generación del 60
incluso las que están en guardería
e inclusísimamente las que están en geriátrico

pero lo que me importa profundamente
de tu poesía y alrededores
es esa profesión – aaah ¿cómo se dice? –
profusión de íconos e índices
¿tú qué opinas del ícono?
¿lo usan todas las mujeres
o es también cosa del machismo?

porque tú sabes que en realidad
lo que a mí me interesa
es no sólo que escriban
sino que sean feministas
y si es posible alcohólicas
y si es posible anoréxicas
y si es posible violadas
y si es posible lesbianas
y si es posible muy desdichadas

es una antología democrática
pero por favor no me traigas
ni sanas ni independientes

(69-70)

[you're/the great poetess/Susana Etcetera?/delighted/I'm Petrona Smith-Jones/I'm associate professor/at the University of Paughkeepsie/which is a teeny-bitsy south of Vancouver/and I'm in Argentina on a grant/of the Whorefar Commission/to compile an anthology/of women writers on the road to develop-ment/developed and also menopausal/although it's a known fact that come what may/all the women that wrote and will write in Argentina/already belong to the generation of the 'sixties/including those in the nursery/and even including those in old folk's homes/but what is deeply important to me/about your poetry and its surroundings/is that profession – oooh, how d'you say it?/profusion of icons and indices/what do you think of the icon?/do all women use it/or is it a macho thing too?/because you know that in reality/what interests me/is not only that they write/but that they are feminists/and if possible alcoholics/and if possible anorexic/and if possible raped/and if possible lesbians/and if possible very unhappy/it's a democractic anthology/but please don't bring me/any sane or independent women]

Again, the resistance to fixed identity refuses the tired process of 'naming' of the academic interview. What emerges instead is a Rabelaisian feast of perceptions and misperceptions; of cultural difference and condescension (working both ways); of institutions and subversions which, of a sudden, switches from Petrona Smith-Jones and her Putifar Comissión to that no less restrictive missionary band, the radical feminist ghetto-mongers. I take for granted that further commentary on this poem would be superfluous, save to point out the heightened awareness in Thénon's text of the dangerous power which any and all institutions design for 'íconos e índices', instruments which are humorously and healthily eroticized as fetish-gadgets of both men and women. The academic interview itself – when the two cultures involved are North and South – might be subjected to a 'dependency' reading of the lop-sided cultural encounter, the illusion of a multi-voicedness which, in fact, excludes dialogue. An uneven, politically correct 'exchange' (where 'Third World' is avoided in the phrase 'on the road to development') leads only to the new imperative, the 'please don't bring me' (polite) order of a new imperialism, the key note of which is a lack of place for the un-colonized. In short, 'la antología' is always a choice; but a choice which merely parades as 'democrática'. Politically, what system can tolerate persons both sane and independent? Completeness, or closed system, is anathema to the disruptive workings of *Ova completa*. Susana Thénon's anthology is entitled not *Obra completa/Complete Works* but *Ova completa/ Complete Ova/Eggs...* and will be, for some, no doubt, completely *ova...* the top. In her cracked-open *oeuf/re*, words are abused, in reversal of language-systems' traditional strategies of power. Thénon, the Classicist, the translator from ancient Greek; the Modernist, the translator of Rainer Maria Rilke; the multi-lingual, the post- whatever not you but *she* will, nonetheless attempts to break free of the -isms, the labelling constraints, to come out of the closet, of *a* language.

> Monolingualism is a curable disease.
> Edward Said

Poetemporality: *À la recherche d'un temps charmant...*

> Once upon a time there will be readers who won't care what imaginative writing is called and will read it for its passion, its force of intellect, and its formal originality.
> David Shields

> La littérature ne permet pas de marcher mais elle permet de respirer.
> Roland Barthes

No, not more French theorizing; *c'est à dire*, for the time being. 'Poetemporality' is a notion deployed by Adam Sharman, in 'Vallejo, Semicolonialism, and Poetemporality', when addressing, in his *Tradition and Modernity in Spanish American Literature*, William Rowe's 'first major attempt to apply the insights of Néstor García Canclini regarding the region's "multitemporal heterogeneity" to poetry' (Sharman, 2006, 86). His meditation, set alongside assertions from David Shields' *Reality Hunger a Manifesto* (2010), will be revisited as pertinent to the temporalities – and the incurably plural languages – at play, respectively, in the passionately imaginative writings of Thénon and Perlongher.

Sharman recalls Rowe's 'insistence on the different temporalities that intersect in Latin America [and] the belief that [Vallejo's] *po(i)esis* is as much socio-political as linguistic, that "la inteligencia poética" can have a bearing on "el imaginario social"' (56). Further, he emphasizes that:

> Rowe does not 'show' the articulations between the poem and the power structure. This is because there are none. There are only 'processes' that run through the two and that the poem itself reveals. By deploying the concept of the plane of immanence [...] Rowe bypasses the need to show the articulations, opening the way to have the text reveal unlimited 'obscure relationships'. (Sharman, 2006, 64)

In the next layer of his argument, he returns to that 'historiographical convention' which assumes 'an endpoint, called "independence", which supervenes' to the effect that 'colonialism as such was brought to an end'. Juxtaposed, is his reminder of an 'alternative perspective [whereby] decolonization never happened, or, as Jorge Klor de Alva puts it, "the postcolonial condition, strictly speaking, has yet to occur"' (88). Once we accept the ramifications of Sharman's take on the case in point – 'To what extent does the complex temporality of Vallejo's Peruvian poems belong to a non-Western culture or a post-colonial condition and to what extent is it a conventional property of modern poetry itself?' (99) – we might, and we shall, extrapolate. Although Sharman was dealing here with Rowe's work on Vallejo and his poetics, the insights on which I presume to draw include the observation that 'The poem is not about a Peruvian social time opposed to modernity, it is about the time of writing' (102). And further, the consequent implication that 'Rowe ignores the question of resignification, which plays such a key part in García Canclini's work' (102).

Resignification will be instrumental to our understanding of the mechanisms and effects of the performances of Thénon and Perlongher as they have been explored thus far; as re-significations in their different and differentiating 'time[s] of writing', in and out of an Argentina of as yet unfinished, unfinishable?, processes. As their inscribing of instance, circumstance, contingency, moment, chrono-topes indivisibly political and personal. (When was the latter not always the former, *malgré* authoritarian assumptions that *we* are the political, you are – within our limits, our borders – *you* are the person/s to be controlled, under surveillance; and, at our say so, removed?) As ever, one is the other.

How, under pressure, might interrupted self-expression find an outlet beyond suppressed demand, the cry, a scream? In what, if any, act of available re-signification? For Sharman: 'we miss the essential if we do not also understand that disruption comes as standard in the personal lyric. It is a generic, conventional feature of lyric discourse, of the time of modern poetry' (103-4). There where disruption was will re-disruption be – re-signifying – crying out for, re-inclusion, re-incorporation, into the body politic from which its separation – and the separation of its language – can be other than a violent dismemberment, or torture, or exile, which at once diminishes, subjects, the whole into abject fragmentation, a form which no prosthesis might restore other than through the pain and the memory of the missing limb, the phantom of an integrity lost... forever? *Do* cry for me...

Argentina... pleads 'Las tías'. While '*Or Sappho made in Shitland*' – for 'el inglés es más práctico' – chortles a '*do it   don't*' (and mind the gap!). From within an aporetic room on, but never of, one's own; from some space of the silenced voice of an abjected outcast, a mere 'poetess'?... No. Only for whomsoever heeds not the source of verbal grace (*poiesis?*) as conveyed by '*verbigracia en las pudendas*'. Where's the shame? where's the blindness? – '¿no ves que es mujer?'/'can't you see she's a woman?' Echoes not; inversion rather, of the feigned madness of a quondam sovereign male's dismissal of Ophelia: 'Do you think I meant country matters?' (*Hamlet*, Act III, Scene 2). Well, maybe I did... and do, don't you see?

Luce Irigaray re-opens the file – the gap – on Freud's 'tache aveugle d'un vieux rêve de symétrie', that 'blindspot of an old dream of symmetry' whereby the 'little female' is assimilated into a-version of 'little male' sexuality, thereby being 'explained away' in Oedipal 'truth' (Irigaray, 1974, 1). Petrona Smith-Jones – 'assimilated', and assimilating 'little female' – would re-close the anth(rop)ologizing gap of North-South divide when self-announced in that double-barreled 'name of the father'-and-mother of 'nursery' cum 'old folk's homes' – what a pair! – 'the University'. Grand, just grand. Père-Mère...?-?

Pa?... ugh! *ipse dixit*; Ma?... *ipsa* keeps it; 'in the family' parlour-parlance: in that *locos/locas* enunciation of unseparated patriarchal/matriarchal discourse of stasis cum stagnation. *Marcher* in such *littérature* might not be permitted; and – *hélas* Roland – *respirer* won't be easy. You'll think it strange when I try to explain, you won't believe me, or my song – as words and breath struggle to come out together, in apparent disorder... oh, yes, *word games*, the clichéd dismissive accusation of the anti-deconstruction cataloguers of cultural re-appropriation, mendacious assimilation, non-inclusion. When the poems of the sisters to be deemed admissible – funded by a no doubt socio-cultural studies-driven Putifar Comissión – are *not* to be 'about the time of writing' (*pace* Sharman) but, 'in reality', unmediated expressions of their writers: 'feminists, alcoholics, if possible anorexics, if possible raped, if possible lesbians, and if possible very unhappy'; such a 'democratic anthology' can only, as ever and here again, make 'sane or independent women'... gag.

ah sí
fácil
word games
tampón de voces tales
mimpide
tra
gar

más fácil que no hacer
o hacer nada
como el tío de dios

como el tío de dios
que no hizo nada

volar delalf abeto

me ahogo

(75)

[oh yes/easy/*word games*/tampon of such voices/stopsme/
swall/owing/easier than not doing/or doing nothing/like God's
guy/like God's guy/who didn't do anything/to fly/from thealph
abet/I smother]

There will always be a *post-*... even after round 15; some supposedly
final bell, knockout or not.

The spontaneous, arguably facile, way word-games stifle the
personal voice which, even in the most extreme heteroglossia, will
struggle to re-affirm its presence, threatens to render Thénon as open
as Jacques Derrida to accusations of self-indulgent *jouissance*. Yet in
'Round 15', she goes down ('me ahogo') struggling. Her attempts to
break free of the constraints, to come out of the closet of language,
'volar delalf abeto', are exhaled in an irrepressibly feminist defiance. If
the text creates a new kind of reader, s/he must be the judge of whether
Thénon's challenge has been 'más facil que no hacer/o hacer nada'...
must decide, too, on what the agape subject 'gags'. In this under-taking,
s/he, caught in the act, smothered in reading/hearing, hardly
breathing, perchance – inseparably – indulges, performs (going
double-Dutch, all Greek to me, or even French), *le scriptible*; in the

118

moment of finding unswallowable *le lisible*... the flavour without savour of unmediated consumption of texts as cultural verifiers.

It has become commonplace, in the wake of the writings of such as Irigaray, to trace the passage from mimeticism to mimicry in the undermining (or overwriting) of male canons. Thénon's re-writable, re-signifying 'Oh, puss' catalyses, speeds up (and down), as agent, stroking and much-to-be welcomed deconstructions of established patterns of patriarchal heavy-handedness; to which it would deny an oft-times punch-drunk voice from again having the last word. Boxing clever, she deploys the inherited tropes of surreal entrapment in her multi-lingual and saturated literary internationalism; not only in 'word games' but also with a characteristic armoury of black humour, revolutionary politics, fantasy, dream and, above all, an alternative erotics of subversive textuality. An ever-struggling *id* – *Ça... oui, ça permet de respirer.*

No less Argentine... indeed, the more inclusively so, as a *machista* 'national' literary culture is subsumed into her poetry so that the male/female positions are relocatable ever within the strategies of social d(omin)ance. The elaborate footwork, the side-steps, of her poems may be seen and heard to perform to the beat of her title/text *Ova completa*, itself an echo (parody) of masculine 'completeness'. Thus, *obra* will function not as 'l'oeuvre' but as 'leurre', the work (or lure) of *his* (and now *her*) pomps and vanities. Colonialisms? There where *id* was [post-] will *ego* [intra-] be?

If, textually, it takes two to tango, I have opted to read and re-write the pairing but fleetingly as Néstor with Susana; Susana with Néstor... *res inter alios acta*. No harm done. *Quis custodiet*? No one is looking.

The overwhelmingly written character of *modernista* poetry cedes terrain to a modern, spoken written language in which local American experience – including the marginal, the vulgar, and the childish – finds its place.

Adam Sharman

We evaluate artists by how much they are able to rid themselves of convention [...] I enjoy [...] the sense of banditry [...] To loot [...] is exciting and dangerous. Let us see who controls the danger.

David Shields

An early-career sabbatical leave in Latin America, scheduled for April 1982, was to begin at the University of Buenos Aires on an invitation to address the topic of Jorge Luis Borges, detective fiction and structuralism. A war intervened. In late November 1997, after the publication of *Latin American Literature: Symptoms, Risks and Strategies of Post-structuralist Criticism* and at the gracious initiative of Ana María Barrenechea and Silvia Delfino, I shared a master class on the topic of a somewhat different approach to a JLB text... Much of what follows was inspired by Ana María's probing interrogation: A characteristic instance of Borges's going transcendental? What of alternative, shall we say, re-historicizing, 'takes' on the Malvinas conflict...?

The gaps to be filled on the conflict and its aftermath were literary and other artistic representations of a key formative event not only in late twentieth-century international relations but also in the discourses of post-colonialism and cultural politics; whence a monograph on fictional accounts and exploitations of, allusions to, and extrapolations from, the Falklands-Malvinas factor, a rich archive of creative works in Spanish, Portuguese, French and Italian, as well as in English, on which virtually nothing had been written. The challenge was to achieve accessibility without diminishing the literary critical edge. The University of Cambridge Distinguished Scholar Workshop of 2006 was devoted to the topic *Comparative Literatures in Conflict Falklands-Malvinas An Unfinished Business* and afforded me the opportunity to hone the contents of the ensuing book in extended classroom debate and discussion with cross-discipline postgraduate researchers and staff. The project formed part of a broader interest in the literatures of war and post-conflict cultures, including the plight of veterans, explored during *Hors de Combat. The Falkland-Malvinas Conflict 25 Years On*, the first international encounter of ex-combatants from Argentina and the United Kingdom, in the context of an academic forum, organized at the University of Nottingham on the eve of publication, in 2007, of *Falklands-Malvinas An Unfinished Business*. Ever since, work in an international network of veterans support and cooperation has involved addressing meetings of the South Atlantic Counsel of the UK House of Lords, the Argentine Chamber of Deputies and Foreign Ministry Diplomat Training Programme as well as Embassies and colloquia in Europe and Latin America. Analysing genres complementary to comparative literature, testimony, cinema, political and cultural theories, informs the forthcoming *It Breaks Two to Tangle: Political Cartoons of the Falklands-Malvinas Conflict*.

VI. OTHERED SELVES: *'OH! WHAT AN UN-LOVELY WAR'*
Heroes of the peace: Villains of the piece
Borges in poetry: Andahazi in prose

> Poetry is to prose as dancing is to walking.
> Paul Valéry

> They were only playing leapfrog...
> *Oh, What a Lovely War!*
> *d'après* and *pace* Joan Littlewood

Transcendental echoes

The first poem by an author of renown to deal with the Malvinas-Falklands conflict was the untitled text that has long-since come to be referred to as 'Juan López y John Ward', published in Buenos Aires in *Clarín* on 26 August and, in a by no means unproblematic translation, in *The Times* of London on 18 September 1982.[1] The poem has been dissected variously and multiply, as part of the Borges critical industry, but it is still pertinent to situate it in the context of the genre of war poetry:

> Juan López y John Ward
>
> Les tocó en suerte una época extraña
> El planeta había sido parcelado en distintos países, cada
>   uno provisto
> de lealtades, de queridas memorias, de un pasado sin
>   duda heroico,
> de derechos, de agravios, de una mitología peculiar, de
>   próceres de bronce,
> de aniversarios, de demagogos y de símbolos.
> Esa división, cara a los cartógrafos, auspiciaba las
>   guerras.
>
> López había nacido en la ciudad junto al río inmóvil.
> Ward, en las afueras de la ciudad por la que caminó
>   Father Brown.
> Había estudiado castellano para leer el Quijote.
> El otro profesaba el amor de Conrad, que le había sido

---

[1] The poem was later published in *Los conjurados, Obras completas* (Buenos Aires, Emecé, 1989), vol. 2, 500.

revelado en un aula de la calle Viamonte.
Hubieran sido amigos, pero se vieron una sola vez cara a
cara, en unas
islas demasiado famosas, y cada uno de los dos fue Caín, y
cada uno, Abel.
Los enterraron juntos.
La nieve y la corrupción los conocen.

El hecho que refiero pasó en un tiempo que no podemos
entender.

(Borges, Clarín, 26 August 1982)

Juan López and John Ward

It was their fate to live in a strange time.
The planet had been carved into different countries,
each one provided
with loyalties, with loved memories, with a past which
doubtless had been heroic,
with ancient and recent traditions, with rights, with
grievances, with its own mythology, with forebears in
bronze,
with anniversaries, with demagogues and with symbols. Such
an arbitrary division was favourable to war.

López had been born in the city next to the motionless
river.
Ward in the outskirts of the city through which Father
Brown had walked.
He had studied Spanish so as to read the *Quixote*.
The other professed a love of Conrad, revealed to him
in a class in Viamonte Street.
They might have been friends, but they saw each other
just once, face to face, in
islands only too well known, and each one was Cain and
each one, Abel.
They buried them together.
Snow and corruption know them.

The story I tell happened in a time we cannot understand.

(Borges, The Times, 18 September 1982;
translated by Rodolfo Terragno)

So be it? Amen? The construction of an opening gambit of Olympian distance, impersonality, objectivity, disinterest, a refusal to take sides, a mere 'naming of parts';[2] thus might the word 'fate' be seen to operate, reiterating a classical trope of juxtaposing destiny with the 'strangeness' of time, as if history were always in excess not only of its writing but also of our understanding of it. The apparent predetermination implicit in the division of the planet into potentially martial factions would make it appear that, not for the first time, here is a Borges text going transcendental; opting for the difference between countries as predestined, unavoidable point of departure on a road to cyclically repeated wars. According to the terms of such an irresistible binary, the only predictable construct would be that of Nationalisms, Histories writ large, official versions, 'loyalties' to be tested, and attested, by check-lists of 'past', 'heroic', 'cherished memories', 'anniversaries'. The writing implements of such a polarized reading of history are meticulously mapped: 'rights' and 'wrongs'.

Thereby a mythology has been produced and, in Borges's representation of it, is shown to be inseparable from proprietary rights and ownership. The reality effects of such strong myths are the hammered bronze echoes of anniversaries, the resonance of demagoguery and the unequivocality of symbols. Only once in the opening sequence of the poem has a 'doubtless' crept in, near-casual prefiguration, its ironizing frame easily missable, of an overt, a sententious and, thus far, it might seem, a dangerously unopposed, omniscient voicing: 'Esa división [...] auspiciaba las guerras' (less meticulously mapped – without, indeed, any cartographers at all – in Terragno's rendering 'Such an arbitrary division was favourable to war').

As in the case of all closed meanings, the planet-wide carve-up into differing Nationalisms, into different signifieds, might indeed have been for too long read as ordained by fate and agreed by men... agreed but arbitrary, and with no positive terms. Read retrospectively, however, the 'different countries' of the opening sequence might be said to require a re-writing of their respective histories in excess of the confining terminology, the straitjacket of those nationalizing ideologies which endow countries with auguries, auspicious or ill, both of, and for, war. It is in this light, therefore, that the wording 'was favourable' might be said to point to an over-dominant metaphysics, the supp-

---

[2] 'Today we have naming of parts. Yesterday/We had daily cleaning. And tomorrow morning,/We shall have what to do after firing. But today,/Today we have naming of parts'. Henry Reed, 'Lessons of the War: I': 'Naming of Parts', 1942, 1.

osedly unavoidable (and historically repeated) resolution of conflicting mythologies of nation through military confrontation.

As the Juan López and John Ward of Borges's text are schooled in the respective cities of their differential fates, the private and public strands of their lives (their perusal of Conrad or Cervantes, their perambulations along the River Plate or through Chesterton's suburbs) are interwoven only to lead them to the particular circumstance of their signifying encounter. This particularity is not just constructed on difference. The specificity of the brief attributions to Buenos Aires (displaced inheritor of an *hidalgo* tilter at dreams) and London (misplaced scene of a bumbling detective theology) is complemented by a prolonged disclosure of, and an openness to, reciprocity and its potential. An encountering without othering is tentatively approached via Juan and John as *literati*, through their readerly preparing for, their conceiving of, the translatability of a mediated other – that Other filtered through literatures, through traditions, through societies, and which consists of cultural difference. The hypothetical status of such *un*reality effects is however confined, consigned, to but a short sentence, 'They might have been friends', before the onset, the onrush, of a more divisive outcome... the inter-bayonetry of that form of cultural transfer which will always set its face against negotiated settlement (of differences). War-war, not jaw-jaw: Missus-Mistah Kurtz; s/he *not* dead... Non-negotiable. Art of darkness. Demagoguery... and its Other; that 'arbitrary' sinking feeling? Governance and, again, its inter-texts, literatures, come together in conflict.[3]

In a 'just once', in sheer instantaneity, the Borges text confronts the meeting of faces though not of eyes. In the borrowed terms of narrative analysis, the only available sphere of action is the double-actant space where each is Cain and each is Abel. For the absolute narrative, transcendent History, can cope with, and will apportion, no blame, no fault, no right, no wrong. In such an ironized story, the Juan/John 'fate' is, inevitably, both to live and to die in 'a strange time', buried together under the cover not of darkness but of a more pervasive, chilling, snowy blankness, and the corruption of a shared, a *same* death, which, macabre aspiration, abolishes the difference of self and other, self in other. A same death which permits no story, no history of their

---

[3] Governorship of 'an island' is promised, in Volume 1 of Cervantes' novel, to Sancho Panza when Don Quijote becomes an emperor or wins honours for some great deed. In Volume 2, the Duke and Duchess create a mock island and governorship for Sancho. D and D? Dictatorship and its other (half), the Dame; read Leopoldo and Margaret?

difference, their common particularity, resolved or dissolved in the illusory coming together of the time and its telling. But is 'a time we cannot understand' merely a conclusive note of resignation to fate, to strangeness, to incomprehensibility? or an invitation to read back through the poem, attempting to listen not to what '*we*' cannot understand but rather to the fact '*I*' tell'?

The excessive relation of the individual's voicing to simultaneous histories-become-History constitutes an invitation to listen again, whether to the Borges poem or to the official spokes*men* of the Thatcher Government, the Ian Macdonalds, the John Notts. What we are asked to hear is a counterpoint to the clipped, flat, matter-of-fact, the received pronunciation intoning, the cultivatedly condescending understatement, on the course and the 'official' discourse, of a history of the excessively famous, of the notorious. Thus the Borges poem subverts, even as it broaches, the construction of dangerous *clichés* of *in*difference; will not allow Juan and John an infamous loss of particular identities whereby they are turned into 'The Unknown Soldier', become transfused by, confused with, a sentimentalizing *dulce et decorum est pro patria mori*... Particular differences between Juan and John should be no less legible now than is that instance of differences at play within *Juan Ló*pez and John *War*d; the projected inscription of Jorge Luis's own initials into a (warred) relationship with the (linguistic) Other overtly inscribed by both trace and excess of intra-textual conflicts.

Counterpoint and excess also serve to characterize the relation of the Borges poem to its Wilfred Owen precursor, 'Strange Meeting'. Direct echoes are muted but an overt interpellation in Borges's opening line, 'extraña'/'strange', convokes both title and the ghosts from Owen's face-to-face encounter in Hell in order to pre-figure his own protagonists' entrenched inseparability in an all too similar 'profound dull tunnel'. Owen's first-person – 'out of battle escaped' only to confront his also dead adversary of but yesterday's jab and parry – is allowed a point of view:

> 'Strange friend,' I said, 'here is no cause to mourn.'
> 'None,' said that other, 'save the undone years,
> The hopelessness. Whatever hope is yours,
> Was my life also'.
> (Owen, 1918, in Silkin, 1982, 196-98)

Borges, however, ethically refraining from any identifying relation with the combatant Owen's option for eerie dramatic dialogue, borrows only the hypothetical. 'They might have been friends' performs the defamiliarization necessary to his own respectful visit to the grave of the predecessor's poem, and his strategic retreat from it. If Borges's Juan and John are not permitted to enter such an exchange as 'I am the enemy you killed, my friend. I know you in this dark', it is because of an *excess*. In appropriating but requiring to go beyond, Wilfred Owen's 'Strange Meeting', the later poem reminds us too that it is written after the era of *La Grande Illusion*: 'but they saw each other just once, face to face'. Concomitantly, Owen's 'Let us sleep now...' finds in Borges's 'Los enterraron juntos' a counterpart but without hint of consolation. 'My hands were loath and cold' derives from a personal voice not available in the Argentine's bleaker rendering of the icy effect of war: 'Snow and corruption know them'. Thus is the final line of the Borges poem calculatedly prepared for. Facts? History? Such events as have rendered *too* famous mere outcrops of the South Atlantic must exceed understanding; must confound nationalistic apportioning of roles of right and wrong; must allow for no making capital out of *H*istory; must refuse the writing of *M*yth.

The Borges strategy, here, as I read it, confirms the view that 'To treat wartime as a parenthesis of history is to depoliticize it, blur the social and cultural complexities of its literature and thought and ultimately make it mythical rather than historical' (Featherstone, 1995, 23). The 'Falklands Conflict' came to represent a particularly dominant metaphysics of presence in the strife-torn early 'eighties. Amongst the scandalously repressed absences of that period of burning UK inner-cities, of strikes and counter-strikes – Brit *versus* grit – was the very term *Malvinas,* itself repressing another by now faint imperial echo, less of Britain's 'naming of parts' than of Brittany's parting with names – St. Malo, whence *Les Iles Maloïnes*. Now, out of France, in a late twentieth-century rivalry of post-imperial but never post-economic colonizing powers, was cast the shadow not of Breton exiles but of bolt-on Exocets. The creation of a meta-geography (and a metal market) favourable to war suggests that the ever bullish economy of Nationalism emerged, in April 1982, as a fragmentary narrative of half-locatable places where, with stunning rapidity, all too recognizable visages of power *chose* to come face-to-face.

Perhaps not apocryphally, the Galtieri-Thatcher struggle over southern (dis)comfort on the rocks – in ten and a half shot weeks to be rendered a blasted wreath-laden *cimetière marin* – is said to have been described by Borges as that of 'two bald men fighting over a comb'. Perchance a loftier intertext, a more resonant, inseparably literary and historical drama of sovereign struggle, is pre-scribed; pre-scripted in a pre-ghostly encounter with ever-the-enemy otherness, unutterable prolepsis of bloody outcome? It is written... as a cyclically sanguinary post- and pre-, a pre- and post-war game; the clash of protagonists – too bold – in a play that dare not speak its name. There where sovereignty was and is – 'en suerte una época extraña' of yore or of now – will wilful conflict ever unsheathed violence be:

Say from whence
You owe this strange intelligence? Or why
Upon this blasted heath you stop our way
With such prophetic greeting.
Act I. Scene iii.

I am in blood
Stepp'd in so far that, should I wade no more,
Returning were as tedious as go o'er.
Act III. Scene iv.

Lay on...

Dancing with death... Exploding genres

Might the poetry of war be said to dance with death? The analogy draws on, in order to depart from, a classic if ever problematic distinction drawn between the genres of prose and poetry. Paul Valéry's assertion that 'one should guard against reasoning about poetry as one does about prose' assumes that the 'walking' performed by narrative fiction reaches 'the place, the book, the fruit, the object of desire' and 'at once entirely annuls the whole act; the effect swallows up the cause, the end absorbs the means and, whatever the act, only the result remains'. Poignantly, in the context of any analysis of the literature of war, Valéry's counter-claim for poetry is phrased as follows: 'The poem, on the other hand, does not die for having lived: it is expressly designed to be born again from its ashes and to become endlessly what it has just been. Poetry can be recognized by this property; that it tends to get itself reproduced in its own form: it stimulates us to reproduce it identically' (Valéry, 1972, 261).

Confronted, in the classroom – or elsewhere in the literary theoretical market-place – by such *a priori* challenges as the ostensible differentiation of, or even the tension between, literary genres, and notions of contrastive claims regarding the risk of 'going transcendental' (Rorty) and a recommended 'Always historicize' (Jameson) in the performance of one's critical reading, of one's putatively re-historicizing 'takes', a provisional suspension of generic terminologies may be – indeed, has been – broached; even pleasurably... *Text*.

> To read is to struggle to name, to subject the sentences of a text to a semantic transformation [...] All subversion thus begins with the Proper Name [...] What is obsolescent in today's novel is not the novelistic, it is the character; what can no longer be written is the Proper Name.
>
> Roland Barthes (*S/Z*)

One of the most violent fantasies born of the Malvinas conflict is the short narrative 'El dolmen' ['The Dolmen'] by Federico Andahazi. It is a fiction constructed on, but rapidly deconstructing, projections of otherness that go beyond the obvious Argentine-British binary. In this case, the other 'Other' is a constructed identity called Irishness. The story will initially draw on the force of this supposedly unifying label only to explode its myth-making power in an ending that confirms how, often, the most effective fictions of fantasy derive from an intensification of the real.[4]

Though the action of 'El dolmen' takes place exclusively in the Islands themselves, it is narrated within a supra-national frame that generates an otherwise inexplicable mystery regarding the relationship and respective motivations of its soldier protagonists, a sadistic officer and an ostensibly masochistic volunteer. The opening paragraph contextualizes the 1982 war by focusing, through an omniscient narrator, on events of extreme violence far removed from the Malvinas but with implications crucial to the tale's eventual plot:

> Fue el mismo año en que los flemáticos servicios británicos convirtieron al líder de la irlandesa Liga de Orange en un cedazo de carnes hecho con veintitrés disparos de una Browning; el mismo año en que las milicias de la Irish Revenge transformaron al general de la Scotland Yard en un puzzle de trescientas cuarenta y ocho piezas imposibles de armar, con los

---

4 No English translation as yet exists, whence the extensive sequences from the text rendered here.

siete kilos de trotyl que pusieron debajo de su flamante Jaguar V12. Fue el mismo año, en fin, en que, siete mil millas al sur, la Real Marina hacía del buque Manuel Belgrano una brasa crepitante que hervía las aguas heladas mientras se hundía de culo hacia el fondo del Atlántico. (Andahazi, 1999, 50)

[It was the same year in which the phlegmatic British Services turned the leader of the Irish Orange League into a meat sieve with twenty-three shots from a Browning; the same year in which the Irish Revenge militias made the Head of Scotland Yard into an impossible to put together jigsaw puzzle of three hundred and forty-eight pieces with the seven kilos of trotyl that they placed under his flaming Jaguar V12. It was the same year, finally, in which seven thousand miles to the South, the Royal Navy turned the ship called the *Belgrano* into a sizzling hot coal which made the ice-cold waters boil as it went down into the depths of the Atlantic.]

Thereafter, the narrative homes in on the relationship between the raw volunteer, Manuel Rattaghan, and Severino Sosa, the Lieutenant commanding his unit in their task of laying mines and digging defensive trenches on their way to Ganso Verde/Goose Green. What we are told of them is starkly contrastive, virtually nothing for the one and, for the other, almost an excess of background detail. Rattaghan has joined up 'con un único y secreto propósito' ['with a single and secretive purpose']. Severino Sosa is 'un correntino semi-literato y aterrado que, hasta entonces, suponía que la Guerra consistía en torturar y matar prisioneros maniatados y quebrados, secuestrar mujeres y saquear casas de civiles desarmados' ['a terror-stricken semi-literate from Corrientes who, until then, had supposed that war consisted of torturing and killing shackled and broken prisoners, kidnapping women and ransacking the houses of unarmed civilians']. In the face of the oncoming British attack, however, Rattaghan's lack of fear, or any other emotion, means that 'Podía adivinarse que su propósito era otro. Que había llegado a Malvinas para librar su propia guerra' ['It was possible to guess that he had another reason for being there; that he had come to the Malvinas to fight his own war'] (50).

El soldado Rattaghan no hablaba con nadie. No parecía mostrar ninguna preocupación ante la llegada del enemigo [...] No mostraba signos de frío ni de hambre ni de miedo, ni siquiera de tedio durante aquellas eternas horas muertas de la espera. (50)

[Private Rattaghan spoke with nobody. He appeared to show no concern at all with the coming of the enemy [...] He showed no hint of cold, hunger or fear, nor even boredom during those never-ending dead hours of waiting.]

Apart from masking his own fear by bullying, threatening and humiliating the troops under his command, the Lieutenant suffered with deep unease the frightening calm of Volunteer 2nd Class Rattaghan:

Miraba a su subordinado con una mezcla de aprensión, recelo y cierto temor que se resumía en un desprecio que pronto habría de desaguar en odio. No hubiese habido forma de hacerle entender al teniente que aquel apellido no era inglés, sino irlandés y que un irlandés – o su descendencia – era una entidad completamente diferente de la de un inglés. (50)

[He looked at his subordinate with a mixture of apprehension, caution and a certain fear summed up in a disdain that was soon to leak into hatred. There would have been no way of making the lieutenant understand that that surname was not English, but Irish, and that an Irishman – or his descendants – was an entity completely different from an Englishman.]

What he did know was the information that the local military command had passed on to him about the volunteer called Rattaghan:

El voluntario Rattaghan tenía un hermano mayor cuyo paradero aquella misma comandancia decía desconocer, aunque se presumía – según un parte del ministerio – que su denunciada desaparición había sido voluntaria y ahora, quizá, se hallara en el exterior o, quién sabe, tal vez hubiera sido muerto por sus propios camaradas de armas marxistas-leninistas. (50)

[Volunteer Rattaghan had an older brother whose whereabouts were said to be unknown although it was presumed – according to someone in the Ministry – that his declared disappearance had been voluntary and now, perhaps, that he was to be found outside the country or, who knows, had possibly been killed by his own Marxist-Leninist comrades in arms.]

What he could not know about was what the younger brother had witnessed in 1976:

> El soldado Rattaghan había presenciado, siete años antes, cómo su hermano había sido sacado de su cuarto, arrastrado por los pelos escaleras abajo hasta la calle y molido a patadas por incontables borceguíes iguales a los que él mismo ahora llevaba puestos y así, medio muerto y a la rastra, lo habían tirado sobre la caja de un Unimog idéntico al que había transportado al soldado Rattaghan a la base aérea. Desde entonces, jamás volvió a ver a su hermano mayor. (50)

> [Private Rattaghan had witnessed, seven years earlier, how his brother had been pulled out of his room, tugged downstairs to the street by his hair and kicked unconscious by countless boots similar to the ones that he himself now wore and so, dragged off half-dead, he had been thrown onto the back of a Unimog identical to the one which had taken Rattaghan the soldier to the airbase. Since then, he had never seen his older brother again.]

The days of waiting provide the furiously shouting Severino Sosa with the opportunity to vent his hyena-fury on Rattaghan by way of rallying the rest of the volunteer force:

> [M]anga de putas, pedazos de mierda, decía, pronto vamos a tener visitas, decía, vamos a ver, imbéciles, cómo se trata a un inglés [...] Rata, rata inglesa hija de puta [...] Entonces Severino Sosa ordenó que lo estaquearan. Crucificado el soldado contra la nieve [...] Rattaghan no despegaba la vista de los ojos de su superior y aun cuando el sisal había empezado a teñirse de rojo, el soldado no había siquiera lanzado un gemido. Permaneció crucificado por el término de doce horas. (51)

> [Bunch of whores, pieces of shit, he would say, we're expecting visitors, so let's see how to treat an Englishman [...] Rat, English rat, son of a bitch [...] Severino Sosa then ordered them to stake him out on the ground. Crucified in the snow [...] Rattaghan never took his eyes off his superior and even when the hemp rope had begun to turn red, the soldier hadn't even groaned. He stayed out there crucified for twelve hours.]

A bar of chocolate goes missing, Rattaghan is blamed and his upper incisors are ripped out and put as a trophy in the Lieutenant's tunic pocket. Some cigars are stolen, Rattaghan takes the rap… and the thirteen stubs of Severino Sosa's daily smokes are put out on his subordinate's balls.

The excesses of *el proceso* and of the 'dirty' war in both reality and fiction, whether echoing the testimonies of 'los chicos de la guerra' ['the kids of the war'] or the episodes of Rodolfo Enrique Fogwill's seminal novel, the first to address the conflict, *Los pichiciegos* [*The Warmadillos*] (1983),[5] are subsumed into Andahazi's unflinching narrative before, on the fifth day, the plot explodes with the advent of the Sea Harrier jump-jet fighters and the effect of their cadmium bombs. Rattaghan is thrown sixty metres and, only when emerging from his temporary deafness and blindness, turns to find the crater of dismembered bodies that were once his comrades:

> De no haber tenido un único y secreto propósito hubiese cedido a la tentación del sueño fatal […] Entonces giró la cabeza y pudo ver un temblor finísimo en la nieve. Como un lagarto, corrió hacia aquel promontorio palpitante y hurgó en la escarcha con la yema – ya insensible – de los dedos; tocó un borceguí; giró sobre su eje ventral y cavó con ambas manos hasta tocar una barbilla pétrea. Entonces pudo descubrir que aquello era su teniente, Severino Sosa. Por primera vez desde su llegada a Malvinas, rió. Rió como jamás se había reído. Enterrado como estaba su teniente, le cacheteó las mejillas y, cegado por la fiebre y el dolor, le dijo sin dejar de reírse, miráme hijo de puta y entonces, el soldado Rattaghan se levantó el labio y le mostró las cuencas vacías de los dientes que le había arrancado el día anterior y miráme hijo de puta, le gritó y le enseñaba las muñecas llagadas por el sisal de la cuerda con la que lo había estaqueado la tarde anterior y miráme hijo de puta, le decía sin dejar de reírse, a la vez que le abría los párpados yermos para que le viera los huevos escaldados. De no haber tenido un único y secreto propósito, lo habría matado ahí mismo. El soldado raso Rattaghan tomó a

---

[5] *El Proceso de Reorganización Nacional* refers to the period of dictatorship stretching from the military *coup* of 24 March 1976 until the official relinquishing of power to the constitutional government on 10 December 1983. *The Warmadillos* is the title I coined for Fogwill's corruscating *Los pichiciegos*, see *Falklands-Malvinas:an Unfinished Business*, 2007, 350.

Severino por las axilas y arrastrándose con los codos y las rodillas, lo desenterró por completo. Lo sentó sobre un peñasco y, sosteniéndole la cabeza por los pelos, le dijo, no te vas a morir ahora hijo de puta, ahora no. (52)

[If he had not had a single and secret purpose he would have given in to the temptation of fatal sleep [...] Then he turned his head and managed to see a very faint shiver in the snow. Like a lizard he crawled towards something sticking out and palpitating and then poked in the frost with his fingertips – by now without feeling; he touched a military boot; he turned on his belly and dug with both hands until he touched a petrified chin. He then discovered that the object was his Lieutenant, Severino Sosa. For the first time since his arrival in the Malvinas, he laughed. He laughed as he had never laughed before. Buried as his Lieutenant was, he slapped his cheeks and, blinded by fever and pain, said to him laughing, look at me you son of a bitch and, then, Private Rattaghan raised his upper lip and showed him the empty cavities where his teeth had been pulled out the day before and look at me you son of a bitch he shouted and showed him the wrists wounded by the hemp of the rope with which they had staked him out the previous evening, he said to him without stopping laughing, as he forced open his unyielding eyelids so that he could show him his scorched balls. If he had not had a single and secret purpose, he would have killed him there and then. Soldier Rattaghan took Severino by the armpits and, dragging him on his elbows and knees, dug him out of the snow completely. He sat him on a rock and, holding him up by the hair, said to him, you are not going to die now you son of a bitch, not now.]

Having filled his knapsack with provisions scattered in the Harrier raid, Rattaghan improvises a travois and embarks on a day-long dragging of the moribund Severino Sosa through the snowy terrain. He glimpses a log cabin:

Cuando faltaban no más de diez pasos para llegar a la casa, exhausto, desfalleciente y casi congelado, el soldado Rattaghan se desmoronó. Cuando abrió los ojos tuvo la alucinatoria certeza de que se encontraba en su casa [...] Sobre la mesa de luz junto a la cama, pudo ver una imagen de Santa Brígida igual a la que tenía su madre en el dormitorio. Más allá [...]

descansaba una Biblia en inglés y, en otro estante, pudo leer los lomos de otros libros ordenados sin demasiado criterio. Había obras de Joyce y de Yeats, de Synge y de Burke, de Goldsmith, de Swift y unos volúmenes de lomos marrones e ilegibles. Hubiera jurado que era la biblioteca de su hermano. Desde su perspectiva, sobre su cabeza, el soldado Rattaghan pudo ver la cruz invertida de un rosario celta. Era cierto – se dijo – que aquel techo de listones de madera tibia y hospitalaria no era el de su casa. Pero lo que le hacía suponer que todo aquello no era más que un desvarío, era el hecho de que estaba escuchando una vieja canción irlandesa en idioma gaélico que únicamente le había escuchado cantar a su abuelo. Se incorporó sobre los codos y entonces comprobó que estaba sobre una cama. Más allá, un hombre alimentaba una salamandra sobre cuyo crisol se cocinaba un guiso. Era un viejo que presentaba el porte de un dolmen. (52-53)

[When there were but ten steps to go before arriving at the dwelling, exhausted, fainting and almost frozen alive, Private Rattaghan collapsed. When he opened his eyes he had the hallucinatory certainty that he was in his own house [...] On the bedside table, he could see a picture of Saint Brigid, the same as the one that his mother had in her bedroom. Beyond that [...] there stood a bible in English and [...] works by Joyce and Yeats, Synge and Burke, Goldsmith, Swift and other volumes with brown and illegible spines. He could have sworn that this was his brother's library. From his perspective, over his head, Private Rattaghan could make out the inverted cross of a Celtic rosary. He was sure – he said to himself – that that wooden ceiling, warm and hospitable, was not the ceiling of his house. But what made him suppose that this was nothing other than his mind rambling was the fact that he was listening to an old Irish song in the Gaelic language that he had only heard sung by his grandfather. He lifted himself up onto his elbows and then realised that he was lying on a bed. Over there, a man was putting fuel on a stove on top of which a stew was cooking. He was an old man with the stature of a dolmen.]

Just as the earlier details of torture and abuse, physical and mental, had derived from both factual testimony and fiction, so the effects of entering a twilight world of potential salvation and enlightenment are redolent of both mythology and lyricism; with echoes of a particular –

and pertinent – precursor intertext.

In Borges's own favourite and perhaps best known story, 'El Sur' ['The South'], a journey towards the land of his forefathers undertaken by the bookish Juan Dahlman is triggered by the ambivalent clause 'Increíblemente, el día prometido llegó' ['Incredibly, the promised day arrived']. Dahlman is thus released, textually, both to leave the sanatorium, where he has been operated on for septicaemia, and to dream his own preferred, heroic, death in the Argentine south as an alternative to a banal end under the surgeon's scalpel. Again, here, in the Andahazi story, the narrative progression, after the loss of consciousness that occurs at Rattaghan's liminal encounter with his own past and with the phantasms of a shared imaginary, hinges on a phrase of ambivalence – 'la alucinatoria certeza' ['the hallucinatory certainty']. Was he indeed 'back home'? Was the picture of Saint Brigid in fact 'the same' as the one that had belonged to his mother? Were the books swearably those of his lost brother? Was the Celtic cross of the rosary an inversion in a doubled sense, a cipher of the text and counter-text in which he was now to live… or die, as harbingered in his own recent crucifixion? Was the 'uniqueness' of his grandfather's song in Gaelic sacred enough never to be reproducible other than in dream or, now, in the convoked reconfiguration of all his concentrated past in the personified dolmen, 'gigantic, proud and of an indifference that could be said to be of stone' (53)? Was he, indeed, re-encountering a long-lost brother? What could be said to be the action of the rest of the story, as was the case in its Borges antecedent, authorizes the reader to opt for a real or a figurative ending… or both:

> 'Puede llamarse afortunado. Apenas tiene una luxación en los hombros y las rodillas, dos falanges quebradas, una costilla fisurada, el tabique de la nariz roto y unos cuantos raspones. Mi nombre es Sean Flanaghan […] En cuanto a su compañero, soy menos optimista', dijo el viejo señalando a la derecha de Rattaghan. (53)

> ['You can call yourself fortunate. You've only got a dislocated shoulder and knee, two broken fingers, a cracked rib, a broken nose and some other grazes. My name is Sean Flanaghan […] As for your companion, I'm less optimistic', said the old man, signalling to Rattaghan's right.]

When told that the missing teeth and the burns to the testicles cannot be war wounds, the young volunteer can only lower his eyes. Con-fronted, however, by the teeth taken by Flanaghan from the

Lieutenant's tunic pockets, by the old man's incomprehension and, at once, by his aiming of a double-barrelled shotgun at Severino Sosa's head, Rattaghan speaks out at last:

Entonces el soldado Rattaghan habló. Le contó lo que jamás había dicho a nadie. Le habló en un inglés clarísimo. Le explicó por qué no podía matarlo y cuál era su propósito en aquella guerra. Primero le contó que su abuelo había nacido en Belfast, que muy joven llegó a la Argentina, que su padre había sido casero de la estancia de los Anchorena, que la abuela había sido institutriz; le habló acerca de su madre y de la imagen de Santa Brígida, igual a la que ahora descansaba sobre su mesa de luz. Y le dijo, también, que había tenido un hermano. Entonces volvió a tomar aliento y habló. Le habló de su hermano mayor, le dijo que se llamaba Patricio, Patricio Rattaghan, que también leía a Joyce y Yeats, a Synge y a Burke, a Goldsmith, a Swift y a otro irlandés que era en realidad argentino, Rodolfo Walsh, que también su hermano escribía y entonces le recitó una poesía, podía recitar todo el libro, le contó que una noche de julio de 1976 un camión del ejército se estacionó en la puerta de su casa, que se bajaron diez hombres armados y se lo llevaron a la rastra, que lo molieron a patadas, que él, Segundo Manuel Rattaghan, escondido tras la puerta, tuvo pánico, que no entendía nada, que, literalmente se cagó de miedo, que, a través de sus ojos infantiles, había visto todo y que jamás se perdonó no haber hecho nada, que nunca más lo volvió a ver. Le dijo que lo torturaba el hecho de que, con el paso de los años, se iba borrando de su memoria la cara de su hermano, pero que había un rostro que jamás había olvidado, que desde aquel día se le aparecía todos los días como un mal pensamiento, como una mosca pertinaz, le dijo que nunca había olvidado el rostro de aquel que daba las órdenes cuando se llevaron a su hermano. Le contó que, desde entonces, no había hecho más que buscar esa cara. En los subtes, en lo colectivos, entre los transeúntes, en todas partes, hasta que un buen día vio aquel rostro en la televisión, en una nota que les hacían a los heroicos soldados del batallón 63.3 que habían sido los primeros en pisar las islas recuperadas, entonces aquel rostro no pudo sustraerse al hambre de gloria y dijo su nombre mirando a cámara: Teniente Severino Sosa. Fue cuando él, Segundo Manuel Rattaghan, decidió presentarse como voluntario al batallón 63.3. Entonces, señalando al hombre que yacía a su lado, le dijo al viejo: 'Él secuestró a mi hermano'. Cuando el soldado Rattaghan hubo terminado de hablar, el viejo lo miró a los ojos y se quedó en silencio. Asintió, se bebió el contenido del vaso de un solo sorbo, se puso de pie. Fue y vino y, finalmente, habló: 'Entiendo su punto de vista, pero si le interesa saber lo que pienso, opino que hay que matarlo ahora'. (53-54)

[Then Private Rattaghan recounted what he had never told anybody before. He spoke in very clear English. He explained why he could not kill him and what he was doing in that war. First he told how his grandfather had been born in Belfast, had arrived when very young in Argentina [...] He spoke about his elder brother, said that his name was Patricio, Patricio Rattaghan, who also read Joyce and Yeats, Synge and Burke, Goldsmith, Swift and another Irishman who was in fact Argentine, Rodolfo Walsh [...] He recounted that one night in July 1976 an army lorry had parked at the door of their house, that ten armed men had jumped out and had dragged him off, kicking him as they went, that he, Volunteer Manuel Rattaghan, hiding behind the door, had panicked, that he had understood nothing; that, literally, he had shit himself with fear, that, through his child's eyes, he had seen everything and had never forgiven himself for doing nothing, that he had never seen him again. He said that he was tortured by the fact that, as the years passed by, the face of his brother was being erased from his memory, but that there was a face that he had never forgotten, that from that day it had appeared to him like a bad thought, like an irritating fly, he said that he had never forgotten the face of the man who was giving the orders when they took his brother away. He told how, since then he had done nothing but search for that face. In the underground, on buses, amongst passers-by, everywhere until one day he saw the face on television, in a report that was being broadcast about the heroic soldiers of Battalion 63.3, who had been the first to set foot on the recovered Islands, then that face could not hold back from its hunger for glory and had stated its name as it looked into the camera: Lieutenant Severino Sosa. That was when he, Private Manuel Rattaghan, had decided to volunteer to join Battalion 63.3. Then, pointing to the man who lay beside him he said to the old man: he kidnapped my brother [...] The old man finally spoke: 'I understand your point of view, but if you want to know what I think, it's my opinion that we have to kill him now.']

After recounting his own story of 'qué hacía un irlandés en el fin del mundo' ['what an Irishman was doing at the end of the world'], of his own escape from Belfast, of the 'troubles', of his militant Catholicism yet opposition to radicalizing the struggle, of his five years in detention, and of the murder of his wife 'la dueña del culo más espléndido de Irlanda' ['the bearer of the finest arse in Ireland'] and only son James in a loyalist bombing, Sean Flanaghan, 'aquel gigante de ojos transparentes, aquel dolmen enorme e inexpresivo' ['that giant with transparent eyes, that enormous and inexpressive dolmen'], breaks down inconsolably before repeating, 'Si quiere saber mi opinión, pienso que hay matarlo. Eso no es un semejante' ['If you want to know my opinion, I think we have to kill him. That is not a fellow human being'] (54).

Waking suddenly at midnight with 'la absurda ocurrencia de que el teniente no sólo se había movido, sino que, en algún momento se había levantado' ['the absurd idea that the lieutenant had not just moved but, at some point, got up', Rattaghan 'dissuaded himself' from the idea of the impossible and tried to sleep: 'Estaba por conciliar el sueño cuando escuchó que decían su nombre. Era la voz inconfundible del Teniente Severino Sosa. Se le congeló la sangre' ['He was about to reconcile himself to his dream when he heard someone saying his name. It was the unmistakable voice of Lieutenant Severino Sosa. His blood froze'] (54). Stopping the old man from tendering water to the Lieutenant, Private Rattaghan whispers into Severino Sosa's ear:

[D]ecíme, hijo de puta, qué hiciste con mi hermano. La proximidad del cucharón parecía devolverlo a la realidad. Por fin dijo: 'No sé de qué me habla, soldado'. Había dicho esto último con un sino de sarcasmo que se traslució en una sonrisa imperceptible, involuntaria. El soldado Rattaghan tuvo la inmediata certeza de que el teniente no sólo sabía de qué le hablaba, sino que sabía de quién le hablaba. Siempre lo supo. Ese era el motivo del odio que le prodigaba desde el día en que lo vio, desde el momento en que escuchó el apellido Rattaghan. Siempre supo que era el hermano de su víctima. Entonces, Segundo Manuel Rattaghan tomó una resolución: lo iba a torturar hasta que hablara. Se acercó a la salamandra y puso a calentar en el crisol el fierro del atizador. El viejo se había sentado en la mecedora y bebía indiferente. El hierro pasó de negro a rojo y de rojo a blanco. Rattaghan lo retiró y lo acercó a la cara del teniente, me vas decir, hijo de puta, qué hicieron con mi hermano. Severino Sosa no hacía más que negar todos los cargos y pedir agua. Conforme se encolerizaba, el soldado Rattaghan, en la misma proporción, descubría que era incapaz de torturar. Ni sabía cómo se hacía ni podría hacerlo aunque supiera. Lloró de impotencia. 'Yo podría hacerlo por usted', dijo el viejo sin mirarlo, 'pero ésta es su guerra'. (54-55)

[Tell me, you son of a bitch, what you did with my brother. The closeness of the knife seemed to bring him back to reality. Finally he said: – I don't know what you're talking about, soldier. He had said it with an inevitable sarcasm that shone through in an imperceptible, involuntary, smile. Private Rattaghan was at once certain that the Lieutenant not only knew what he was talking about, but also that he knew who was talking. He had always known that this was the reason for the hatred that he had shown him from the first day he had seen him, from the moment that he had heard the surname Rattaghan. He had always known that he was the brother of his victim. Then Volunteer Manuel Rattaghan took a firm decision: he was going to torture him until he told. He approached the stove and put the iron poker in to heat in the flames. The old man had sat down on the rocking chair and, indifferent, was drinking. The iron went from black to red and from red to white. Rattaghan pulled it out and held it close to the Lieutenant's face; you're going to tell me, *hijo de puta*, what they did with my brother. Severino Sosa only denied all the charges and asked for water. As he got angrier and angrier, Private Rattaghan discovered too that he was incapable of torturing anybody. He didn't even know how to do it, nor could he have done it even if he had known how. He wept in his powerlessness. 'I could do it for you,' said the old man without looking at him 'but this is your war.']

The self-knowledge and the powerlessness of the one, Private Rattaghan, are un-mirrored in the knowledge and re-empowerment of the other, Lieutenant Severino Sosa:

Entonces Severino Sosa, con una voz inédita, afable y calma, empezó a hablar. Voy a decirle, soldado qué fue de su hermano, pero antes quiero agradecerle que me haya salvado la vida. El corazón de Rattaghan se sobresaltó primero y luego latió con ansiedad. El viejo se incorporó sobresaltado por una inquietud indecible. Le voy a decir qué pasó con su hermano, siguió diciendo el teniente, pero quiero que sepa que jamás voy a olvidar que si no hubiera sido por usted, soldado, ahora yo estaría muerto. El viejo buscaba algo desesperadamente. Soldado, voy a decirle de una vez qué fue de su hermano, pero antes quiero que sepa que estoy en deuda con usted; sucede, dijo, que odio tener deudas, entonces sacó el brazo por debajo de las cobijas y extrajo el rifle de doble caño del viejo, levantó el arma y apuntando al pecho de Segundo Manuel Rattaghan dijo: esto fue lo que pasó con su hermano, entonces disparó. En el mismo momento en que Sean Flanaghan corría hacia el soldado, Severino Sosa volvió a disparar al centro de los ojos del viejo. Cayó como lo hiciera un dolmen, sin quebrarse, sin emitir una sola queja. (55)

[With an unprecedented, affable and calm voice he began to speak. I shall tell you, soldier, what became of your brother but first I want to thank you for having saved my life. Rattaghan's heart missed a beat and then quickened with anxiety. The old man stood up surprised by an unspeakable disquiet. I'm going to tell you what happened to your brother, the lieutenant said again, but I want you to know that I shall never forget that if it hadn't been for you, soldier, I would now be dead. The old man was desperately looking for something. Soldier, I'm going to tell you now what became of your brother, but first I want you to know that I am in your debt; as it happens, he said, I hate being in debt, he took his arm from under the covers and pulled out the old man's double-barrel rifle, then raised the gun and pointing at the chest of Volunteer Manuel Rattaghan said: this is what happened to your brother, then he pulled the trigger. In the same moment that Sean Flanaghan ran towards the soldier, Severino Sosa shot again this time between the eyes of the old man. He fell as a dolmen would fall. Without breaking, without emitting a single complaint.]

The meaning of the text falls, too, piece upon piece, dolmen-like, into place; but not into any space of fulfilment. Uncomplainingly. Passively. For dolmens will ever invite, permit, demand re-inscriptions, the projection of countless and endless meanings upon their petrified semblance of presence. As absence of plenitude, the dolmen may nonetheless serve any purpose; may witness, but bear no witness to, either reality or dream; either justice or injustice. Always in difference, ever indifferent to what a self-constructing protagonist might project onto it.

The effectiveness of 'El dolmen' as a short story, technically, derives from a Borges-like double trajectory that takes the reader simultaneously into and away from the inhuman abuses of war. Yet, unlike the case of the author of 'Juan López and John Ward', the risk for Andahazi is decidedly not a 'going transcendental' in his literary treatment of the war. On the contrary, the story, whether it be read as narrating the dream sequence of a combatant already moribund on the field of battle or a twist-in-the-tail though straightforward account of unrelieved brutishness, attests rather to the failure of any transcenddental enterprise; to the pointlessness of exacting an expiatory confession rather than punishment; to the futility of investing in the past in order to solve problems of the present; to the Judaeo-Christian insidiousness of three-fold but inverted, pernicious, denials; to the senselessness of any identity construction composed only through religion, nation, literature or myth; to the wilful blindness of seeing a 'beyond' made up of the all-too-familiar titles of the Bible and works by Joyce and Yeats, Synge and Burke, Goldsmith and Swift whilst failing, or being unable, unwilling, to decipher 'other volumes with brown and illegible spines'.

Whereas the Juan López and John Ward, and the self (JL) and the soldier (warred), respectively, of the Borges poem rely on the collapsing of different identities into similarities, the non-dolmen (the man of action) that is not Juan, nor John, but *Sean* is strikingly *un*like his near-namesake Rattaghan in that he *would* have killed Severino Sosa. And his key explanatory words are 'Eso no es un semejante', otherwise translatable as: '*That* is not a... *simulacrum*' (my italics and suspension of *dis*belief). The depersonalized actant of an abject military – *Severino Sosa* – is not by coincidence inscribed with the initials SS. Transported criminality, Nazi crypto-*Schulz*Staffel or otherwise, may be re-ciphered but is not acceptable, is not to be re-inscribed, in Argentina.

Yet the self-sacrificing pursuit of truth has not led Manuel ('God is with us', made man, and crucified) to discover the facts of what has happened to his disappeared brother; rather to decipher his own, his new, his final testament, his costly lack of the will, or the zeal, either to exact revenge or to deliver justice. In contrast, the Old Testament severity of judgment ('a tooth for a tooth', two teeth for two teeth) of the Irish nationalist Sean stands erect but outside the hybrid Rattaghan story – it is not Flanagan's war. His anti-colonialism has been played out elsewhere, against the English, and ideologically. The Rattaghans, in contrast, are – were – Argentines, tasked with their part in constructing legality from *within* the nation. Theirs is the imperative to oppose a recidivist totalitarian criminality, putatively still suffused with a proto-Nazi and, in moments of undisciplined and unbridled militarism, an ill-hidden past; to resist that cyclical intra-colonial re-enactment of the repressions performed upon a nation from the outside *and* from the inside, inseparably. For, as Thénon's 'Amen'-'Omen' slippage had proposed, the alternative, when resignation turns into fatalism, will be abjection.[6]

As yet, Rattaghan resistance is performed neither resignedly nor fatalistically, not ideologically but personally (albeit also always political, however sub-consciously); it is not Flanagan's *war* but it is Manuel's private *conflict*. As such it cannot but bode failure, the abject ceding, out of the inability to kill, to eradicate the inhuman, because of a weak, irrelevantly motivated, humanity; a (sur)rendering of one underground man to another. *Ecce homo* or – 'from behind the stove, incognito' – *rat, again*? The most enticing reminiscence of precursor texts is Dostoevsky's:

> antithesis of the normal man [...] it feels insulted [...] and wants to revenge itself [...] it will suffer a hundred times more than the one on whom it revenges itself [....] But it is just in that cold, abominable half despair, half belief, in that conscious burying oneself alive for grief in the underworld [...] in that acutely recognized and yet partly doubtful hopelessness of one's position, in that hell of unsatisfied desires turned inward, in that fever of oscillations [...] that the savour of that strange enjoyment of which I have spoken lies. (Dostoevsky, 1918, 57-58).

In the Argentine nation's notes from underground is inscribed its ruling *junta*, lording it over a cowering populace; tools whether guilty or innocent, complicit or conscripted and, here, problematically albeit involuntarily, volunteering for *a*, but inseparably, *the* cause.

It is not only theory that travels un-smoothly but also practice. 'Truth and Reconciliation' is an instrument of post-conflict that cannot be presumed to work in any society not (yet) prepared to confront, let alone change, its continuing brutality, its cyclical, repetitive, repression and killing... *its* perceived Truth, *its* 'due obedience', *its* 'final point' (the 1987 laws of 'Obediencia Debida' and 'Punto Final', decreed by President Raúl Alfonsín, relieved the Argentine military of all legal responsibilities). Thus, Andahazi's radical turn at once historicizes as it textualizes, throws up, and into question, the impossibility *and* the possibility of impunity; the in-commensurate relationship of justice to injustice; the (in)comprehensibility but also the continuing threat of the inhuman.

---

[6] Recall 'Poema con traducción simultánea Español-Español', chapter I.

Antjie Krog, in *A Change of Tongue*, opens her South African-derived meditation on 'A Translation' with an echo of Jacques Derrida: '... for the notion of translation we would have to substitute the notion of transformation; a regulated transformation of one language by another, of one text by another'. She continues, in a manner pertinently evocative of the challenge posed, on a different continent and in different transition – and certainly far removed from some putative Latin American rainbow nation – by Andahazi's radically transformative demolition of the ominously lapidary text of Argentina's monolithic 'Gran Relato':

> Take the word 'forefather'. Or would you use the word 'ancestor'? Does it carry the same content? A foreign culture can only be perceived by means of comparison with one's own culture, the culture of primary enculturation. There can be no neutral standpoint for comparison [...] The concepts of our own culture will thus be the touchstones for the perception of otherness. (Krog, 2003, 267; 271)

'El dolmen' thus poses a challenge to all constructs of peace and reconciliation that, in the politics of the post-conflict, eschew eradicating, jurisprudentially, that uniform process of militarist, or other semi-literate, ideology whereby the human is subjugated to any State or National interest. Such a dolmen – 'gigantic, proud, and of an indifference that could be said to be of stone' – that static, unchanging, stoic-escapist configuration of an ancient, but undecipherable knowledge, or wisdom, or venerability, is but a myth to be exploded.

*

Coda: was there a text in this class?

Tremendismo and/or (sur)reality effects

Curiosity kills the cathol(ist)ic prowler when, on return to the scene of the crime which is already and always *text* – the fiction excluded from that n^{th} Book of the Republic of post-Plato literalists, unmediated realists all – an 'English Protestant' re-opening of discursive manipulation raises its sectarian binary head:

> Mientras los ingleses protestantes y los irlandeses católicos se mataban sin tregua ni piedad en el Reino Unido, cinco mil

millas al sur la Real Armada hacía del buque Manuel Belgrano una brasa crepitante que hervía las aguas heladas al hundirse de culo hacia el fondo del Atlántico.

[While the English Protestants and the Irish Catholics were killing each other with neither pause nor pity in the United Kingdom, five thousand miles to the south the Royal Armada turned the ship called the *Manuel Belgrano* into a sizzling hot coal which made the ice-cold waters boil on sinking bottom up into the depths of the Atlantic.][7]

Thus reads the contrastive opening of an otherwise identical earlier – Buenos Aires, Bar La Academia, 1986-marked – version of the *Blanco y Negro* publication of 28 March 1999 'El dolmen' analysed thus far. 'Them' versus 'them'; at colonially unchanging loggerheads, brought into focus as a backcloth to a 'United', sovereignly authorized, historically echoing 'Armada' *not* 'Marina task-force aimed at an 'us' (dis)embodied in the sinking – notoriously unifying – of the *Manuel Belgrano*... synecdoche of a suddenly re-authorized 'Argentina'. Close enough to the history of the military adventurisms to be *vraisemblable*; but lacking, we now observe, 'un effet du réel'?, a function naming 'falsely', and deployed, we shall see, 'to subject the sentences of a text to a semantic transformation' whereby 'subversion thus begins with the Proper Name' that 'cannot be written'... as such. Whence the difference, the differences in the later aperture-cum-aporia, the sole corrective swerves from the previous ostensibly realist narrative referentiality, previously storied as grounded in history, as 'historicized' via a post-1968 Ulster (*pace* another Fredric).

For there is not and never was an 'irlandesa Liga de Orange'; nor a militia of the 'Irish Revenge'; and a 'general de la Scotland Yard' must wait to be appointed, perchance, if and when the British police force were one day militarized... Fictionalizing with (sur)reality effects, of pronounced *in*-verisimilitude, would appear to be the name of this game.

> When the solidarity of the old disciplines breaks down – perhaps even violently [...] performances, 'limit works', exist [...] at the limits of 'enunciation, rationality, readability etc.' [...] Texts are radically symbolic, 'off-

---

[7] Cf. the 1999 and the 1986 texts of 'El dolmen'.

144

> centre, without closure', playful, offering *jouissance* [...] Texts help us glimpse a 'social utopia'... [a] transparency of linguistic relations if not social ones, a 'space where no language has a hold over any other'.
>
> Roland Barthes ('From Work to Text')

Pondering not motive *qua* intention – 'trust the tale not the teller' – but motifs (heavy versus light) of the amended shock-tactic overture to a symphony of violence, indices of a calculated literary style of brutalism, provoked revisionist further analysis. Spot the *différance*... as a number of telling Barthes insights are played out: 'violently'; 'at the limits of "enunciation, rationality, readability"'; 'radically symbolic, "off-centre, without closure"'; and, riskily, 'playful, offering *jouissance*'... dare it be suggested?

A decade or more of classroom-shared readings of and reaction to the fiction, poetry and song, drama and film from the United Kingdom, Argentina and elsewhere, including France, Italy, Ireland, the United States and Brazil, addressed in my *Falklands-Malvinas: An Unfinished Business* of 2007, had already thrown up a peculiar contradiction. Only in Argentina was there either, principally, no knowledge of, or ostensible interest in, 'El dolmen'. There, when and wherever I broached the text and mentioned its author, the reaction was one of blithe unawareness or a rather sniffy indifference... I soon gained the impression that the name Andahazi itself sufficed to provoke – 'en ciertos sectores'– the opposite of D. H. Lawrence's admonition: whence 'We don't know the tale but wouldn't trust the teller'...[8]

While 'cinco mil' corrected to 'siete mil', 'Real Armada' replaced by 'Real Marina', 'al hundirse' becoming 'se hundía', might have merited minor (geneticist) attention, it is the only other textual shift, namely, of the extended opening two sentences, that invites immediate re-thinking; above, below and beyond previous analysis... and access to a 'transparency of linguistic relations if not social ones, a "space where no language has a hold over any other"'. Whence a Barthes-derived challenge to that class of reader or readers primed to pass through the

---

[8] Only subsequently did I spot the small-print footnote (p. 55) to the *Blanco y Negro* version dated 28 March 1999 and that was always used in class; it refers to 'su primera novela *El anatomista* – acusada de *escabrosa* desde ciertos sectores' ['his first novel *The Anatomist* – accused in certain sectors of being *scabrous*']; my italics.

presumed *lisible* of the real towards the *scriptible jamais hors-texte*, whereby a short apparently culture-specific 'Argentine' chronotope is subjectable to deconstructive re-writability, in an inverted transcendental, downwards, *requete* hellish, *re-re-lectura*.

Federico Andahazi would not be the first in the aftermath of a prolonged conflict, a *process* of state-sponsored brutalism – whether projected to last a thousand years, or incompetently conducted, albeit at the cost of at least thirty thousand disappeared and broken lives without number, that did endure, alas, for some three thousand days – to risk an aptly 'scabrous' (we shall echo but to reinforce, not refute) wherefore *De profundis* literary discourse. Here, in particular, the text plumbs the depths of a *junta*-inspired-and-incited depravity... and, extrapolating, *pace* Roland, fathoms a 'social *dys*topia' as it swerves anxiously away from an influential precursor (say, *leaning*) towards a *soi-disant* voyage to the end of the Right?

An instance is the style promulgated in the novel said to be the second most-sold in Castilian after (also John Ward's?) the *Quixote*, Camilo José Cela's *La familia de Pascual Duarte*, in the train of the Spanish Civil War. *Tremendismo* has been associated thereafter with an exaggerated lingering on the grotesque, gratuitously cruel and psychopathically murderous character of Cela's eponymous protagonist and, by unavoidable extension, of the Francoist State that had rendered the narrative readable as an all-too-realistic fiction.

Is Andahazi's option for the 'poor' style of *tremendismo* pitched merely to sensationalize? And, retrospectively, is the surreptitious meta-referential 'glimpse' of 'another Irishman who was in fact Argentine, Rodolfo Walsh' some gratuitous sleight of hand concealing-revealing the bogus relevance of that 'en realidad' which, textually, both separates and conjoins nationalities? Does such a hyphenated sense of belonging – ascribed to the extra-textually secret police-murdered author of the mixed genre testimony-fiction-investigative journalism of 1957, *Operación masacre* – matter?

Or, there where SS-*jouissance* was, might *le plaisir du texte* radically reveal and invite resistance to the sado-masochist dominance of a Fascist pervert prototype's torture and extermination of its stubbornly plural internal other through the cyclical *intra*-banality of evil?

> Up to your waist in water,
> Up to your eyes in slush –
> Using the kind of language,
> That makes the sergeant blush;

Who wouldn't join the army?
That's what we all inquire,
Don't we pity the poor civilians
sitting beside the fire.
Chorus
Oh! Oh! Oh! It's a lovely war,
Who wouldn't be a soldier eh?
J. P. Long and Maurice Scott, 1917

The poetry of heroism appeals irr-
esistibly to those who don't go to war,
and even more to those whom the war is
making enormously wealthy. It's always
so.

Louis-Ferdinand Céline

That art and politics must somehow stand speechlessly, ingenuously, apart is contradicted by artists prepared to take on the establishment, head on or via between-the-lines subversions less than welcome in societies embroiled in, or in the recuperative period after, traumatic conflict. The literary and cinematographic representation of the 1982 Malvinas-Falklands war was never going to avoid controversies. Such tensions informed discussions after talks I was invited to give on *De eso no se habla/We Don't Talk About It*, María Luisa Bemberg's internationally acclaimed film of 1993; hardly surprising in respect of the director's playing on and with a metaphorical micro-Argentina, self-dwarfed and aggrandised by the glamour of the eternal outsider in a destructive marriage of grotesque but unsustainable deceptions. Her cinematography epitomised, I suggested, Theodor Adorno's proposal for understanding the effects of war:

> It is now virtually in art alone that suffering can still find its own voice, consolation, without immediately being betrayed by it [...] It is to works of art that has fallen the burden of wordlessly asserting what is barred from politics. (Adorno, 1985, 313)

To engage with neo-, post-, and intra-colonial relations in a production not to be determined as categorically suitable for either cultural, or aesthetic, or historical, or political analysis *separably* was irresistible: be it – were it – at the memorable 1997 Colloque de Cérisy-la-Salle, *La part du féminin dans le surréalisme*, in 'Est-ce bien de cela qu'on parle? En deçà et au-delà du surréel féminin en Argentine'; at the1999 UNC Córdoba debates on *Las marcas del género: configuraciones de la diferencia en la cultura*, in '*De eso no se habla… ¿o sí?*'; at the Institute of Romance Studies, London, in 1999; or at the *Congreso Internacional de la Asociación Española de Semiótica*, in 2000. At issue whenever the putative inseparability of the discourses of art and politics was raised, not least in respect of Argentina and indeed Latin America generally, was whether as much heat as light resulted. Cliché, yes; but just another false binary? Read on...

VII. INFANTILIZING THE NATION
María Luisa Bemberg's *De eso no se habla... ¿O, sí?*
Yes, *I do... n't want to talk about it*

> - A este pueblo no puede venir
> ningún circo.
> - ¿Por qué?
> - Porque nunca vino uno...

Sí cómo no...

Spoken emphasis? Written equivalence? A conflated metaphysics of presence *as* absence? What is to be talked about, written, filmed, or silenced? Who owns culture? Who decides what is discursively appropriate? And with what moral conscience at stake? What acceptabilities, respectabilities, correctness? What medium, what genre, might most effectively plumb and project the collective imaginary? And with what degree of interference? Even at an explicit juncture of a nation's coming to terms with its present, and with its suppressed or 'absent' recent past, it will always still be necessary to pursue questions of proprietary rights, of ownership.

It is pertinent to ask such questions with regard to cinema in post-dictatorship Argentina in general and, in particular, to María Luisa Bemberg's 1993 film *De eso no se habla*. Amidst the moral seriousness of a culture still adjusting to the psychological implausibilies of *Punto Final*, that guillotine law whereby military (and other) personnel 'acting under orders' sought to avoid, and indeed might have succeeded in avoiding, having to face due legal process, Bemberg's carnivalization of a mother's corralling of her dwarf-daughter might have struck the cinema-going public as jarringly frivolous. Certainly, the plot turns on the problematic enforcement of a presumed *Obediencia Debida*, and undermines many a national shibboleth in the process. It does so, however, within the confined imaginary of a tiny rural community. Ostensibly, the film pays no heed whatsoever to a contemporary archival 'madre' or 'abuela' thematics, deemed appropriate, by many critics, both locally and internationally, to the ethical imperative of searching the national conscience. What the film did achieve for its director was a late-career international box-office success. Casting the ageing but ever-irresistible (and marketable) Marcello Mastroianni opposite the accomplished Luisina Brando and the debutante Alejandra Podesta, Bemberg constructs an uncommon variation on the romantic triangle consisting of the outsider Ludovico d'Andrea, the widow

Leonor, and the daughter 'la pequeña' Carlota. The question arises, however, as to whether the director, in making a comparatively high-budget film in international co-production, was somehow less authentically Argentine – and concomitantly less prone to reflect its politico-cultural reality and ideological preoccupations – than her more cash-strapped 'national' counterparts? In a recent, uncompromising, study, 'Del cine-testimonio al cine-testamento' (1997), Ximena Triquell pursues the implications for a national cinema of involvement in international co-productions:

> Los resultados son dispares. Mientras resulta un medio sumamente eficaz para financiar filmes que de otro modo no podrían realizarse, la necesidad de proveer películas para un mercado internacional implica, en numerosos casos, limitar las complejidades de la trama, para atenerse a recetas fáciles de éxito seguro [...] En este desolador panorama resulta sorprendente encontrar realizadores aún interesados en hablar sobre la historia reciente. (Triquell, 1997, 65-6)

> [The results are uneven. While it is a highly effective way of financing films that would otherwise never be screened, the need to produce films for an international market implies, in many cases, limiting the complexities of plot, in order to hold on to easy recipes for guaranteed success [...] In this desolating panorama it is surprising to find directors still interested in speaking about recent history.]

She goes on to single out Adolfo Aristarain, Lita Stantic, and Jeannine Meerapfel as directors who, in the period from 1991 to 1993, 'dibujan esa grieta por la que, en la homogénea apatía del cine argentino de la primera metad de esta década, se insinúa esperanza' (66). Triquell's criteria for the effective capturing of *lo acaecido, lo ocurrido* – key terms in her arguments concerning history and the real – raise 'cuestiones complejas, tanto sobre los hechos (las condiciones que hicieron posible la represión, la actitud pasiva de la población ante lo que sucedía, etc.), como sobre la posibilidad de representación de lo ocurrido y la forma más adecuada para hacerlo' ['complex questions, as much regarding the facts (the conditions which made possible the repression, the passive attitude of the population towards what was happening, etc.), as about the possibility of any representation of what happened and the most adequate way of so doing'] (67). As her title suggests, and as her Genettian analysis confirms, primacy of place is given to 'un recorrido a través de la memoria'; but, she insists, this must be a 'trip through memory' which fulfils certain conditions: 'así, si bien se regresa al mismo lugar de donde se partió, éste já no es el "mismo"' ['and so, although there is the return to the starting point, it is no longer the "same place"'] (69).

Triquell's option for a national-testimonial mode of effective engagement with Argentine society of the post-*proceso* era commits her to a preference for depicting directly recent political reality and its effects or, at the very least, to reading the national cinema in militant terms. In *Magical Reels* (1990), John King points out that, acutely aware of both the source and the nature of the censorship which bedevilled the distribution of her early film *Señora de nadie* (1982), and its treatment of sexual politics, María Luisa Bemberg soon adopted a system of encodings, generic and cultural, to convey other effects:[1]

> We must beware of using sixties rhetoric to condemn the very different realities of the 1980s.[2] María Luisa Bemberg also successfully worked within the codes of melodrama in 1984 with *Camila*, which was a huge box-office success [...] The film also undermines the stereotypes of women, enshrined in such

---

[1] 'Bemberg's treatments caused initial problems with the censors: "When I wanted to do *Señora de nadie*, there was a military regime in power, and they told me that it was a very bad example for Argentine mothers and that we couldn't put a *maricón* in the film. The colonel said he would rather have a son who had cancer than one who was homosexual, so I couldn't do it. I had thought that both a homosexual and a separated woman were marginals, and so in the film they get together". *Señora de nadie* was premiered the day before the invasion of the Malvinas/Falklands, a military adventure that would help accelerate the demise of the military government. By mid-1982, the regime was crumbling and the transition to democratic government was under way' (King, 1990, 90-1).

[2] A clue to the predominating critical climate out of which such prescriptiveness has emerged is spelt out by John King: 'Solanas and Getino theorized their concerns in a seminal, bombastic essay "Towards a Third Cinema", which has had a significant impact in Latin America and in the Third World. The essay covers four themes: cultural neo-colonialism in Argentina, the dependent nature of the Argentine film industry, the Third Cinema, and militant cinema as a crucial aspect of Third Cinema. It argues that in Argentina and in the Third World generally, film makers must pose an alternative to both the first cinema, Hollywood, and the second cinema, the "auteur" cinema, which does not commit itself to popular struggle [...] This then is the cinema of liberation, the Third Cinema, a production strategy and a political strategy, which is a mixture of Third World and Peronist "Third Way" rhetorics' (King, 1990, 87-8).

codes as the nineteenth-century American 'Cult of True Womanhood', a blend of piety, purity, domesticity and submissiveness, or in the idea of the 'fallen woman', a character who populates literature and film and who must be punished for the transgression of sexual mores. (King, 1990, 96)

L'effet du (sur)réel

In the analyses which follow, as well as looking at functions of the real in *De eso no se habla* and its representation of a sleepy and apparently 'out-of-time' Argentine small-town society, I shall also draw attention to the inseparability of reality effects and what I choose to term surreality effects. I shall look to the surreal as a space of both comedy and transgression, a face of both the risible and the monstrous. I shall ask whether, in the suppression of such a face, it is only the sexually threatening subversive that is subjected to moral censorship; or whether such repression is always also inseparably, though differentially, political. Specifically, and in terms of sexual politics, I shall suggest that Bemberg is alert to cinema's parallel role to that of literature in responding to a challenge expressed, for Latin America, by the Mexican writer and critic Elena Poniatowska:

> Women writers have not changed their calendar; the centre of their solar system is still man, and the rules of life are still those dictated by patriarchal society. Latin American women's literature still has not discovered itself: an infinite variety of genres awaits us in the future. We come onto earth to recognize our faces, as the Nahuatl philosophy says. One side of our faces has been the slow discovery of women writers [...] And if society rejects them, it will be because they will have rejected society first; then the waters will follow, not only the amniotic fluid that gives life to the foetus, but all the waters that come from unknown, unsuspected, sources, a great waterfall will splash over us with all its strength, all its violence, all that women have kept inside them for years of repression, and also – why not say it – for years of convenience. (Poniatowska, 1996, 158-61)

Such a challenge might be viewed as one taken up by Bemberg within the context of a cinema which enlists effects of *épatement* in order comically to inconvenience patriarchies – and, why not say it, complicit matriarchies? At a virtually unbridgeable distance from the production of many contemporary cinematographers in Argentina, *De eso no se habla* might be more pertinently approached as Bemberg's exploiting of *l'effet du surréel*. As for the filter of such a strategy, the role played by the cinema of Luis Buñuel may be seen, still, as primary. The unsettling of the constructs of personal and national identities via tropes of displacement, ellipsis, incongruity, and indeterminacy has been a familiar legacy of the early cinema of the surreal since the 1920s. To heed Buñuel's response to the Surrealists' Paris discussion of the 1920s is also, however, to broach ethico-political values and an artistic method which Bemberg might be said to have adopted here. Namely, a stance *against the prevailing orders* of an Argentina ever in *desfasaje*, ever out of phase with its self, its selves:

> What fascinated me most [...] in all our discussions at the *Cyrano*, was the moral aspect of the movement [...] It was an aggressive morality based on the complete rejection of all existing values. We had other criteria: we exalted passion, mystification, black humour, the insult, and the call of the abyss. Inside this new territory, all our thoughts and actions seemed justifiable; there was simply no room for doubt. Everything made sense. Our morality may have been more demanding and more dangerous than the prevailing order, but it was also stronger, richer, and more coherent. (Buñuel, 1994, 107)

The strains of subversion upon which *De eso no se habla* primarily draws – passion, mystification, black humour, the insult – debunk the not so discreet sham of a very Argentine bourgeoisie. The *effects* of using motor cars or dress-fashions, whether lifted from now the '20s or '30s, now the '40s or '50s, set but do not fix the action of Bemberg's film in a particular moment of national reality. The bourgeois time-frame with and within which it operates allows for a shuttle between, say, the 1930s and more recent reference. To-ing and fro-ing in time, to-ing and fro-ing in space, the film exploits the unstable locus of identity-construction of both nation and individual. Inward and outward looking, provincially conservative and all-too-easily impressed by imported cosmopolitanism, a small town develops its Janus-faced posture towards both the (*criollo-hierba mate*) national and the (Italian-filter) cosmopolitan exotic. Importation, however, brings both added value and a levy to be paid, whether in the province or in the capital.

Uneven modernities

In 'The Last Snapshots of Modernity: Argentine Cinema after the "Process"' (1996), Elia Geoffrey Kantaris problematizes crucially both the cultural circumstances and the aesthetic complexities of what I have referred to as an Argentina ever out of phase with its self, its selves:

> Argentina [...] suffers what we might call a 'delayed modernity' which reaches deep into the totalizing core of Peronism with its blend of the neo-fascist personalist rule, the quasi-socialist championing of workers' rights and income redistribution, and the nationalist promise of industrial greatness on the backs of the ordered and mobilized masses. Yet what is the relevance of this delayed modernity to the Argentina of the 1980s, just emerging from the latest and bloodiest of its military dictatorships? One answer might be to view the period of military rule which began in 1976 as the violent culmination of the process of transition from the industrial modernization of the Peronist state-led economy of the 1940s and '50s [...] to account for the social cost of that 'Process' (*la deuda interna*) [...] Argentine culture begins a profound re-examination of the ideologies and the promises of this delayed modernity, scanning the horizon for a flash of light, for some clue of its cultural co-ordinates and of the direction in which to proceed. (Kantaris, 1996, 222-23)

Plus ça change... for the benefits of sophisticated self-scrutiny, it seems, are still, in the '90s, double-edged: '"Our culture is a disaster when it comes to self-image", says Pablo Chapur' (Faiola, 1997, 14). Behind the old canard about *porteños* thinking they are French, wishing they were English, speaking Spanish but being Italian, lie notoriously more sinister faces and masks:

> Experts cite a uniquely Argentine struggle with self-image and personal identity. In Buenos Aires [...] more people undergo psychoanalysis per capita than anywhere else in the world [...] Here the pressure to be thin like a model has become overwhelming [...] 'You don't find Argentine girls aspiring to be lawyers or doctors these days. They all want to be models' [...] Argentina's leading super-model, Mancini, lapsed into a coma for several days in December after liposuction on her already tiny frame. The cases of men with eating disorders are also rising markedly. 'I had a sense that unless I was totally thin, my

friends would tease me or I wouldn't get a girlfriend', said Martín, aged 18. He was admitted to the hospital three months ago when he became afraid to swallow because 'my saliva had too many calories'. (Faiola, 1997, 14)

The surreal effects of this 1997 news story – none too distant from either a Buñuel sequence or an '80s Almodóvar pastiche of one – evoke a socio-political reality and a cultural climate out of which emerged the apparently out-of-era film *De eso no se habla*.[3] To re-echo Poniatowska, 'splashing over us with all its strength, all its violence' and, I would add, its surreal *effectiveness*, 'all that women have kept inside them for years of repression, and also – why not say it – for years of convenience', has vitriolically penetrated that carapace of women's own reluctance 'to admit that they were writers as if saying so would annihilate their capacity for being women and would transform them into some kind of freak' (Poniatowska, 1996, 60). The freak-show at which women have been put on display by men is, in turn, comically exposed by Bemberg.

A tell-tail show

The film displays, but subversively transforms, a community's perceptions of freakiness and, as the title emphasizes, screens the unvoiceable. What can and cannot be said, as well as alternative modes of expression and of social performance, elaborated whether by way of enforcement or resistance, will be the subject of, and under, analysis. First psychologically, and then politically. *De eso no se habla* – no doubt in the shadow of a pastiched French father – might be said to shake an unpalatable cocktail of *ça parle* and *le nom du père*. But apart from provoking trigger-happy interdictory responses via Jacques Lacan, and clichédly facile re-appropriations which reinforce the very masculist structures they might seek to subvert, Bemberg's film also invites the critic to enter analysis through a surreal imaginary which is both feminine and Jewish. In *Freaks: Myths and Images of the Secret Self* (1978), Leslie A. Fiedler plots a suitable *Map of Misreading*, in Bloomian terms, for the anxious swerve Bemberg takes – away from the

---

[3] Out of time, out of space; and it might seem out of place to hear Roland Barthes (par Roland Barthes): 'Mutation du corps (à la sortie du sanatorium) [...] Depuis, débat perpétuel avec ce corps pour lui rendre sa maigreur essentielle (imaginaire de l'intellectuel; maigrir est l'acte naïf du vouloir-être-intelligent)' (Barthes, 1975, 34).

'cine testimonial' of the Argentine mainstream. In the chapter 'Dwarfs: Changing the Image', he asserts:

> After millennia of ghettoization, they have dared to dream of forging themselves into 'the most cohesive class of people since the unification of the Jews'. Jew and Dwarf? How often that conjunction has occurred to me as I, a Jewish non-Dwarf, have pursued their history. (Fiedler, 1978, 89)

Bemberg's treatment of Argentine society as one which unsuccessfully chooses to represent itself as pursuing its history monologically, repressing such conjunctions as might display cultural differences of race, class, gender, and other tensions at play within the nation, begins ludically. The principal female protagonists of the film, Doña Leonor and her 'monstrous' daughter-dwarf, Carlota, contribute to plays on names which, throughout, are both multiple and suggestively multi-lingual. Whether or not in a refined rejection of the neighbours' *sobriquet* for 'Carlotita', Leonor, and at the little girl's insistence, in echo of her clucking tutor, Monsieur Poussineau, calls her beloved and artistically accomplished creation (or is it *confection*?) 'Charlotte'. However, her French-lettered precaution cannot protect her, or us, from the (mis)conception enshrined within the *chatte* of her little *harlot*. Yet before indulging further such free-associations of automatic linguistic, visual, and cultural fore-play, the analyst might return to the Kristevan fluidity of the opening sequence of Bemberg's adaptation of the original Julio Llinas short story.

The virtually closed sign-system of the all-female first scene – Carlota's second birthday party – is only potentially intruded upon by maleness, in the figure of the young servant Mojamé (*sic*), whose latent 'Arabian' function is not to be revealed, in Bemberg's treatment, until the very end of the film. It is as if the widow and her daughter were, until this primal moment, at one and as one. There had thus been no need for Leonor to heed the epigraph which, to the sound of laughter (whether of joy or of mockery we do not know), appears on the semiotically 'empty' screen of quasi-amniotic darkness: 'This tale is dedicated to all people who have the courage to be different in order to be themselves'.[4] Emergence into language occurs via whispers, the hidden-behind-the-hand pointers of other mothers only finding voice

---

[4] The epigraph appears in English in the internationally released version of the film, which has English subtitles. It is some four minutes shorter than the original and excludes the M. Poussineau French lesson.

in the indirectly expressed solidarity of the neighbour with a deaf-mute daughter. But Doña Leonor refuses to accept the monstrosity of this second birth(day) – and the narrator is afforded his first opportunity to hold up the vanity-mirror of (masculine?) omniscience: 'Por mi parte creo poder asegurar que todo empezó ante un espejo, en una noche de luna' [For my part I think that I can state with certainty that it all began in front of a mirror, on a moonlit night]. The semiotically fluid phase of a 'perfect' Carlota is superseded by the performative *stade du miroir* of the – for Leonor – party-dressed but potentially unstressed Carlo*tita*. Only that evening, first before her own mirror and later under the cover of darkness, does Leonor react: 'Mojamé, Mojamé, ¡Despierta!'. Invoking the aid of her dormant but ever-present Muslim puppet-prophet, in the ineffectual absence-in-death of her late (and 'incomparable... as a Catholic') husband Azumendi, she enters – in an inspired Bembergian inversion of *Kristallnacht* – upon her pastiched iconoclasm. Proleptically repressing configurations of a threatening *petit guignol*, she smashes and buries some (markedly Aryan) garden gnomes, property of the village priest's German-speaking mistress, the widow Schmidt (and, no less, of an Argentine collective imaginary?). There follows the *Inquisición* of her book-burning (*Gulliver's Travels*, *Snow White*, *Tom Thumb*). The near-silence of the sequence is broken only by the mock-shock gravity of the Protestant Frau... '¡Despierte, padre!', more bathetic than any Lacanian invocation of *le nom du père*, not least because of the *usted* form of the imprecation... and the fact that Padre Aurelio has kept on, in clerically sober monochrome, his (white) underwear and (black) socks. When we next see Leonor, in his sacristy, she is firmly rejecting the ineffectual assertion of the Law of the Father by the fornicating Aurelio. She is obliged to confront this parody of Aurelius as merely time-serving and to assume control of him and his flock. For what had previously been intoned only by an as yet apparently extra-diegetic narrator, 'Ya no tenía alguna duda, el orgullo de su vientre, la luminaria de sus ojos, la alegría de su corazón... era enana' ['No longer did she have any doubt, the pride of her womb, the light of her eyes, the joy of her heart... was a dwarf'], having found overt and intra-diegetic influence in Padre Aurelio's reference to 'la *pequeña* Carlota', now prompts the female interdiction (*un non de mère*?) of Leonor's first but emphatic barrier to her daughter's entry into language: 'De eso no se habla'. And, the male-voice narrator assures us, San José de los Altares would obey: 'De ese asunto no se hablaría más' [On that subject nothing more would be spoken]. *Supplementing* the metaphysics of taboo, he adds: 'De haberse hablado del asunto se hubiese dicho que Doña Leonor pretendía *suplir* la brevedad de su hija con el prestigio de las artes y de las letras' ['If the matter had been spoken about one might have said that Doña Leonor was trying *to make up* for the shortness of her daughter through the prestige of the arts and literature'] (my emphases). And so pass thirteen years.

In the libidinal economy of a but temporarily interrupted feminine superstructure, namely, a matriarchally-imposed conspiracy of silence, a base but tell-tale market is very soon seen to operate, as Leonor provides for Charlotte in and through her *Almacén La Carlota*... the village store, display-case, exhibition-site, place of exchange, cross-roads of fateful encounters. Soon, too, (a ludic Vico, bearing the insight that poetry is born of our ignorance of causes?) Marcello Mastroianni's Ludovico d'Andrea intervenes. As, upstairs, the now late-adolescent Carlota sits reading in bed, Ludovico plays out, downstairs, that parlour-game of chance and of popular culture which gives rise to the saying 'la vida es una tómbola' ['life is a lottery']. As teller of tales, as charming man caller, he thrusts his hand into the semi(er)otic pouch and manipulates a code of numbers: '15 - la niña bonita' ['the pretty girl']; '21 - la mujer' ['woman']; '71 - la casa' ['home']; '40 - la danza' ['dance']; '33 - la edad de Cristo' ['the age of Christ']; '48 - il morto che parla' ['dead man talking']; '77 - las piernas de la mujer' ['the woman's legs']. With him at Leonor's *tómbola* table are Padre Aurelio, Frau Schmidt, Doctor Blanes and the latter's wife, Mercedes, Ludovico d'Andrea – the classically elegant Italian outsider – deciphers the village luminaries and their secrets as adroitly as he deals out their respective counters. A pronounced complicity prefigures the breaking of Leonor's imposed code of silence... the '*eso* de que (no) se habla' would appear, for the townsfolk, to be but the thinnest veneer. As they leave, Frau Schmidt says to Padre Aurelio '¿Me acompaña, Padre?'. 'Sí, cómo no. Con mucho gusto', he intones. Mercedes, in contrast, for once fails to entice Ludovico back home for his night-cap *copa*... but only because her husband is present (if not on call). Signor d'Andrea prefers – on this particular Tuesday, to visit another, less private, house. Not only has he declared himself – as philosopher of tango – to his respectable *tómbola* partners: 'En mi vida tuve muchas, muchas minas, pero nunca una mujer!' ['In my life I've had many, many, girls but never a woman']. He now also shows the poker-playing eminences of the *quilombo* that he is a discriminating and witty brothel poet: 'Sólo vengo por Myrna'. He only comes for Myrna... but Thursday is normally his night. Tuesday that of Don Saturnino, wheel-chair bound, stroke-victim mayor who cannot speak (left-side... *por eso no habla*) and whose concupiscent mumbles (*de eso*) are decoded by his long-suffering but short-sighted son. So Myrna takes the handles and wheels away the dignitary: 'vuelvo en seguida' ['I'll be back shortly'] she sneers in a wry aside to a d'Andrea already waiting to slip into the mayor's position...

Soon the gamester is in the *Almacén*, dispensing his imported gifts of, and for, seduction. In the case of 'la enana', his present is a macaque. The monkey's tail is in Charlotte's lap... just as the exotic tales of far-off lands are on Ludovico's tongue. And, in the background, hovers the passive Mojamé, whose differential racial role is, at this stage, still denied in his '¡No soy eso!' [I'm not that!]' rejection of the womanly midget's ethnic teasing, 'seguro que tus padres eran árabes' ['it's sure that your parents were Arabs']. But any full-frontal Eastern promise latent in Mojamé is deferred (or stimulated?) by Leonor's rasping interjectory '¡Que se mueva!' ['Get a move on!']; a deferral replicated by Ludovico's ill-apprehended substituting of a Shetland pony for the (Arabian) steed which Leonor seeks for her daughter's fifteenth birthday, unconscious rein-cum-spur to the play-boy Ludo's curiosity-cum-voyeurism. 'Anduve buscando pero aquí no hay animales de esa categoría' ['I went searching but here there are no animals of that quality'], she explains. Though Leonor is angry enough to whip away first the Shetland pony and then her own dark mare (-and-trap?), *Cuerva* (ill-omen?), she is more than appeased when d'Andrea gives to Carlota the requisite white stallion, pointing him toward the fanlight from where he will (but Nevermore?) view her daughter's first mounting: 'le puse una escalera...' ['I put a ladder up for her...']. The trotting mare of Leonor underlines her role, in this sequence, as a *trotaconventos*, as a complicit (however unconscious) go-between.

The more Ludovico – according to Padre Aurelio, performing the pomps of Satan – peppers his narrative with references to Cayenne, Devil's Island, and the exotic real, the more Carlota transforms his discourse into the erotic surreal. What she holds in her lap is not only a sexual threat, a tell-tale tail to be uncurled, but also the prehensile knack to make a monkey out of both her mother and the small-town repressions of San José de los Altares. Evoking imaginative 'selvas y orquídeas' ['forest and orchids'] *à la* Douanier Rousseau, in the public place of the *Almacén* which bears her name, only in the private space of the barn-cum-show-ring does she bare the mane of her white stallion. Never side-saddle but ever astride, face painted and head turbaned, prolepsis of – for her if not for a perceptive (no less *voyeur*?) audience – pleasure to come. If this enclosure is a mirror-stage, then Bemberg has also provided her, again on a birthday, the fifteenth, with a mirror-state. For Charlotte is caught by her mother performing tentative first dance-steps to the 78 rpm strains of Bizet's *Carmen*... to the accompaniment, and in the company, of her own captivated image. She is soon unafraid to emerge from the frame of Doña Leonor's interdictory control, opting to take her bow standing (short) not seated (erect), prior to her first public performance *qua* pianist, of Schumann's *Étude* opus 68. (*Qua* penis, she might also be said to perform as the shrunken fetish-object of the glowing widow's previously unfulfilled desire.)

Leonor, in anguished witness to her daughter's growing libidinal awareness, but blind to Carlota's construction, before the mirror, of a positive self-image, tears the buttons from her dress, in proleptic (mamma's?) mourning for her 'lost' daughter-cum-whore-imitator. The 'coming out', as woman, of the girl-mutant Carlota provokes the resistance of all of San José de los Altares. From Mothers' Union frumps to bordello queens, through a bevy of the town's dignitaries and gargoyles, young and old, a freak's parade of Buñuelian proportion provides the bourgeois 'normality' against which Ludovico's own struggle is to take shape. He fails to die (in an 'engineered', self-sacrificing, duel with his cuckolded Dr Blanes); he cannot (forever) run away; he is himself, *mutatis mutandi*, entrapped. While the town and even Leonor read his 'madness' as love for the widow herself, Ludovico craves Carlota: 'Puede considerarlo mal gusto pero no es cosa de broma... La deseo como nunca he deseado a otra mujer' ['You may consider it bad taste but it's no joking matter... I desire her as I've never desired another woman'], he confides to a protesting Aurelio. The crescendo of incredulous mockery only enhances Carlota's immunity to derision, only strengthens the mother-daughter role-reversal: '¿Estás contenta?' – 'La Felicidad no lo es todo' ['Are you happy?' – 'Happiness isn't everything']. Her entry into marriage will not be unconditional. She will not thus be framed... or fulfilled, by a however infatuated (Ludi-crutch?) player with his own desire...; a besotted collector of miniatures.

Neither the paroxysms of death (Don Saturnino's) nor the hysterical at-the-altar laughter (Doña Leonor's) that punctuate the wedding ceremony are at all climactic for Carlota. For her, penetration of the social imaginary is but a moderately pleasurable phase; and the broken membrane of a sexuality explored is soon revealed as being but a release into mourning. No Ludovico, no status, no available otherness can sate desire, nor defer the greyness of small-town envelopment. For, thus far, Carlota, Carlotita, Charlotte, 'la pequeña', has been performed upon; re-designated; assigned. In bed, she might mirror the off-the-shoulder black negligé(e) of her mother but never the *maja vestida* pose. From a chronicle of Eros to Thanatos foretold. The shock of her mother's grave-tending inkling of an ominous world-beyond – heralded by an elephant's trumpeting clarion-call to the circus ring of distant plenitude – poignantly prompts the overt interdiction, spoken to Ludovico, now in the driving-seat as mayor and as husband: 'Que no vaya a la función'. For Leonor, past passive role-playing, as Azumendi's unsatisfied wife, has bred present active pay-rolling, as mother of the far from reluctant debutante Charlotte. For Carlota, such symbolic orders, however imposed, cannot stunt the development either of the powerful (and therefore, for the townsfolk and no doubt for many an audience, sexually threatening) woman, or of the artist within. Her creativity, her practised flair, her (w)horsewomanship, her poise and, no less, her sensitivity, have radiated towards a distant circumference of self-definition... whence the pull of the ring.

Poniatowska's plea, again, rings out: 'when women realize that a woman is an extraordinary being, full of grace and harmony [...] they will give us their intimacy with the earth and with themselves [...] they will not be afraid of losing their men because they have won themselves'. 'Years of repression' (the town's but *not* Carlota's acceptance of the matriarchal Leonor's interdictory 'de eso no se habla') and, 'why not say it?, years of convenience' (Ludovico's and the patriarchal San José de los Altares' turning of Carlotita into a diminished commodity within and beyond her *Almacén*) have come undone. The garb of mayor's wife respectability ill fits the creative and performative genius cultivated in Carlotita the listener, Carlota the player... as the imposition of both a French and many another imported discourse eventually extinguishes the *ersatz* 'Charlotte'. The closing phase of Bemberg's film draws ever more strongly on the Buñuelian heritage of *épatement*, reminiscent of *Tristana* in Carlota's shrinking before the monster of bourgeois confinement. Even more overtly does it exploit a bestiary inhabited by, and inherited from, surrealist women artists. It is as if the Doña Azumendi who 'paints' her mutant daughter were a composite of both a Leonor and a Leonora. Fini cats, Carrington horses – projected figures of symbolic entrapment in the depiction of a markedly Argentine framing of repressed sexuality – are transformed by the addition, the super-imposition, of Carlota's monkey-business. It is as much with relief as with resignation that Ludovico d'Andrea reacts to the loss of his midget-but-far-from-child bride. Fulfilling the prediction of his beloved *porteño* tango, 'Caminito', which he had sung to Charlotte's piano accompaniment shortly after first appearing in the town, he could have an active role only 'hasta que se fue' ['until she went away'] ... Then he must brave the storm to release (himself from) her (as) white stallion. Metonymic or metaphorical escape? Both... before drowning, say some, or, say others, haunting the Hamburg circus in unrequited search (for, *d'après* Borges, his three-legged *gata*?),[5] the withdrawal ('para siempre') behind the shutters of her failed representation of Charlotte (as *finísima*?) is preceded by lingering camera-shots of a momentarily caged yet soon-to-perform 'great' animality... the elephant (indelible cultural memory?) in chains, the lion (irrepressible sexuality?) behind bars.

An *imprimatur* for a story of gypsy release through the Fellini-evoking wandering circus might be read into Carlota's fleeing from a marriage without appetites. As she walks past the performers' caravans, the men dismantle the Big Top; the women let down and untangle their washed hair in a refiguration of an earlier brothel-scene. A climate of loosened binding is broached and articulated by the dwarf's response to the ring-master's 'Bene?'... 'Bene. Benissimo', she retorts. Passage to a new, augmented, life through a different, superlative, language? From a parodically Italian Argentina to an ever-other El Dorado?... From a ring-mistress to but further taming by a whip-master? Or, *à la* Charlot(te), vaudeville-style, via *La strada* (however incompletely, perhaps only *8½*?), to Babel? Or just, in an escapist's illusion, to the *Circo Houdini*? But who is telling this tale? Not Bemberg herself, *qua* a Pierre Menard, reproducing exactly, in this case, Julio Llinas' 'original' story... but rather – and for observers even half-alert to the Hispanic narrative tradition – as with *Don Quixote*, an entirely 'other' narrator: one who had once said 'no soy eso'; another (self-concealing?) Arab in the Cervantine line of Cide Hamete Benengeli. Only in the final sequence does Mojamé Ben Ali reveal his narrator's identity, indulging a shift from intra- to extra-diegesis. He, too, at last, has entered language, has found the voice to utter his own name... but at what price? Explicitly, he is left behind, to narrate. Yet even he will miss out on Carlota's new story, her unending stories... wistful Arabian inheritor only of a tradition of male dependency on that most surreal of female tale-tellers Sheherezade. Implicitly, he has whetted (or wetted? for *mójame* = moisten me) the young girl's appetite for acting out her own, differently embedded, emplotment. But thereby – in, and out of, Carlota's lap – hung the tail.

De eso se habla, si...

If... si...

---

[5] Cf. 'No hay que buscarle tres pies al gato' ['It's no use searching for three-legged cats']. Two plus that monkey's tail... or paw? Remember? Mourning becomes the *animot*.

If only... si solamente...
But only if... pero solamente si...
Not (yet) yes. No (todavía) sí.

The effectiveness of Bemberg's handling of the questions I have raised, regarding proprietary rights and access to, and for, other faces, alternative voices, might be seen and heard to displace that affirmative accent on realist modes of representation which has habitually bedevilled totalitarian societies. More exquisite than the cultural cadavers which her film dissects are the respective gazes, the plural, indefinite, diffuse, and (not to be confined within national borders) exportable perspectives performed in discourses of *si*... but not of *sí*. The missing accent leaves room for other slants, other cuts, other anatomies, other archives, other disciplines, other punishments... analogous instances of Argentina's infantilization of its self and of its own other(s) within.

The film's propensity for *desfasaje* has already been noted. A non-specific chronotope operating as 'somewhere in a not-so-recent Argentina' allows Bemberg to play with more than just the hardly subtle name of the small town of San José de los Altares. A most (un)holy family eventually gets to the altar, locus of repetition of that ambiguous controlled laughter which opened the film's soundtrack and preceded the emergence of its first images from out of semiotic darkness. '¿Es risa? o es emoción?' ['Is that laughter? Or is it emotion?'] – the vengeful neighbour's *bofetada*, the opportune slap in the face which silences Doña Leonor's hysterical guffaw is more effective than it is enlightening. The very possibility of, the necessity for, a release of subversive force is countered by the community's apparently ineluctable option for silencing any expression of it.[6] Whilst it is

---

[6] Cf. Anna Reid: 'Unable to articulate and produce words, the purpose of language is questioned and, unable to control the movements of her body, the only sound she emits is uncontrolled laughter'. She takes up Foucault's argument that 'language always seems to be inhabited by the other, the elsewhere, the distant: it is hollowed out by distance'. She continues in a treatment of fiction relatable to the present reflections on cinematic strategies: 'By revealing the fragmentary nature of historical discourse upon which the contemporary national discourse is based, the nation-state is delegitimized [...] new or different forms of expression need to be found in order to express the past and its influences on the present [...] History defines the past – and often the present – and is often used as a means of social control. If so many had been excluded from history, how can History be defined and to what extent, as a written document, is it valid?' (Reid, 1998, 86, 87, 90).

tempting to juxtapose the neurotic and the psychotic as modes of analysis appropriate to the film's action, it is only as provisional categories that such readings of the behaviour of Carlota and Doña Leonor, respectively, might be applied. Neurotically, Carlota might be seen as striving to bridge the gap between the village's perception of her, as Carlotita, and her putative place in the symbolic imaginary, as a 'self-outed' performer, as a fulfillable Charlotte... Psychotically, Doña Leonor, regressively, repetitiously, polishing the (*plata*?) name-plate of the late husband's erect but stone monument, rubs herself into a paralysis which, in turn, she seeks to impose upon the small town's future and her (metonymic) daughter's development; in the psychotic case, the symbolic imaginary, *qua* other must be erased... But the three dots indicate necessary incompletion. As I indicated in my opening remarks, the unstable locus of identity-construction is, inseparably, both individual (*frotteuse*?) and national (or *de la Plata*?).

Do you know the way to San José? Or through the barriers to its (or Argentina's) self-representation? One guideline is the rich varietal sound-track of Nicola Piovani. Apart from Carlota's mirror-response to Bizet's *Carmen*, her Schumann recital and the Mendelssohn *Wedding March*, the musical dialogics of the film are a crafty play on popular sentiment... a pastiche of escape into national stereotyping. Filiberto's 'Caminito' and Carlos Gardel's rendering of 'Milonga sentimental' puncture the haunting revisiting of Italian neo-realism via Greco's and D'Arienzo's 'El Flete'. However, a meta-musical score never distant from memory is Carlota's metronomic practising of her scales, superficially at one with, but ultimately resistant to, the ideological layerings placed upon such music's social performance. Occasionally, the music stops:

> Leonor: -Mi pobre marido, que en paz descanse, jamás supo alcanzar a la mujer que se escondía detrás de la dócil y fiel esposa. Y ahora temo que esa mujer no existe.
> Ludovico: -Charlotte tendrá no sólo un marido fiel sino apasionado.
>
> [Leonor: -My poor husband, may he rest in peace, could never reach the woman hiding behind the docile and faithful wife. And now I fear that that woman doesn't exist.
> Ludovico: -Charlotte will have not just a faithful but a passionate husband.]

The ironizing, Satiesque accompaniment to this scene is abruptly syncopated, giving way to the inseparable interruption of reality and of surreality into Leonor's consciousness. As if in a game of musical chairs, she is left silently unseated. Any lapse into sentimentalism, however, will be rapidly combated by a '90s commentary, the parodic – circus beat – intervention of Fito Paez (youth-cult present) masquerading as wedding musician very much *à la* Visconti, eroticizing the clichéd Thanatos in a grotesque pastiche of a scene inherited from *Death in Venice* (death-cult past). Visually, the illusion of a happy-ever-after finale is momentarily indulged. Contrapuntally, marital bliss is parodied as the doll-like newly-weds are waltzed though the mechanical strains of their first coupling. The earlier, compulsive, reaction of Leonor to the sugar figurines atop their wedding cake – biting off and swallowing the heads and hiding the little bodies in her bra – is brought back into sinister, matriarchal, focus.

A socio-political intertext of the devices to which an 'abandoned' provincial Argentine woman will resort in order to keep 'her' man in power (in spite of his overt proclivities for the adolescent girl) begins (and for many viewers will have already long begun) to speak historical and ideological memory through the interstices, gaps, and interruptions of Leonor's controlling desires. Controlling but not always controlled. Perhaps having realized that infantilization of the other and of the self might function inseparably ('juntitas las dos' is her hope for their future), she is momentarily stunned to but discover a passion which Carlota must confront. Political rather than libidinal interest soon takes over in Leonor's ambition for her (stunted) future (offspring): 'ahora tengo que pensar'. From this point, the narrative exposes ever more overtly threads of a social imaginary dyed, though not exclusively coloured, with memories of Ev(it)a Perón.

Cultural memory

Memoria – memory, memoir. One of the dominant words, and discourses, of Latin American intellectual and artistic *milieux* of the last decades, the *memoria* has represented a coming to terms with the dictatorships, the dirty wars, the torture, and the pain of the years of militarism. The *memoria* has claimed, and usually been given, the status of a genre apart, a somehow authentic – authenticated – textualizing of testimony curiously regarded as exempt from discursive troping; tropes which, if recognized, might render it susceptible to the critical analysis traditionally reserved for the primary texts of literary and cinematic production. In this instance, it will not be necessary to deploy, say, Hayden White's multi-layered dissection of the heavily troped discourses of history. Taking up the invitation of applying to the *memoria* not even a Machereyan but simply a Bembergian detection of, and playing with, generic gaps and silences, it is tempting to view *De eso no se habla*, amongst other possibilities, as an instance of the counter-memoir: 'y de aquel día *memorable* en San José de los Altares de ese asunto no se hablará más' ['and from that *memorable* day forth in San José de los Altares that subject will not be spoken of'] (my emphasis). One might then ask whether a critical-institutional preoccupation with remembering can be any freer of symptomatic gaps than are successive acts (and expressions) of forgetting.

It won't be easy

You'll think it strange when I try to explain how I feel, that we still need the tropes after all the memoirs... You won't believe me. All you will see are the facts you once knew, although they're dressed up to the nines, at sixes and sevens with you.

I had to let it happen, I had to change Ximena Triquell's 'cuestiones complejas, tanto sobre los hechos [...] como sobre la posibilidad de representación de lo ocurrido y la forma más adecuada para hacerlo' ['complex questions, as much regarding the facts (...) as about the possibility of any representation of what happened and the most adequate way of so doing']. To re-deploy her terms, the passage from *testimonio* to *testamento* certainly involves an act of the will... but in several senses: from testimony to legacy – and via that *recorrido de la memoria* which cannot exclude another will, the will of desire. Triquell's demand regarding place, however, is also, of necessity, fulfilled: the place of *lo acaecido, lo ocurrido*, can never be the 'same' as the space, the locus, of retrospective enunciation. If she, and we, are committed to re-opening the archives in search of 'las condiciones que hicieron posible la represión' ['the conditions that made repression possible'] or to scrutinize 'la actitud pasiva de la población ante lo que sucedía' ['the passive attitude of the population towards what was happening'], we might listen again to a muted *eso*... An integral part, albeit deferred, of 'proc/*eso* no se habla'?

Half someone else's

A process of speaking (or not speaking) the Nation will always risk (mis)representation. *El pueblo un(id)o* – notwithstanding the disruption latent in the desire thrust into its midst – is determinedly represented as *One*. And the other articles of constitution of the *pueblo* are, no less, those borrowed from a Faith long-Suffering, ever-Militant and would-be Triumphant: *Holy, Catholic, Apostolic*. But the other of language (in which, for Bakhtin, under different but still totalitarian pressures, the word was always half someone else's), must always be pursued dialogically.

The word	**[...someone else's]**
Doña Leonor to Don Saturnino *Recuerda que yo no tengo un hombre a mi lado.*	[Azumendi? D'Andrea? Duarte? Perón?]
Doña Leonor on Don Saturnino *Se murió, Mojamé. Nadie tiene que darse cuenta de nada.*	[Let them eat steak... Oblivious. *A la sombra de...*]
Commissioner of Police to Doña Leonor *Nos hemos quedado un poco acéfalos*	[...]
Doña Leonor to Padre Aurelio *Podríamos recaudar dinero para los niños huérfanos y al mismo tiempo producir un evento cultural*	[*La Fundación Ayuda Social María Eva Duarte Perón*] [*La Ciudad Infantil*]
Doña Leonor to Carlota *Pero voy a ser la primera...*	[First Lady... to die]
Narrator on Ludovico d'Andrea *Obedeciendo a impulsos patrióticos se había enrolado en alguna guerra... o la huida se debía a deudas de juego.*	[Italy? 1939-1945?] [...a gamble]
Padre Aurelio to Ludovico d'Andrea *Lo único que te pido es que no altere la paz de este pueblo.*	[Concordat... appeasement?]
Ludovico d'Andrea to Doña Leonor *Con todo respeto debo decirle que el alcade soy yo. Yo he autorizado la*	[Towards a 'third Position'... *and* foreign capital]

presencia de estos artistas que van
a abonar un impuesto que acabo de
crear por nuestra pobre comuna.

Ludovico d'Andrea to Carlota
Estás libre de ir. Hay tiempo.   [And as for freedom? And as for
                                            fame?]
Carlota to Ludovico d'Andrea
No hace falta.   [They are illusion]

Half and half?

Evenness will only operate in theory. In cultural and political practices, disproportion and its spaces remain to be accounted for. But merely to posit a third factor is as insufficient as it is, predictably, just another category. In a 'special report' for *Screen* (1997), 'The Changing Geography of Third Cinema', Michael Chanan provided ample evidence that then current positions in film criticism were as passionately disputed as in any other arena:

> The real issue lies elsewhere, in the perennial problem about the relationship, or rather mismatch, between theoretical endeavour and the terrain of praxis. This issue is part of the problem: if the question is the practice of Third Cinema, then this is not conducted according to a theory, it responds directly to everyday exigencies. And this applies to both means and ends, both to the political target and the route taken by the process of production [...] the point of reception is polyvalent. The global conditions of postmodern culture make it possible for margins and interstices across the globe to become aware of each other. This is even more acute in the case of, let us say, a North African film-maker exiled in Paris who makes a film about the marginality of his fellow exiles which is then seen, sporadically and intermittently, on screens all around the world; or an Argentine exile who returns to make a film funded by a European television station about the course of the continent's political aspirations. The result is perhaps the extension of Third Cinema into a new space akin to what Teshome Gabriel has recently called nomadic cinema. This much is theory. Perhaps it is necessary to reiterate the point which Getino made in his Notes on Third Cinema, written ten years after the original manifesto: the value of theory is always

dependent on the terrain in which praxis is carried out. Which suggests that what we need now is a new geography. (Chanan, 1997, 187-88)

Chanan's metaphor for Third Cinema interrogates the spatial. My (adjacent) trajectory has traced not a mental re-mapping of some theoretical thirdness but a performance within that shuttle-space between cultures in which any third term can be but provisional. Its representation will always be unsettled by contestatory voices and images ever seeking to appropriate uneven post-modernities. Such post-modernities, as all modernities before them, can be no less disproportionate then the political modernizations which produce, accompany, contradict but do not always control (or infantilize) them. *De eso sí se habla... ¿o no?*

It is without doubt the most intriguing and provocative, and will undoubtedly create camps of for and against with a lot of bemused people saying 'How did it all come about without our noticing it?' What you and the others have done is to dig deep and ask: 'If you do not know what I am about, can you tell me what you are about?', and that produces a lot of guilty shuffling of feet, as at Exeter this spring.

Robert Brian Tate, 1 December 1984

When thirty six years on the hand-written version of this personal thank you note fell from my copy of the *Festschrift* volume presented on his retirement to the distinguished Hispanist mediaevalist and historian R. B. Tate, the reference to the annual conference of the Association of Hispanists of Great Britain and Ireland, held at the University of Exeter, was a reminder of where 'it' had started. Appointed from the École Normale Supérieure in Paris to the newly established inaugural post in Latin American Studies at the University of Nottingham, I had delivered my first public lecture as a member of the AHGBI to what was then a predominantly peninsularists' grouping, in a context where all but one of the university departments in the subject area were headed by early-period specialists.

It was but fifteen months since Gabriel García Márquez had delivered his Nobel Prize acceptance speech on *The Solitude of Latin America*. Shortly after my presentation came the dead hand on my shoulder of the eminent dictionary philologist... and the peremptory 'If you want to make it in this discipline, don't think you can get away with treating us like this, young man'. Thus spake Sirrah Bluster. *Discipline and Punish* misread? No; unread. *What you will* has ever been the food of love, music to my ears, played on and with – 'Free-play of fore-play: the fiction of non-consummation. Speculations on *Chronicle of a Death Foretold*' – here reproduced and, recently, supplemented. Not least, thanks to Brian Tate, Robert Pring-Mill, Arthur Terry and Peter Russell, early-period and all-period luminary humanists all; to such mentors of profound and lasting generational shifts in the discipline, notably in the proliferation across the UK of Latin American Studies, gratitude.

Thirty years to the month after the original publication, in *Gabriel García Márquez: New Readings* (McGuirk, 1987), a chance encounter, in Cartagena de Indias, in August 2017, prompted a return to the primal scene of writing, and composition of the chronicle of a text retold, here appended in an extended 'Speculation – word play. A game of the name'. An off-the-shelf invitation to talk on the legacy of the earlier book in the Librería Ábaco y Café, kindly proffered by the irrepressible fount of GGM love and lore, Iliana Restrepo Hernández, led to an impromptu short presentation to a gathering of its *littér-ateurs habitués* in the magically unreal setting of the Ohlala Bistrot. Shortly before, at the very gates of Getsemani, a passing observation on Colombian usage, casually dropped by a Cambridge colleague, Dr Rory O'Bryen, had op-ened my ears to the episcopal take that was to inform the after-play performed firstly in Colombia, days thereafter, and now here. My thanks go to Iliana and to Rory for reminding me that, like deconstruction, like non-consummation, these decades on, and *pace* J.D., im-'Pure speculation is still waiting'.

VIII. FREE-PLAY OF FORE-PLAY IN
CRÓNICA DE UNA MUERTE ANUNCIADA
Freud, Derrida and García Márquez
Chronicle of a Death Foretold as fiction of non-consummation
Unbecoming 'Speculations – On Freud'

> In his text something must answer for
> the speculation of which he speaks... I
> also maintain that speculation is not only
> a mode of research named by Freud, not
> only the subject of his discourse, but also
> the operation of his writing, what he is
> doing in writing what he is writing here,
> that which makes him do it and that
> which he causes to be done, that which
> makes him write and that which he
> causes to be written.
>
> Jacques Derrida

García Márquez's text, *Crónica de una muerte anunciada* also opens with an epigraph; from the sixteenth-century Portuguese playwright Gil Vicente: 'La caza de amor/es de altanería' (translated by Gregory Rabassa as 'the hunt for love is haughty falconry'). A first speculation concerns the multiple punning which opens the novel, for 'altanería' means height, high flight, falconry, haughtiness and pride; 'de amor' might also mean 'of love' and the second 'de', too, might mean 'of' or 'for'. To the Colombian ear, 'la caza (casa) de amor(es)', too, might prefigure the brothel of María Alejandrina Cervantes. 'Opens the novel', then, in all senses, invites open reading rather than interpretative closure. This analysis of *Chronicle* draws upon several of the speculations applied by Derrida to Freud's *Beyond the Pleasure Principle* and, in its turn, extends the mirroring process of speculary reflection by adducing others. The guiding principle of the interaction between this study and the host-text is Derrida's wish to mark the intersections of the various speculations: 'If we wish to interlace, in another style with other questions, the networks of a so-called internal reading [...] the networks of autobiography, of auto-graphy, of auto-thanatography, and those of the "analytical movement" inasmuch as they are inseparable from it, we must at least, we must at least begin by marking, in the reading hastily called "internal", the places that are *structurally* open to the crossing of the networks' (Derrida, 1978, 86). Thus, this text will take the form of a series of overlapping speculations.

Speculation – speculary reflection

> Q. How did the writing of *Chronicle of a Death Foretold* come about?
>
> A. The novel is set 30 years ago and it's based on a real event, an assassination that took place in a town in Columbia. I was staying very near the participants in this 'drama' at a time when I'd written several short stories but still hadn't got my first novel published. I realized straight away that I'd got hold of some extremely important material, but my mother knew about this and asked me not to write this book while some of those involved were still alive, and then she told me their names. So I just kept putting it off. There were times I thought the 'drama' had ended, but it continued to develop and things kept on happening. If I'd written it then, I'd have left out a great amount of material which is essential to the understanding of the story. (*Cencrastus* 7, 1982, 7).

The mirroring of a 'real event' by a first-person narrator involved in, though recounting retrospectively, the 'drama' which shook Sucre, a small Colombian town, some thirty years previously, invites corroboration, not least beause of the *chronicling* promised by the title and by the presentation of testimony collected from eye-witnesses, participants and even the protagonists themselves. When the *chronicle is* published by the country's, the continent's, most famous author, the topical interest increases. Thus, the invasion of Sucre by journalists shortly after the publication of García Márquez's book in 1981 resulted in a typically pseudo-literary event, a flood of interviews, opinions and memoirs drawn from those involved. The journalistic impact of the novel, however, is not merely *post hoc;* for García Márquez, the professional newspaperman, exploits the generic ambiguity of his text: 'For the first time I have managed a perfect integration of journalism and literature... journalism helps maintain contact with reality, which is essential to literature. And vice-versa: literature teaches you how to write... I learned how to be a journalist by reading good literature' (Grossman, 1982, 71-72). 'Maintaining contact with reality' poses the perennial problem of realism. Yet, in another interview, the author admits the complication already implied, above, in his use of the word 'drama':

> A. It's interesting to see now that the novel which finally emerged has nothing to do with the reality of the situation.
>
> Q. Are any journalistic techniques used in the novel?

A. I've used a reporting technique but nothing of the actual drama or those taking part remains except the point of departure and the structure. The characters don't appear under their real names nor does the description tally with the real place. It's all been poetically transmuted. The only ones who retain their real names are members of my family because they've allowed me to do this. Of course, some of the characters are going to be recognized, but what really interests me, and I believe this must also interest the critics, is the comparison between reality and the literary work.

Q. Aren't you laying the novel open to a guessing game of who's who?

A. That's already happened. When the novel appeared a Bogotá magazine published an article written from where the events took place with photographs of who was supposed to have taken part. They've done a job which in journalistic terms, is, I think, excellent, but there's one snag: the story that the witnesses are now telling the journalists is totally different from what happens in the novel. Perhaps the word 'totally' is wrong here. The starting point is the same but the development is different. I'm pretentious enough to believe that the 'drama' in my book is better, that it's more controlled, more structured. (*Cencrastus* 7, 1982, 7)

When he uses the words 'drama', controlled, more structured, poetically transmuted, García Márquez betrays not only an author's awareness of the existence of what Derrida called 'the places that are *structurally* open to the crossing of the networks' but, at the same time, a reader's propensity to interpret, even to offer value judgements ('my book is better'). He does not go farther than a 'reading hastily called [by me] "internal"', a reading which merely acknowledges the impossibility of mimesis. Thus, 'we [as reader] must begin by marking the places *structurally* open to the crossing'. In the process, 'we do not aim for either priority or originality. We merely formulate formulate speculative hypotheses to explain and describe the facts that we observe (Derrida, 1978, 88).

Fact	**Fiction**
Miguel Reyes Palencia marries and discovers his wife is not a virgin. He returns the bride,	Bayardo San Román marries and discovers his wife is not a virgin. He returns the bride, Ángela

Margarita, to her parents after striking her and abusing her verbally. His friends give him a knife to kill her with. He refuses but offers her the knife to kill herself.	Vicario, to her parents' home where her mother, Pura, strikes her repeatedly.
However, the girl is forced to name her love, Cayetano Gentile Chimento, who is pursued and killed by her brother.	The girl is forced to name her lover. She names Santiago Nasar, who is pursued and eventually killed by her twin brothers, Pedro and Pablo.
García Márquez knows the protagonists. He does not himself witness the events. He promises his mother not to publish while protagonists are alive. She releases him from his promise. He writes *Chronicle* but says he will not publish until the Pinochet regime in Chile falls.	The narrator knows the protagonists and attends the wedding celebrations. He misses the actual crime because he is in the brothel of María Alejandrina Cervantes. The narrator 'pieces together' various eyewitnesses' versions of the death of Santiago Nasar and interviews the principal surviving protagonists.
He publishes *Chronicle* in 1981.	The narrator constantly refers to his text as a 'chronicle'.

The first two references to self on the part of the narrator in *Chronicle* are of different temporal orders. 'Yo estaba reponiéndome de la parranda de la boda en el regazo apostólico de María Alejandrina Cervantes' ['I was recovering from the wedding revels in the apostolic lap of María Alejandrina Cervantes'] (11) refers to the narrator at the time of Santiago Nasar's death: 'cuando volví a este pueblo olvidado tratando de recomponer con tantas astillas dispersas el espejo roto de la memoria' ['when I returned to this forgotten village, trying to put back together the mirror of memory from so many scattered fragments'] (14) points to the *construction* of the present narration, nearly thirty years later. The mirror is broken. But as scattered as the fragments are the instances of 'I'. The intervening instances are also chronicled in the text: 'Yo conservaba un recuerdo muy confuso de la fiesta antes de que hubiera decidido rescatarla a pedazos de la memoria ajena [...] En el curso de las indagaciones para esta crónica recobré numerosas vivencias marginales [...] Muchos sabían que en la inconsciencia de la parranda le propuse a Mercedes Barcha que se casara conmigo [...] tal como ella misma me lo recordó cuando nos casamos catorce años después' ['I had a very confused memory of the festivities before I decided to rescue them piece by piece from the memory of others [...] In the course of the investigations for this chronicle, I recovered numerous marginal experiences [...] Many know that in the unconsciousness of the binge I proposed marriage to Mercedes Barcha [...] as she herself reminded me when we were wed fourteen years later'] (71-72). Thus, apart from the collective nature of the fragmented memory, we are confronted with the literary convention which Philippe Lejeune has called the 'autobiographical contract', that is, 'the affirmation in the text of the "identity" between the names of the author, narrator, and protagonist, referring in the last resort to the *name* of the author on the cover [...] manifesting an intention to "honour the signature"' (Lejeune, 1982, 192-207). (Lejeune uses Gérard Genette's categories of point of view; and, by these, *Chronicle* (almost) assumes the homodiegetic form of the 'eye-witness' account. Almost bequeathes a supplement). García Márquez's signature is honoured, in the first instance, by the presence in the text of Mercedes, his own wife, and later, by that of Margot his sister, Luis Enrique, his brother, Luisa Santiaga his mother, and Gerineldo, his illustrious forebear. Yet analysis is further complicated by the mother's refusal to greet Bayardo San Román's father, General Petronio San Román, 'héroe de las guerras civiles del siglo anterior, y una de las glorias mayores del régimen conservador por haber puesto en fuga al coronel Aureliano Buendía en el desastre de Tucurinca [...] un hombre que ordenó dispararle por la espalda a Gerineldo Márquez' ['hero of the civil wars of the past century, and one of the most glorious of the Conservative regime because he had put to flight Colonel Aureliano Buendía in the disaster of Tucurinca [...] and a man who gave orders for Gerineldo Márquez to be shot in the back' (55). For when we decide on the nature of the autobiographical contract, in this instance, it is not enough to follow Lejeune's view 'that all questions *of faithfulness* (this is the problem of [...] resemblance) depend in the last analysis on the question of *authenticity* (this is the problem of identity), which in itself is formulated in terms of the name of the author' (Lejeune, 1982, 203). Here, as elsewhere in *Chronicle,* the narrator refers not only to García Márquez's family as his own but also to García Márquez's fictional creations from other, earlier novels, in this case, *Cien años de soledad.* The crossing of networks, therefore, problematizes genre distinctions: autobiography, fiction and journalism. It also, concomitantly, highlights intertextuality: that is, the suggestion (beloved of García Márquez) that all his writing is but one text – *signature*. The extended signature loses the presence(s) of self (selves) – Being – 'in the differential character of the language system and the arbitrariness of signs' in order *not* to succumb ultimately, as do Saussure and Husserl, 'to the metaphysics of presence' (Leitch, 1983, 44).

Derrida's neologism *différance* is articulated by Vincent Leitch as: '(1) "to differ" – to be unlike or dissimilar in nature, quality, or form; (2) "differre" (Latin) – to scatter, disperse; and (3) "to defer" – delay, postpone'. *Chronicle* splits the narrating presence into dissimilar natures, qualities and forms of 'I'. *Chronicle* scatters and disperses 'the fragmented mirror of memory'. *Chronicle* defers, delays, postpones the *writing* of 'a death foretold'. 'This is obviously what makes it threatening and necessarily dreaded by everything in us that desires a realm, the past or future presence of a realm' (Derrida, 1973, 153).

Here, the realm of speculary reflection. And the writing achieves such a loss: 'Años despues, cuando volví a buscar los últimos testimonios para esta crónica [...] Las cosas habían ido desapareciendo poco a poco a pesar de la vigilancia empecinada del coronel Lázaro Aponte, inclusive el escaparate de seis lunas de cuerpo entero que los maestros cantores [...] habían tenido que armar dentro de la casa, pues no cabía por las puertas'. ['Years later when I came back to search out the last pieces of testimony for this chronicle [...] Things had been disappearing little by little despite Colonel Lázaro Aponte's stubborn vigilance, including the full-length wardrobe with six mirrors which the master craftsmen [...] had had to assemble inside the house since it would not fit through the door' (139). The possibility of speculary reflection cannot exist outside the locus of the single, original *event:* here, the house of the widower Xius, where Ángela's non-virginity is discovered on the wedding night.

And what of the 'I'? '"Era una insistencia rara", me dijo Cristo Bedoya. "Tanto, que a veces he pensado que Margot ya sabía que lo iban a matar y quería esconderlo en tu casa"' ['"It was a strange insistence", Cristo Bedoya told me. "So much so that sometimes I've thought that Margot already knew that they were going to kill him and wanted to hide him in your house"'] (34). Not so strange while the certainty of authorship, of a future narrator to 'tell the tale', exists. But Margot's faith in concealing Santiago with the narrator conflicts with the narrator's own uneasiness regarding the self as a purveyor of writing: 'Mucho después, en una época incierta en que trataba de entender algo de mí mismo vendiendo enciclopedias y libros de medicina por los pueblos de la Guajira [...] Al verla así, dentro del marco idílico de la ventana, no quise creer que aquella mujer fuera la que yo creía, porque me resistía a admitir que la vida terminara por parecerse tanto a la mala literatura. Pero ella era: Ángela Vicario veintitrés años después del drama' ['Much later, during an uncertain period when I was trying to understand something of myself by selling encyclopaedias and medical books in the towns of Guajira [...] on seeing her like that, in the idyllic frame of the window, I refused to believe that that woman was the one I thought she was, because I didn't want to admit that life would end up so closely resembling bad literature. But it was she: Ángela Vicario twenty three years after the drama' (142).

The strange insistence is the notion of mimesis, the idyllic frame of bad literature which a deferred voice, a writing, will not admit.

Speculation – whodunnit?

> dans la langue il n'y a que des différences, sans termes positifs
>
> Ferdinand de Saussure

Alguien que nunca fue identificado había metido por debajo de la puerta un papel dentro de un sobre, en el cual le avisaban a Santiago Nasar que lo estaban esperando para matarlo, y le revelaban además el lugar y los motivos, y otros detalles muy precisos de la confabulación. El mensaje estaba en el suelo cuando Santiago Nasar salió de su casa, pero él no lo vio, ni lo vio Divina Flor ni lo vio nadie hasta mucho después de que el crimen fue consumado. (26)

[Someone who was never identified had pushed under the door an envelope containing a piece of paper warning Santiago Nasar that they were waiting for him to kill him and telling him, as well, the place, motives and other precise details of the plot. The message was on the floor when Santiago Nasar left the house but he didn't see it, nor did Divina Flor, nor anyone else, until long after the crime had been consummated.]

'Place', 'motives', 'details of plot', 'crime': the language of detective fiction. Since *Chronicle* manifests many traits of the detective genre, it is critically enticing to answer the question 'whodunnit' by speculating on the sign(s) provided by the text; in short, and in Saussurean terms, by regarding the genre as *langue* and the individual utterance, *Chronicle,* as *parole*. Given the traditional elements of victim, motive, weapon, criminal(s), and the refinements of legal trappings, policeman, autopsy, prosecution and judge, the sign, read as crime-novel, is virtually transparent. But the element 'missing' from the whodunnit model is mystery. The fact that the text reveals victim, criminals and motive so early has a concomitant effect on narrative sequence.

Instead of the syntagmatic progression associated with the detective genre which its subject matter evokes, namely a classic typology of enigma–pursuit–solution (Todorov, 1977, 46), *Chronicle* depends, rather, on an associative structure, again in Saussurean terms, in its generation of meaning. Thus, drawing for a moment on Roland Barthes' *S/Z*, the hermeneutic (enigma) and the proaretic (action) codes, since they involve the apparatus of resolving a given sequence of actions, may be construed, here, as misleading the reader into identifying the utterance of *Chronicle* with the language of detective fiction.

To what 'language', therefore, does *Chronicle* belong? Bearing in mind Barthes's fifth code, the referential, which points to the cultural setting of the text, it is perfectly possible, in the Spanish American perspective, to highlight and explain an associative structure of narrative. In the process, the semic code, relating to the development and understanding of character, and the symbolic code which controls symbolic and thematic interpretations, might be used to situate *Chronicle* in the system of *pundonor*, or 'honour code', literature. In this system, there is no deciphering of mystery or solution of crime; it is rather a matter of observing 'poetic' justice at work. Ángela Vicario's lost honour, revealed only on her wedding night, must be recuperated, along with that of her family. Thus, the virtual complicity of the deceived husband and Ángela's mother when he returns the bride: 'Bayardo San Román no entró, sino que empujó con suavidad a su esposa hacia el interior de la casa, sin decir una palabra. Después besó a Pura Vicario en la mejilla y le habló con una voz de muy hondo desaliento pero con mucha ternura. "Gracias por todo, madre", le dijo. "Usted es una santa"'. ['Bayardo San Román did not enter but pushed his wife gently into the house without saying a word. Then he kissed Pura Vicario on the cheek and spoke to her in a very deep and dejected voice but with great tenderness. "Thank you for everything, mother, you are a saint"'] (76-77). His subsequent withdrawal from the action and Pura Vicario's physical and mental punishment of her daughter are as little of a surprise to the reader, in *pundonor* tradition, as the subsequent assumption of the duty to kill Santiago Nasar, the named lover, by Ángela's brothers. Once the 'tragedy' of dishonour occurs, the action of the narrative is irreversible. Society and reader await a known outcome, whence the 'foretold' nature of death.

There do remain, however, in *Chronicle,* elements not of mystery but of the unexplained. The most obvious, and one central to any reading of the cultural code, is that of the possibility of Santiago Nasar's innocence. Very early, the text offers an 'open' or unread sign of such a possibility, namely, the (*pace* Hardy) anonymously delivered 'note under the door'. Unread by Santiago Nasar, the note, it will be remembered, told him 'the place, motives and other precise details of the plot':

> It is clear that it cannot be *exposed*. We can only expose what, at a certain moment, can become present, manifest; what can be shown, presented as present, a being – present in its truth, the truth of a present or the presence of a present. (Derrida, 1973, 130)

The above refers not, specifically, to Santiago Nasar's unread letter; it is Derrida's own formulation of *différance,* that 'which is neither a *word* nor a concept' but which refers to 'the *play* of differences' (Derrida, 1973, 130). My argument is that Santiago Nasar's letter is an instance of *différance* at work, unread, unexposed. Thus, 'the precise details of the plot', though pointed towards by the *unread* text of the note under the door, will not be revealed by the *read* text of *Chronicle. Chronicle* refutes the cause and effect and teleological structure of the detective story (it begins and ends with the death); equally, it denies the placing of the *punto* (point, full stop) to *honor*; that is, it 'opens' a closed system, the *pundonor*. For the *pundonor* is a language, too: and 'in language there are only differences, without positive terms' (terminologies and terminations). That *Chronicle* itself constitutes a *trace,* a note slipped under the door of a closed system of writing (of the *Tess* era?), will be my fifth speculation, the free-play of a reading, a re-reading of 'thanatography'.

Speculation – money-making

The millionaire launching of Gabriel García Márquez

José Vicente Kataraín, director of 'La oveja negra' publishing house in Bogotá, explained how they obtained the García Márquez contract, negotiating in Barcelona with Carmen Balcells, holder of the Colombian's publishing rights. 'We managed to produce, publish and sell one million copies of the complete works in two years, an unprecedented figure in so short a time. Because of this success, the company competed with a number of foreign publishers to launch *Chronicle of a Death Foretold*. Spain and Argentina are publishing another million, besides ours, that is, two million copies are on the Spanish-speaking market. By the end of the year, with world-wide sales, in thirty two languages, it will be the most successful publication in history. 'The director says that they needed forty five aeroplanes to export the novel, bearing in mind that a 727 normally carries eight tons of cargo. By the author's request, the format of the book is light and easy for the reader; the large lettering is similar to that of a children's story. He also wanted it to be economically priced in order to reach the maximum readership. (Hernández de López, 1981, 64)

'Autobiography, auto-graphy, auto-thanatography'; writing about the self, writing the self, writing of the death of the self. The 'crossing of networks' has been confined, so far, in this 'reading hastily called "internal", [to] the places *structurally* open to the crossing'. Thus, in Derridan terms, the *presence, being* and *voice* of García Márquez are deconstructed by the *difference, trace* and *writing* of *Chronicle*. While, as argued above, the signature need not succumb ultimately to the metaphysics of presence, it is the aim of the present speculation to situate *Chronicle* in an economics of signature. In this respect, the argument will draw upon Pierre Macherey's 'view of the author as someone who works upon a world of signs and codes from the inside, so that he or she is "written" by the language in the act of writing it'. That world entails 'a theory of reading which sees texts as necessarily *incomplete* and contradictory and which is crucially concerned with *ideology*' (Forgacs, 1982, 146).

However much García Márquez might complain of the traumatic impact of the sudden fame and responsibility thrust upon him by the success of *One Hundred Years of Solitude* (Mendoza, 89), the public demand for the authenticity of his signature, for 'recognizability', impinges on 'the world of signs and codes' from which *Chronicle* is produced: not only in the occasional cross-reference to Colonel Aureliano Buendía or to a Petra Cotes, but also in the replicated Buendía dynasty of the Vicario family – Poncio, the father, 'sentado solo en un taburete en el centro del patio' ['seated alone on a stool in the centre of the patio'] (73), Pablo 'que aprendió el oficio del oro en el taller de su padre y llegó a ser un orfebre depurado' ['who learned to work with precious metals in his father's workshop and became an elegant goldsmith'] (134), Pedro who 'se reintegró [...] su patrulla se internó en territorio de guerillas cantando canciones de putas, y nunca más se supo de ellos' ['re-enlisted [...] his patrol went into guerilla territory singing whoring songs and they were never heard of again'] (134) and Pura, the mother, Ursula reincarnate. The list of possible parallels is long, from the comic, Pedro Crespi impact of the newcomer, Bayardo San Román, to the elaborated inclusion of a certain Gabriel, this time the name on the cover rather than the Paris-bound friend of the last of the Buendías, Aureliano Babilonia.

The temptation to counterfeit the successful currency of a previous best-seller constitutes another speculation; a speculation, as Derrida has it, 'in the sense of the production of a surplus value and in the sense of calculation or gambling on the stock-market or issuing more or less fictitious bills' (Derrida, 1978, 92). To José Vicente Kataraín and to Carmen Balcells, no doubt, praise-worthy – but, no less, prize-worthy. Nobel prize-worthy. (And were I writing in French, I should not resist the temptation either. *Prix Nobel*, Nobel prize... and Nobel *price*).

Yet this is no condemnation. For, it must be recalled, it is nothing other than a theory of reading – in this case, my own reading of 'someone who works upon a world of signs and codes from *the inside*' (my italics). How the signature *García Márquez* 'is "written" by the language in the act of writing it' yet remains 'necessarily *incomplete* and contradictory' will be the substance of my next, ideological, speculation.

Speculation – free play

> The self, like the world, is a text [...] readers who are astonishingly eager to see shattered or social selves in novels and poems are a good deal more reluctant to acknowledge the consequences of such a deconstruction for their own relations to texts [...] neutrality itself is a fiction [...] and the literary critic, whose avowed subject is fiction, need not find this embarrassing. (Benn Michaels, in Tomkins, 1980, 199-200)

The fantastic enterprise of the last Buendía, in *One Hundred Years of Solitude,* of reading his own destiny in the very act of fulfilling it, may be taken as one metaphor of the erroneous reading-practice of the assumption of realism. Aureliano Babilonía's fate is sealed by his attachment to a supposed link between the text he is reading and his own act of reading it. For him, that link is one of a transparent, mimetic relationship, a 'realist' characterization *par excellence*. For this reason, his reading is *closed*; he has no second chance in the closed cycle of one hundred years, the final chapter of which he himself constitutes. Since this might be construed as García Márquez's attack not merely on the notion of realism but specifically against the reading practice which renders it possible, it becomes necessary for the reader – now liberated from the notion of text as speaking mirror – to redefine the link, the relationship. Apparently audaciously, then, by returning to a supposedly documented event, *Chronicle* cuts the umbilicus, renders non-fiction fiction, but not simply, dismissively, as in the throw-away (Borgesian?) notion that 'all writing is fiction' but rather in terms of *reading,* that reading-practice which insists on perpetuating the confusion of transparent realism. In short, *Chronicle*'s reference is plurivalent; despite having paid the fares to Sucre of all those journalists. Concomitantly, there can be many answers to the question(s) 'whodunnit?':

> 'Anda, niña', le dijo temblando de rabia: 'dinos quién fue'. Ella se demoró apenas el tiempo necesario para decir el nombre. Lo buscó en las tinieblas, lo encontró a primera vista entre los tantos y tantos nombres confundibles de este mundo y del otro, y lo dejó clavado en la pared con su dardo certero, como una mariposa sin albedrío cuya sentencia estaba escrita desde siempre. 'Santiago Nasar', dijo. (78)

> ['Come on, girl', he said, trembling with rage, 'tell us who it was'. She hesitated no more than the time it took to say the name. She sought it from within the darkness, found it at first sight amongst the many, many confusable names of this world and the other one, and she pinned it to the wall with her well-aimed dart, like a butterfly with no will of its own, whose sentence had been written forever. 'Santiago Nasar', she said.]

Fulfilling the promise that my fifth speculation would constitute a pursuit of the trace left by the note slipped under the door of a closed system of writing, I come to the necessary free-play of any, of all, reading. Of my reading. Of a reading prompted both by the title of 'a death foretold' and of Derrida's notion of 'auto-thanatography', but one of the many networks of reading. I begin with 'confusable names'.

The lay-out below, while less than arbitrary, is nonetheless an unembarrassing non-neutrality. It may serve to focus attention on the free-play of names which follows.

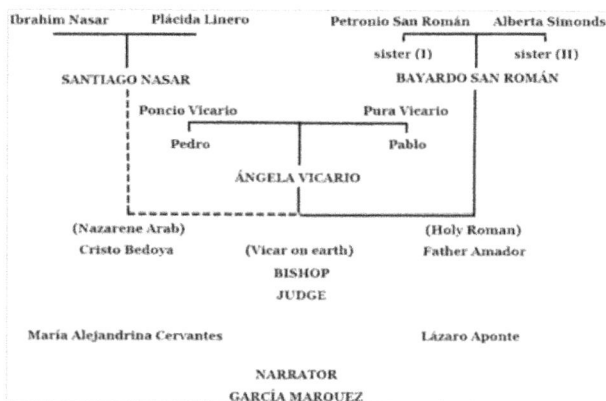

From within the darkness' of 'the many, many confusable names of this world and the other one' comes the name Santiago Nasar. Born of the Arab intruder Ibrahim, master of falconry (16), deflowerer (19), and of the Christian mother, inaccurate decipherer of dreams, Santiago Nasar is the outsider, 'como todos los turcos' ['just like all Turks'] (162), 'the stranger in the house' of a Holy Roman dominance. I echo the 'Stranger in the House' proposition of Tony Tanner's *Adultery in the Novel*: 'Western Literature as we know it starts with an act of transgression, a violation of boundaries that leads to instability, asymmetry, disorder, and an interfamilial, intertribal clash that threatens the very existence of civilization' (Tanner, xi). Part Nazarene, victim 'with no will of its own, whose sentence had been written forever', whose fate it is to die against the tree, the wooden door of his own house, in the helpless proximity of his placid mother. Part saint (if martyr), but SANT-IAGO... thus, part perpetrator, 'distiller' of doubt – the doubt which destroys the Moor. Notorious womanizer, would-be deflowerer both of Divina Flor (18-19) and of the church for his own funeral (69), he is sacrificed by raisers of hogs who cannot bring themselves to kill *named* pigs, except when these are called after flowers (86). Yet there is a complication:

> Para la inmensa mayoría solo hubo una víctima: Bayardo San Román. Suponían que los otros protagonistas de la tragedia habían cumplido con dignidad, y hasta con cierta grandeza, la parte de favor que la vida les tenía señalada. Santiago Nasar había expiado la injuria, los hermanos Vicario habían probado su condición de hombres, y la hermana burlada estaba otra vez en posesión de su honor. El único que lo había perdido todo era Bayardo San Román. 'El pobre Bayardo', como se le recordó durante años. (134)

> [For the immense majority there was only one victim: Bayardo San Román. They assumed that the other protagonists of the tragedy had fulfilled with dignity, and even with a certain grandeur, the part which, as a favour, life had assigned them. Santiago Nasar had expiated the insult, the Vicario brothers had shown they were men and their ridiculed sister was once again in possesssion of her honour. The only one who had lost everything was Bayardo San Román. 'El pobre Bayardo', as he was remembered for many years].

The text at once echoes the *pundonor* and, at the same time, points to a double victim. If not an exact doubling, an overlap. Bayardo/'boyardo'? ...

the word used to describe Santiago Nasar, by the narrator but in reported speech, as follows: 'Victoria Guzmán [...] no perdía ninguna ocasión de preservar a la hija contra las garras del boyardo'. ['Victoria Guzmán [...] lost no opportunity to protect her daughter from the claws of the boyar'] (110). The play is multiple, throwing up an ambivalent social code which both anticipates and accepts a *droit de seigneur*, throwing open the question of characterization. For it is arguable that Santiago Nasar and Bayardo San Román function inseparably, *actantially,* as fallen-aristocrat co-ordinates in a system of honour-code writing. Further, that the *actant* is to be understood classically, in Greimas's sense of *the sphere of action*, a cultural sphere which is constituted not by the 'real-life' protagonists of Sucre, a *characterization*, but by an elaborate play of names and of binaries, of punned pairs.

Speculation – word play. A game of the name

> The 'anagram' should not be defined as a regulated dislocation lacking completeness, but as an indeterminable multiplicity, a radical undecidability, which undoes all codes. (Leitch, 1983, 10)

In the 'juxtaposition of Santiago Nasar/Bayardo San Román, an anagrammatical free-play breeds saints and martyrs ('y ardo'/'and I burn'), Christians versus Moor, incomplete Nazarene, Holy Roman obedience to a severe marriage-code. And the play remains incomplete, always leaves a trace:

> Cuando se alivió el sol, dos hombres del municipio bajaron a Bayardo San Román en una hamaca [...] Magdalena Oliver creyó que estaba muerto.
> '¡Collons de déu !', exclamó, '¡qué desperdicio !'
> [...] el brazo derecho le iba arrastrando por el suelo [...] de modo que dejó un rastro en la tierra desde la cornisa del precipicio hasta la plataforma del buque. Eso fue lo último que nos quedó de él : un recuerdo de víctima. (137-38)

> [When the sun was less fierce, two men carried Bayardo San Román down on a hammock [...] Magdalena Oliver thought he was dead. 'Collons de déu!' she exclaimed. 'What a waste'. [...] his right arm was dragging on the ground [...] so that he left a trail from the edge of the precipice to the deck of the boat. That was all that we had left of him: the memory of a victim].

The silent mark traced on the memory by the limp victim's hand of a droopy *seigneur* finds an accompanying, coded (Catalan) voice: 'God's balls!'– the coming together of religion and sexuality. What a waste... (Or dis-perdition?).

A less profligate sphere of chronicled action is that of sexual politics. And the complicity of church and state: 'What is important in the work,' Macherey writes, 'is what it does not say' (Forgacs, 1982, 149). It does not say much of the bishop, a Christ's *vicar(io)* on earth. His role is one of neglect. An absence [...] who 'odia a este pueblo' ['hates this town'], 'echará una bendición de compromiso, como siempre' ['will toss us a dutiful blessing, as ever'] (17) and (almost) visits to p[r]ick up the tribute of *machismo* – 'la sopa de crestas era su plato predilecto' ['coxcomb soup was his favourite dish'] (30).

> Plácida Linero tuvo razón: el obispo no se bajó del buque [...] Por aquella época, los legendarios buques de rueda [...] estaban a punto de acabarse [...] Pero éste era nuevo [...] En la baranda superior, junto al camarote del capitán, iba el obispo de sotana blanca con su séquito de españoles [...] Lo que pasó [...] fue que el silbato del buque soltó un chorro de vapor a presión al pasar frente al puerto, y dejó ensopados a los que estaban más cerca de la orilla. Fue una ilusión fugaz: el obispo empezó a hacer la señal de la cruz en el aire frente a la muchedumbre del muelle, y después siguió haciéndola de memoria, sin malicia ni inspiración, hasta que el buque se perdió de vista y sólo quedó el alboroto de los gallos. (11)

> [Plácida Linero was right: the bishop did not get off the boat [...] About that time, the legendary paddle-steamers [...] were coming to the end of their days. But this one was new [...] On the upper deck, next to the captain's cabin, walked the bishop in his white soutane with his retinue of Spaniards [...] What did happen [...] was that the ship's hooter spurted forth a jet of steam as it passed in front of the port, and left soaked those who were closest to the bank. It was but a fleeting illusion: the bishop began to make the sign of the cross in the air in front of the crowd on the pier, and thereafter went on doing it from memory, with neither malice nor inspiration, until the boat was out of sight and all that was left was the racket of the cocks.]

Crowing in echo of precursor apostolic betrayal, the excited cockerels ostensibly bear witness to a clearly long-standing dereliction of vocation. Dipping further into 'sopa' and 'dejó ensopados' – and notwithstanding the *castizo* cortège of the elevated company dis-grace the bishop is seen to be keeping – the prying linguist will surmise... Might this cleric's episcopal ejaculation have had more to do with the hot soup preference than with the proffering of his one-handed tepid seme of blessing? Far fetched...? Okay. In respect of the coxcomb, however, and pertinently, a related point was raised, in a fortuitous 2017 Cartagena de Indias encounter with Rory O'Bryen – mimic on a par with Nasar, in an 'almost magical talent' ['talento casi mágico'] (106) for imitation, and Colombianist of standing – revealing that 'la cresta de gallo' also indicates HPV [VPH *in situ*]; transmissible disease or compromising metaphor of genital visibility that, hands down, beats the bishop's going through his duty-bound motions? Benediction? Sign of the crotch...

The ins and outs of the Christian-in-half-name-only Santiago affair, and of its lastingly traumatizing impact on the townspeople, would not be a matter either to be influenced or brought to a head by patronizing ecclesiastic power. On the very point of arrival, yet pulling off again, safe, hierarchically aboard, far from coming ashore to consummate his ordained episcopal function, to succour the faithful and the attendant sick, surrounded rather by, and complicit with, the watchful orthodoxy of an indelibly still-colonizing 'retinue of Spaniards', the white-cassocked prelate shows himself unwilling to go the whole way. At the pier-head, steadfast whilst sprayed in parodic antiphon of the *Asperges me*, undrooping supplicants stand resigned, denied the sprinkled indulgence to bend the knee before His Worship's outstretched hand.

Too much to swallow? Remember that, *d'après* Jacques, 'we merely formulate speculative hypotheses to explain and describe the facts that we observe'. Spot the (in-) *différance* as instinctively sniffed out, to be shunned, *in saecula saeculorum*, by the latest hierarch of a Church prematurely – *sicut in coelo, et in terra* – if rather ostentatiously Triumphant; ever alert, and Militant, in the face of a Suffering faithful, here co-habiting with, oblivious to, dangerous heterodoxies of mixed race, of impure blood, of hybrid naming...

> Santiago Nasar se puso un pantalón y una camisa de lino blanco, ambas piezas sin almidón [...] Era un atuendo de ocasión. De no haber sido por la llegada del obispo se habría puesto el vestido de caqui y las botas de montar con que se iba los lunes a El Divino Rostro, la hacienda de ganado que heredó de su padre, y que él administraba con muy buen juicio aunque sin mucha fortuna. (11-12)

> [Santiago Nasar put on a shirt and pants of white linen, both unstarched [...] It was his attire for special occasions. If it hadn't

been for the bishop's arrival, he would have worn the khaki outfit and riding boots in which he went on Mondays to The Divine Face, the cattle ranch he'd inherited from his father, and which he administered with very good judgment but without much luck.]

Though in garb deemed 'de pontifical por si tenía ocasión de besarle el anillo al obispo' ['as pontifical in case he chanced to kiss the bishop's ring'] (17), the (announced) victim's ceremonial attire, on balance, by taking both his names into account, might be otherwise ciphered. *Ojalá*. For textual indeterminacy will betray an uncloseted Arabic-speaking private joker, overheard word-playing publicly in an impious language; self-presenting – 'de' – as pontiff-*like*, in putatively mocking *imitatio*. Or, proleptically, pre-shrouded in white (albeit not muslin)?

> Cristo Bedoya le dio una palmadita en la espalda [...] Santiago Nasar no le contestó, sino que se dirigió en árabe a Yamil Shaium y éste le replicó también en árabe, torciéndose de risa. 'Era un juego de palabras con que nos divertíamos siempre', me dijo Yamil Shaium. Sin detenerse, Santiago Nasar les hizo a ambos su señal de adiós con la mano y dobló la esquina de la plaza. Fue la última vez que lo vieron. (165-66)

> [Cristo Bedoya clapped him on the back (...) Santiago Nasar didn't reply, but said something in Arabic to Yamil Shaium, and the latter answered him, also in Arabic, twisting with laughter. 'It was a play on words we always had fun with,' Yamil Shaium told me. Without stopping, Santiago Nasar waved good-bye to both of them and turned the corner of the square. It was the last time they saw him.]

Consigned, constricted, to the fellowship of Castilian ('hablar en cristiano'), the reader will join the townsfolk (and I'll say it in plain English) in never knowing what, in the language or even in the gesture, was so funny (or mocking, or blasphemous?) on this day ordained for contemplation of the bishopric's incumbent. *Adiós*, too, is but a sign... *not* the last word.

Words ill-chosen shall yet have consequence: 'Thou shalt not take the name...'. 'El Divino Rostro': *bad* judgment; *no* luck. And *do* recall those riding boots routinely worn, though on this day not; a requisite removal of leather before orthodox Muslim burial...? Cleansing? *Limpieza* may have been shown on the surface but *sangre* will be spilt. An eleventh commandment: 'Thou shalt not be found out' in the street; or turning the corner of the square... the conventional, the orthodox. 'I also maintain that speculation is not only a mode of research [...] but also the operation of writing' (*in principio erat*).

For it is written. There is, was, nothing to be done. Certainly not by the would-be saviour Bedoya (*tonto, bobo*), 'stupid, clownish', in his frantic, incompetent, and failed attempt to live up to Clotilde Armenta's confidence that 'en este pueblo de maricas sólo un hombre como él podía impedir la tragedia' ['in this town of faggots only a man like him could prevent the tragedy' (174). Cristo's *Exodus* lesson (7.19), 'and there will be blood', was to take him away; from blundering young medical student to surgeon of renown: 'llegó a ser un cirujano notable' (155). This we are led to credit by a hardly reliable narrator's insistent option, amongst friends, for *histoire*; less plausibly by the *récit* that renders *Bedoya* Clown via the name-never 'in vain' letter of the text of the Chronicle's story. Just so... Justice? Nominally, Colonel Lázaro Aponte, like Lazarus, given a *second* chance to preserve life:

> 'Los vi hace dos minutos y cada uno tenía un cuchillo de matar puercos', dijo Cristo Bedoya. 'iAh carajo', dijo el alcalde, 'entonces debió ser que volvieron con otros !'. Prometió ocuparse de eso al instante, pero entró en el Club Social a confirmar una cita de dominó para esa noche, y cuando volvió a salir ya estaba consumado el crimen. (175)

> ['I saw them two minutes ago and each one had a pig-killing knife', Cristo Bedoya said. 'Oh, fuck', the mayor said, 'they must have come back with two others'. He promised to take care of it at once, but went into the Social Club to confirm a date for dominoes that night, and when he came out the crime was already consummated.]

And what of our Peter and Paul? Since Poncio (Pontius) Vicario, Ángela's father, is too senile to act – 'la vista se le acabó de tanto hacer primores de oro para mantener el honor de la casa' ['having lost his sight doing so much delicate work with gold-jewellery in order to maintain the honour of the house'] (50) – his hands are washed of active responsibility. Thus, the binary, clichéd duo of instrumentality, Pedro and Pablo, vicarious defenders-cum-propagators of an un-thought-out faith and a social code sanctioned by a community unwilling or unable to combat the 'foretold' nature of their act.

> Nunca hubo una muerte más anunciada. Despues de que la hermana les reveló el nombre, los gemelos Vicario pasaron por

el depósito de la pocilga, donde guardaban los útiles de
sacrificio, y escogieron los dos cuchillos mejores: uno de
descuartizar, de diez pulgadas de largo por dos y media de
ancho, y otro de limpiar, de siete pulgadas de largo por una y
media de ancho. Los envolvieron en un trapo, y se fueron a
afilarlos en el mercado de carnes [...] Los primeros clientes eran
escasos, pero veintidós personas declararon haber oído cuanto
dijeron, y todas coincidían en la impresión de que lo habían
dicho con el único propósito de que los oyeran [...] 'Vamos a
matar a Santiago Nasar', dijo. (83-85)

[There had never been a death more foretold. After their sister
revealed the name to them the Vicario twins went to the shed in
the pig-sty where they kept their sacrificial tools and chose the
two best knives: one for quartering, ten by two and a half, and the
other one for trimming, seven by one and a half. They wrapped
them in a rag and went to sharpen them at the meat-market [...]
There were only a few customers at such an early hour but
twenty-two people declared that they had heard everything and
all were agreed that the only reason they said it was to be
overheard [...] 'We're going to kill Santiago Nasar,' he said.]

This Nasar-ene is to be killed by his own friends and drinking
companions; his own disciples collude in a Gethsemane-cum-Damascus
confusion of sleepy inactivity, despite the twins' manifold statement of
murderous intent. And the second requirement for mortal sin,
'responsibility', they admit, too:

'Lo matamos a conciencia', dijo Pedro Vicario, 'pero somos
inocentes'.
    'Tal vez ante Dios', dijo el padre Amador.
    'Ante Dios y ante los hombres', dijo Pablo Vicario. 'Fue un
asunto de honor.' (80)

['We killed him in full awareness of what we were doing,' said
Pedro Vicario, 'but we're innocent.' 'Perhaps before God,' said
Father Amador. 'Before God and before men,' said Pablo
Vicario. 'It was a matter of honour.']

The instrumentality of the twins' actant-status is underscored by several
elements. First, the shift from 'Fact' (Margarita's one brother) to 'Fiction'
(Ángela's twin brothers); second, the play of 'apostolic' naming, duty and

innocence; and third, the anti-realist characterization of Pedro and Pablo, expressed either through their reduction to mere wielders of the knife, so often a fetish-object of the narrative, or, more uproariously, through their hilarious inseparability:

> 'Estuvo como media hora cambiándose la gasa con que llevaba envuelta la pinga', me dijo Pablo Vicario. En realidad no se demoró más de diez minutos, pero fue algo tan difícil, y tan enigmático para Pablo Vicario, que lo interpretó como una nueva artimaña del hermano para perder el tiempo hasta el amanecer. De modo que le puso el cuchillo en la mano y se lo llevó casi por la fuerza a buscar la honra perdida de la hermana.
> 'Esto no tiene temedio', le dijo: 'es como si ya nos hubiera sucedido.' (99-100)

> ['He (Pedro) spent about half an hour changing the gauze he had his prick wrapped in', Pablo Vicario told me. Actually he hadn't spent more than ten minutes doing that, but it was something so difficult and so enigmatic for Pablo Vicario, that he interpreted it as some new trick on the part of his brother to waste time until dawn. So he put the knife in his hand and dragged him off almost by force in pursuit of their sister's lost honour. 'There's no other way', he told him. 'It's as if it had already happened.']

Culmination of the brothers' only 'disagreement' (99), namely, as to whose responsibility had been the final, fatal decision, this passage at once constructs, reconstructs and deconstructs the *pundonor* sphere of action. Irreversible, vengeful action at the hands of blood-relatives; delay, agonizing (though hardly expressed as a matter of conscience) before the act; and, finally, the grasping of the *instrumento...* the tool of honour-code responsibility. 'Knife' . . . or 'prick'?

Speculation – *cherchez la femme!*

Sexual politics centre on Ángela Vicario, already broached in mention of Poncio, Pura, Pedro and Pablo. The axial, unresolved question is not whether Santiago Nasar was her seducer; that comes subsequently. Virgin or non-Virgin (technically)? Despite her unscheming refusal to cover up her own, undisclosed knowledge of why her hymen is not intact, the wedding night frankness that triggers the honour-code action, it is society that asks not how? but who? The how?, possibly more interesting, would surely have made for a shorter narrative; as it is, in Derridan terms, it is an *espacement,* a hidden spacing, opened wide and dwelled upon. But this instance of *aperture* gives rise to the wrong question – who? For Ángela's society (a kind of traditional 'readership'?) is ill-equipped to reason, only to react. Thus, when forced (verbally; that is all we know) to name a perpetrator, she plucks from the darkness not only a 'son of man', whom she names *thrice,* but the name of *man:* 'a butterfly with no will of its own, whose sentence had been written forever'.

Once, the Angel of the Annunciation had visited upon a Pure, Vicarious, virgin-instrument (Mary) the weight of bearing the Nazarene. Now, the roles of angel and vicar are subsumed into but a single *actant,* the one 'sphere of action' where, vicariously, Ángela both announces and condemns. Her hand bears (bares) the responsibility of authorship – 'he was my author' ('fue mi autor'). She names Santiago Nasar responsible for what her own finger has traced, has written, in blood. After his death, in ink, her hand is able to write in full, if feverishly (almost two thousand letters). Her hand weaves the fabric of writing, the seemingly endless act of *écriture* which serves to cover up her act of (carnal) self-knowledge and self-penetrating analysis. It is a more original cover-up – addressed to her saintly (or unresponding) Román-tic – than the traditional method of linen sheets with the stain of honour ('la mancha del honor') recommended by her girl-friend *confidantes*; a more writerly (*scriptible*) display of the ink-and-tear stained sheets of her lengthy but ever one-way correspondence.

Thereafter, all is but a play of names, the ploy of plural, inter-changeable victims; the aperture of a social membrane, pointed at and pierced by her penetrative, accusing finger, and a fabric falsely woven to cover up the long-standing 'gap' of honour, of honour-code, of honour-code writing. A fabric now undone by the readerly (*lisible*). A reading which refutes *whodunnit?* A feminist misprision of the 'macho' code?

Speculation – reading

> The writing changes the very surface of what it is written on. This non-belonging unleashes speculation. (Derrida, 1978, 92)

The instability of the writing surface, of the scene of writing, unleashes myriad unstable readings, incomplete, uncompletable speculations, investigations, guess-work(s), narrations. Internally, the text contains many readers, many readings. Father Amador, vicarious and obscene pathologist, haruspex, picking over (and out) the entrails of the dead

Santiago Nasar in a Rabelaisian fusion of name and functions; gruesome priest, amateur physician. The instructing judge, incapable of clinical, dispassionate reading:

> El nombre del juez no apareció en ninguno, pero es evidente que era un hombre abrasado por la fiebre de la literatura [...] Las notas marginales, y no sólo por el color de la tinta, parecían escritas con sangre. Estaba tan perplejo [...] que muchas veces incurrió en distracciones líricas contrarias al rigor de su ciencia. Sobre todo, nunca le pareció legítimo que la vida se sirviera de tantas casualidades prohibidas a la literatura, para que se cumpliera sin tropiezos una muerte tan anunciada [...] En el folio 416, de su puño y letra y con la tinta roja [...] escribió una nota marginal: *Dadme un prejuicio y moveré el mundo*. Debajo de esa paráfrasis de desaliento, con un trazo feliz de la misma tinta de sangre, dibujó un corazón atravesado por una flecha. Para él, como para los amigos más cercanos de Santiago Nasar, el propio comportamiento de éste en las últimas horas fue una prueba de su inocencia. (158-61)

> [The judge's name didn't appear on any of the pages of the brief, but it was evident that he was a man burning with the fever for literature [...] The marginal notes, and not just because of the colour of the ink, seemed to be written in blood. He was so perplexed [...] that often he fell into lyrical distractions contrary to professional rigour. Above all, it never seemed legitimate to him that life should make use of so many coincidences forbidden to literature merely to achieve without obstacle a death so clearly foretold [...] On folio 416, in his own handwriting and in red ink [...] he wrote a marginal note: *Give me a prejudice and I will move the world*. Under that disillusioned paraphrase, with a felicitous sketch in the same blood ink, he drew a heart pierced by an arrow. For him, as for Santiago Nasar's closest friends, the latter's own behaviour in his last hours was a final proof of his innocence.]

At play, here, is slippage; away from one text as verifiable presence and towards a margin where another *trace,* a parallel *écriture* not confined to ink but extended to blood, is generated by the 'unprofessional' doodling of the arbiter of justice. It constitutes the arbitration of a judgement not as to Santiago Nasar's implied innocence (the function of social justice which the unnamed judge supposedly represents) but on the political power derivable from prejudice. A case, perhaps, of Louis Althusser's 'symptomatic reading':

> When we write, we do not just record what we see and fail to record what lies outside our field of vision; rather, we see all the elements of reality about which we write, but our written text cannot always make the right connections between them. A text thus tends to present reality partially or incoherently, leaving gaps. Through these gaps, however, an informed reader can see what the text was hiding from itself. (Forgacs, 1982, 149)

Not only does the judge's marginal note offer an Althusserian 'symptomatic reading', it performs (without signature) the function of supplementing the narrator's version of events. Politically manipulated, 'life' can 'make use of' the 'coincidences forbidden to literature'. A theory of production, then, derives from such 'making use'. But this judge, exceptionally, appears to stand aside, helpless and 'perplexed', from society's manipulated 'world' (his *Give me...* is, after all, an unfulfilled imperative). He is, rather, 'a man burning with the fever for literature' and, as such, a duplication of that other, most important of readers within *Chronicle*, its own narrator:

> María Alejandrina Cervantes había dejado sin tranca la puerta de la casa. Me despedí de mi hermano, atravesé el corredor donde dormían los gatos de las mulatas [...] y empuje sin tocar la puerta del dormitorio. Las luces estaban apagadas, pero tan pronto como entré percibí el olor de mujer tibia y vi los ojos de leoparda insomne en la oscuridad, y después no volví a saber de mí mismo hasta que empezaron a sonar las campanas. (110-11)

> [María Alejandrina Cervantes had left the door of the house unbolted. I took leave of my brother, crossed the passage-way where the mulatto-girls' cats were sleeping [...] and pushed open the bedroom door without knocking. The lights were out, but as soon as I entered I caught the smell of warm woman and saw her insomniac leopard's eye in the dark and then I knew nothing more of myself until the bell began to ring.]

The narrator withdraws from the scene of action at the actual time of Santiago Nasar's death, into the brothel, 'la casa de misericordias' 'the house of mercies' (74), which sucks the equally 'fevered' male protagonists, sporadically, away from a social reality of 'prejudice' into a temporary oblivion:

Fue ella quien arrasó con la virginidad de mi generación. Nos enseñó mucho más de lo que debíamos aprender, pero nos enseñó sobre todo que ningún lugar de la vida es más triste que una cama vacía. Santiago Nasar perdió el sentido desde que la vio por primera vez. Yo lo previne: *Halcón que se atreve con garza guerrera, peligros espera.* Pero el no me oyó, aturdido por los silbos quiméricos de María Alejandrina Cervantes. Ella fue su pasión desquiciada, su maestra de lágrimas a los 15 años, hasta que Ibrahim Nasar se lo quitó de la cama a correazos y lo encerró más de un año en *El Divino Rostro*. (105-6)

[It was she who did away with my generation's virginity [...] Santiago Nasar lost his senses the first time he saw her. I warned him: *A falcon which takes on a warrior crane, merely risks a life of pain.* But he didn't listen, bewildered by the chimerical whistling of María Alejandrina Cervantes. She was his unbridled passion, his mistress of tears at fifteen, until Ibrahim Nasar whipped him out of her bed and shut him up for over a year on *The Divine Face*.]

Withdrawal from the scene of action to a scene of writing. For this is no ordinary brothel, but the brothel of chimerae, of enchantment, of withdrawal into the literature of its Madame Cervantes, mother (Mary), classical (Alexandrine) lap of adolescent consolation, spontaneous sensuality and anathema to conscience or guilt – or contemplation of the Divine Face (nominally, the Nasars' ranch). Therein, discourse is literary, proverbial, picking up yet never closing the falconry theme of Gil Vicente's epigraph. Therein, activity is but play, the loss and confusion of presence, of identity:

Santiago Nasar tenía un talento casi mágico para los disfraces, y su diversión predilecta era trastocar la identidad de las mulatas. Saqueaba los roperos de unas para disfrazar a las otras, de modo que todas terminaban por sentirse distintas de sí mismas e iguales a las que no eran. En cierta ocasion, una de ellas se vió repetida en otra con tal acierto, que sufrio una crisis de llanto. 'Sentí que me había salido del espejo', dijo. Pero aquella noche, María Alejandrina Cervantes no permitió que Santiago Nasar se complaciera por última vez en sus artificios de transformista, y lo hizo con pretextos tan frívolos que el mal sabor de ese recuerdo le cambió la vida. (106-7)

[Santiago Nasar had an almost magical knack for disguises, and his favourite pastime was to confuse the identities of the mulatto-girls. He would rifle the wardrobes of some to disguise others, so they all ended up feeling different from themselves and the same as the ones they weren't. Once, one of them saw herself repeated in another so accurately that she burst into tears. 'I felt as if I'd been taken out of the mirror', she said. But that night, María Alejandrina Cervantes wouldn't let Santiago Nasar indulge himself for the last time in his transformer's trickery, and with such frivolous excuses that the bad taste of that memory changed her life.]

The scene of writing as brothel, as evasion, as oblivion, as loss of identity (or a 'metaphysics of presence') is denied, fatally, not only to Santiago Nasar, 'changing his life' (to death) by depriving him of his indulgence in 'transformer's trickery'. It is denied, too, subsequently, to the narrator. Yet differently, obversely, in another mirror-image. For Santiago Nasar passes from scene of writing to scene of action; the narrator is expelled from his scene of (would-be) action – 'se detuvo de golpe, tosió de muy lejos y se escurrió de mi vida. "No puedo", dijo: "hueles a él"' ['suddenly she stopped, coughed from far off, and slipped out of my life. "I can't", she said. "You smell of him"'] (126) – to a deferred (thirty years) scene of writing; and to the 'transformer's trickery' which is *Chronicle*.

Notwithstanding this expulsion, all literariness is not lost to the narrator. His absence from the scene of action, of the death, permits him a decentring of point of view, away from omniscience, towards the 'piecing together' of a narrative which is always but another reading. 'El juez instrutor buscó siquiera una persona que lo hubiera visto, y lo hizo con tanta persistencia como yo, pero no fue posible encontrarla. En el folio 382 del sumario escribió otra sentencia marginal con tinta roja: *La fatalidad nos hace invisibles*. ['The investigating judge looked for even one person who had seen him, and he did so with as much persistence as I, but it was impossible to find anyone. On folio 382 of the brief, he wrote another marginal pronouncement in red ink: *Fatality makes us invisible*'] (180). For the anonymous judge (reader), entry into investigation (speculation), for the narrator (reader), entry into María Alejandrina's (house of speculation), for Santiago Nasar, entry into the antipode of brothel – the house of Flora Miguel and arranged marriage (speculation) – all are forms of non-omniscience. It is the 'fatality' of their status in the text – in literature – which makes them invisible. Invisible readers. Readers without signature, who have not written.

Speculation – writing

It engages a new speculation. 'The details of the process by which repression turns a possibility of pleasure into a source of unpleasure are not yet clearly understood or cannot be clearly represented (described, expounded, pictured); but there is no doubt that all neurotic unpleasure is of that kind – pleasure that cannot be felt as such'. (Derrida, 1978, 96; the internal quotation is from Freud's *Beyond the Pleasure Principle*)

He who has written, who speculates (money makes) with signature, is Gabriel García Márquez. But does the deconstruction of this series of speculations reduce his writing, his discourse, to that signature alone? 'The widespread opinion that deconstruction denies the existence of anything but discourse, or affirms a realm of pure difference in which all meaning and identity dissolves, is a travesty of Derrida's own work and of the most productive work that has followed from it' (Eagleton, 1983, 148). García Márquez's signature begins with death (García Márquez, 1947; 1948). This novel is the chronicling of a death. At play, perhaps, is the 'neurotic unpleasure' of death which, dwelt upon, returned to again and again, becomes, is, the 'pleasure that cannot be felt as such'. Thus, through writing, the difference operates; in the overlay of apparent opposites – pleasure, unpleasure – there is a residue, a remainder. And that remainder, here, for me, writing on García Márquez, as for Derrida writing on Freud, takes the form of a question: 'How does death wait at the end, at all the ends [...] of this structure, at all the moves of this speculation?' (Derrida, 1978, 93).

Chronicle of a Death Foretold rehearses from prediction to event the narration of the death, *The Passion,* of a banal Nasar-ene. In the dramatic set-piece of pinning against wood, the end announced throughout – which everyone knows, which no one prevents, which, retrospectively and by piecing together conflicting versions, everyone would mythologize, reliving, exaggerating and exulting in their own part – *Chronicle* rewrites another chronicle: the dominant chronicle of Spanish American consciousness. Yet it would be a travesty of García Márquez to affirm but the 'neurotic unpleasure' of a death (recalled) turning to 'a possibility of pleasure' – the pleasure of the text, the *jouissance* of the 'literariness' of death, and no more than that. For meaning does not dissolve; it multiplies and concentrates. In the process, it deconstructs all possible mythification of a Santiago Nasar; he of absent father (Ibrahim) and of present (dominant, irrelevant, pure) mother responsible, thinking him 'upstairs' already, for the closed door to salvation; he who transmutes an 'Eloi, Eloi, lama sabachthani?' to an 'Ay, mi madre!', repeating not an augury of despair against the Father (Psalm 22), but despairing of his mother's futile auguring, of her failure to decipher his own repeated dreams of trees (10).

Santiago, Hispanic patron-saint, 'Matamoros' ('Moor-killer' but, here, only of the self); false, *ersatz* Nazarene, victim of a Holy Roman (San Román)-descended code, a religion, a society (Catholicism) and its culture, its customs, its politics, its history. A history of 'stained' honour, of hypocritical sexual ethics; a history, an *écriture* written (unofficially, in the margin) in blood. *Crónica de una muerte anunciada* deconstructs a version of the New Testament; it cannot but do the same for the original.

Pure speculation is still waiting.

Jacques Derrida

From 16 to 18 August 2004, in Rio de Janeiro, Jacques Derrida attended his last major international conference: *Pensar a Desconstrução. Questões de Política, Etica e Estética.* The following is the full version of an abbreviated English text provided for him to accompany the original Portuguese. The decision not to update or re-edit the text for this chapter has been taken – *de tout coeur* – in order respectfully to maintain the integrity of the contemporary meditation. The closing epigraphs are taken from Derrida's public response to, and exchange with, the speaker.

IX. DERRIDA TRANS(AT)L(ANTIC)ATED: SPECTRES OF *MAR...*
Mythology as Excess in (via) Fernando Pessoa, João Guimarães Rosa and Chico Buarque de Hollanda

Em tudo um Além...
Fernando Pessoa

Nonada
João Guimarães Rosa

More than a year ago, I had chosen to name the 'specters' by their name starting with the title [...] *'Specters of Marx'*

Jacques Derrida

On 'starting with the title...'

How am I to name my spect-*res* by their name? 'More than a year ago' came the invitation to meditate on the impact of the writing of Jacques Derrida on the practices of Lusophone literary critical traditions. The project was to mark Derrida's 'last' visit to Brazil. Specter or spectre? Was I to spell out the (transatlantic) difference? *To be or not to be* me?. *Whether 'twas nobler in the mind to sweep – perchance to scream –* my *outrageous* (mis)*fortune* aside and to *say we end the heartache and the thousand natural shocks that* vanity *is heir to by opposing* Lusophonia with the *proud man's contumely* for national institutional literatures... *there* was *the rub*. Thus *the insolence of office* more than the *patient merit of the unworthy* took me less to Brazil than to *the undiscover'd country from whose bourn no traveller returns* without the insight that *conscience does make cowards of us all,* if we *lose the name of action* by scorning *enterprises of great pitch and moment.* Had not Jacques himself reminded us that, always, *the time is out of joint* and, no doubt, place, and identity, too? And so, it was a memory of that phantasm of Lusophone writing that ever *puzzles the will* of the comparativist that I could not *turn awry.*

In the interval, as a tracer of the post-Derridan supplements of the post-Marxian era of the post-Berlin Wall, I too have 'remembered what must have been haunting my memory' and that, still 'a specter is haunting Europe' (Derrida, 1994, 4); a *revenant*, perhaps, returned from worlds once called new, along routes which, once opened, once explored, traced lines of two-way traffic, supplemented soon by other possibilities, interferences, other travellers, other voices, interpell-ations. It is on a note, and through an instance, of interpellation that I wish to return to my then dilemma. Prompted by a (chance?) hearing of two versions of a popular song by the Brazilian composer and lyricist Chico Buarque de Hollanda, I was plunged in difference, alerted to *différance*; the agency of the difference between the two led me to ponder (many) a third term. *To be or not to be* locked in national(ist) binaries? How was I to choose a way through the entangling roots, an itinerary from amongst the meandering routes, a methodology from amidst the competing reflections, of five hundred years' post-maritime and pre-revolutionary gestures? And so I opted to return to my own first contacts – 'we must begin wherever we are [...] in a text where we think we are' (Derrida 1976, 162) – with a Portugal of just-prior to the Revolução dos Cravos; and with a Brazil still locked into military dictatorship. I also knew that 'there was a ghost waiting there' (Derrida, 1994, 4); nay, ghosts.

To sea or not to see…

Tanto mar

Foi bonita a festa, pá
Fiquei contente
E inda guardo, renitente,
Um velho cravo para mim
Já murcharam tua festa, pá
Mas certamente
Esqueceram uma semente
Nalgum canto de jardim
Sei que há léguas a nos separar
Tanto mar, tanto mar
Sei também quanto é preciso, pá
Navegar, navegar
Canta a primavera, pá
Cá estou carente
Manda novamente
Algum cheirinho de alecrim.

(Chico Buarque de Hollanda, 1976)

[So much sea/The party was lovely, pal/I was happy/And, stubborn, I still hold on/To an old carnation just for me/They rained on your party, pal/But they certainly/Forgot one seed/In some garden corner/I know we are leagues apart/So much sea, so much sea,/I know too how much we need, pal/To navigate, navigate/Sing out the springtime, pal/Here something is missing in me/Send again/Some whiff of rosemary]

The particular historical and social circumstances of Chico Buarque's composition require little elucidation. It was first performed in the Bar Canecão in Rio de Janeiro, by the composer himself and Maria Bethânia, just two years after the overthrow of Portugal's near half-century of dictatorship. My reflections on the interpellations of the song's performance arise from my insistent conviction that literature highlights the differences which cultural studies explore. I shall therefore speculate on the mechanisms exploited by Chico's song-text in its calling from one locus of enunciation to another, or others, not in a language of homogeneity but in voices of difference, addressing the other in a discourse of the other, through a 'pá' of fraternity, companionship, solidarity, yes, but which, as a marker, does not and could not conceal the differential lexis of a term hardly used in Brazilian Portuguese other than to evoke and to mimic the everyday conversational discourse of its European counterpart.

As well as such differential lexical markers as 'pá', 'inda', and 'renitente', the song exploits other cultural and iconographic ciphers of Portuguese national identity past and present. The most obvious is that of the carnation, still freshly associable, in Chico's 1976 version of the song, with the Revolução dos Cravos of April 25 1974; whence the play on 'murcharam' as the effect of counter-revolutionary political forces in Portugal; and on 'primavera' as the spring both of that particular revolution and of the eternal possibility of rebirth, of fresh flowers and an as yet hypothetical flowering of a future political freedom.

In dialogue with the Portuguese history of the mid-1970s is a complex of Brazilian voicings, no less politically charged but, of necessity, and under censorship, more encoded, less overt. From a Brazil in the throes, if not at the nadir, of military rule, under The Emergency Powers of *The Fifth Institutional Act* and the dictatorship of President General Ernesto Geisel, comes the cry: 'Cá estou carente'. Thus, 'guardo [...] um velho cravo para mim' points, ostensibly, to the cherished hope that one day there will be an equivalent Brazilian spring of bloodless revolution. But to the complexities of 'Tanto mar' I shall return, after I have named *my* spectres... the *revenants* of a personal Lusophone spectrology: Fernando Pessoa and João Guimarães Rosa.

The interpellations which underpin the song-text of Chico Buarque at once pose questions of how nations and, as a corollary, national literatures relate, write and speak to each other. Through what filters does Brazil conceive of Portugal, or Portugal conceive of Brazil? Through the gauze of *H*istory with a capital H? – an intellectual construct in which both have participated and, indeed, have shared a reciprocal forging of, and in, the other? Heeding such as Frantz Fanon's 1960s' warnings of the dangers of constructing notions of nation derived exclusively from the past, critics have been circumspect, no less, about the shaping of so-called 'national' literatures. For Fanon, intellectual constructs have been largely ineffectual in shaping nations, and he proposed that, in mobilizing images into a national imaginary, we do well to look less at literary than at political struggles and revolutions. Suspicious of memory which assumes national forms, Fanon unleashed critical memory to come to terms with what has often been criminal nationhood:

> With the exception of a few misfits within the closed environment, we can say that every neurosis, every abnormal manifestation [...] is the product of [the] cultural situation [...] Only for the white man is the Other perceived on the level of the body image, absolutely as the not-self – the unidentifiable, the unassimilable. For the black man [...] historical and economic realities come into the picture. (Fanon, 1986, 152, 61)

To identify the prevailing model against which Fanon and other, broadly Marxist, re-thinkers of cultural practices were reacting, in what I might figuratively and provisionally term a horizontal-Utopian trajectory, it should suffice to recall Richard Rorty's warning against the lures of the transcendental. In comparative literary analysis, for instance, there would, characteristically, be a gestural pointing to a 'real world' (often a national-specific one) before the critic opted to 'go transcendental'. A pertinent example, admittedly somewhat contrived, illustrates paradigmatically that style of criticism which trades in archetypes, habitually at the cost of sacrificing specificity. While used to grandiose claims being made for the propensity of great modern writers to absorb into their literary production the spirit and genius of their classical precursors (Joyce with Virgil, Eliot with Dante etc.), I have nonetheless been intrigued by an extreme, Lusophonist's, case... mined from the (l)ore of Minas Gerais. In his *recherché* proposal, 'Grande Sertão: Lusíadas', the Brazilian critic Joaquim Branco performs, for the purposes of my argument, an exemplary instance of that 'going transcendental' whereby a but minimal gesturing at cultural difference is offered before the synthetic process of reading Luís de Camões into João Guimarães Rosa begins in earnest. The bracketed subtitle is eloquent: '(De como o vaqueiro Riobaldo encontra o velho Gama, nos mares bravios do sertão-linguagem)'. I might (generously?) attribute a tongue-in-cheek hyperbole to Branco's (clarifying?) juxtaposition:

> E enquanto Camões fixa os limites do reino lusitano: *'onde a terra se acaba e o mar começa'*, Guimarães Rosa explica: 'O sertão é do tamanho do mundo [...] Sertão é quando menos se espera, digo [...] Sertão é o sozinho [...] Sertão é dentro da gente [...] As ciladas armadas por Baco contra os portugueses são aliviadas por vários deuses e deusas, que orientam os navegantes sempre a porto seguro. São as mesmas emboscadas preparadas pelos jagunços do Hermógenes, Ricardão, Antenor ou Silvino Silva, contra os heróis do sertão: Riobaldo, Diadorim, Joca Ramiro, Medeiro Vaz [...] No mar, a expedicão do Gama: *'Relâmpagos medonhos [...] Feros trovões, que vêm representando cair o Céu dos eixos sobre a terra, consigo os elementos terem guerra'* [...] Companheiros e jagunços, de repente, o amor fecha a mata e entrelaça os amigos, no tiroteio, e *'o diabo no meio do redemoinho'* [...] Por que Guimarães Rosa e Camões? Porque a *harpa submersa* no mar corresponde ao cavaquinho e à viola dos *gerais*. A Babel. A Babel mímica/rítmica d'*Os Lusíadas* verseja tanto quanto o *blá-blá-bel* nas barbas do Netuno-sertanejo (Riobaldo). Por isso, o *approach*/enfoque – *Grande Sertão: Lusíadas.* (Branco, 1998, 21-22)

> [And while Camões fixes the bounds of the Lusitanian realm: *'where the land ends and the sea begins'*, Guimarães Rosa explains: 'The sertão is the size of the world [...] Sertão is when we least expect it, I say [...] Sertão is being alone [...] Sertão is inside us [...] The Portuguese are saved from the traps that Bacchus sets for them by gods and goddesses, who always guide the navigators to safe haven. They are the same ambushes laid by the *jagunços* of Hermógenes, Ricardão, Antenor or Silvino Silva, against the heroes of the *sertão*: Riobaldo, Diadorim, Joca Raminor, Medeiro Vaz [....] At sea, the expedition of da Gama: *'Fearsome lightning [...] Fierce thunder, that come to represent the Sky falling from its axis upon the earth, with it the elements at war'* [...] Comrades and jagunços, suddenly, love seals off the forest and interlocks friends, into the gunfire,

and *'the devil amidst the whirlwind'* [...] Why, Guimarães Rosa and Camões? Because the *harp submerged* in the sea corresponds to the *cavaquinho* and to the guitar of the *gerais*. Babel. Mimic/rhythmic Babel of *The Lusiads* puts into verse as much the *bla-bla-bel* in the beard of the Neptune-*sertanejo* (Riobaldo). Whence, the approach/focus – *Grande Sertão: Lusíadas.*]

Whilst we might smile (in recognition of our own generalizing excesses?) at Branco's 'going elemental', his detection within 'a briga dos ventos' of transcendental forces somehow conveyable from their respective literary locations towards a realm of abolished difference, we might also detect a virtual pastiche of archetypal criticism. Precisely the vertical, the heaven-hell, axis of analysis, the blanking out of *différance*, against which Fanon and his like have railed? However, in the reflections which follow, I shall ponder not only the paradoxical limitations of finding, pervasively, 'em tudo um Além' (Pessoa, 1974, 384) but also the limits of Utopian solutions, whether Fanon's critical memory or later, comparable injunctions such as that of Frederic Jameson always radically to historicize analysis, given that 'the structure of the psyche is historical, *and has a history'* (Jameson, 1981, 62; my italics). As both my title and use of an opening epigraph from Derrida's *Specters of Marx* might have suggested, I situate my own institutional voicing in that other interpellation which I hear as the dialogical tension between historical-empirical and mythologising-idealist methodologies.

Spectrality

In proposing this title, *Specters of Marx*, I was initially thinking of all the forms of a certain haunting obsession that seems to me to organize the *dominant* influence on discourse today. At a time when a new world disorder is attempting to install its neo-capitalism and neo-liberalism, no disavowal has managed to rid itself of all Marx's ghosts. Hegemony still organises the repression and thus the confirmation of a haunting. Haunting belongs to the structure of every hegemony. (Derrida, 1994, 37)

The 'dominant influence on discourse today', as I hear it, is the 'haunting obsession' of, and with, Cultural Studies. In its most contagious manifestations, the recognition and celebration of difference for difference's sake constitutes a neo-hegemony, indeed, a 'new world disorder' which lends itself to the transnational interests of both the new capitalism and the neo-liberalism of which Derrida speaks. But is it sufficient to situate, to celebrate, to erect cultural differences – and the recognition of them – into some hegemony of the late twentieth-early twenty-first century? To admit even the possibility would be to indulge, in repetition, a lure-laden game of blocks and shocks.

Derrida has remarked upon the (post-Communist) 'eschatological themes' operating, in blocks, *à la* Fukuyama: 'end' of history, 'end' of Marxism, 'end' of man, even 'end' (or apocalypse, now?) of philosophy (Derrida, 1994, 14). The shocks, as undergone by literary and other criticisms, have left fragmentation, micro-discourses, symbolic values, strategies of conversion (*à la* Baudrillard, *à la* Bourdieu) to *proliferate*: post-, post-, post-... But if 'haunting belongs to the structure of every hegemony', including these neo-ends and neo-posts, through what medium will its spectres be manifested? How, and by whom, will they be named? In *Specters of Marx*, he returns – though I doubt that he has ever left it – to literature. The opening epigraph (Derrida, 1994, xxi) becomes, always was, his obsessive concern:

> The time is out of joint.
> *Hamlet*

I, too, meditate on out-of-jointness as I engage in the naming of my spectres from Portugal and Brazil; and, as the medium which might highlight, and also take me beyond, the mere recognition of their differences, I reflect not on their respective, but on aspects (aspects *are* spectres) of their particular, literatures.

Any spectrum of time represented as a span between origin and end, between *arché* and *telos*, encounters in the spectrum-spectre play a haunting, a revisiting, a *revenance,* whereby out-of-jointness unsettles all possibilities of linear progression, of direct access to historical, cultural and any other reference or meaning. The spectrum of communication does not cease to exist but inhabits other figures, figurations, configurations, (con)junctures, (dis)junctures, joints and out-of-joints. Marxism, no less, seeking 'always [to] historicize', has to confront time conceived of other than as othered; other than as alienated in the archaeo-teleological discourse of a Utopian trajectory. And must do so in the contemplation of the multiple spectres of Marx, of Marxian thinking and practices, of revolutions... flowered, flowering or still to flower:

Before knowing whether one can differentiate between the specters of the past and the specters of the future, of the past present and the future present, one must perhaps ask oneself whether the spectrality effect does not consist in undoing this opposition, or even this dialectic, between actual, effective presence and its other. (Derrida, 1994, 39-40)

And, so, when I (am inclined to, or decline to) name my spectres as Fernando Pessoa and João Guimarães Rosa, am I not naming spectrality effect(s)? Any supposition that I might gain access to them or to their work exclusively in, or via, an engagement with the Portuguese and Brazilian historical or literary historical conjunctures in which their writings occur is bedevilled by excess, in mixtures of reality and unreality effects. In his *Psychoanalysis and History: Negation and Freedom in Freud*, Michael S. Roth has identified both these named practices as 'frameworks through which we can make sense of our pasts'. Psychoanalysts are 'prepared to find several motives for one and the same mental occurrence whereas what seems to be our innate craving for causality declares itself satisfied with a single psychical cause' (Roth, 1987, 9; 66).

Like analysis, literature can resist causalities in, for example, representing the mixed motivations of our anxious reachings for, our callings towards, our interpellations with, the other place, the other culture, the other voice:

Não sei se é sonho, se realidade,
Se uma mistura de sonho e vida,
Aquela terra de suavidade
Que na ilha extrema do sul se olvida.
É a que ansiamos.
Ali, ali
A vida é jovem e o amor sorri.
Talvez palmares inexistentes,
Áleas longínquas sem poder ser,
Sombra ou sossego dêem aos crentes
De que essa terra se pode ter.
Felizes, nós? Ah, talvez, talvez,
Naquela terra, daquela vez.
Mas já sonhada se desvirtua,
Só de pensá-la cansou pensar,
Sob os palmares, à luz da lua,
Sente-se o frio de haver luar.

Ah, nesta terra também, também
O mal não cessa, não dura o bem.
Não é com ilhas do fim do mundo,
Nem com palmares de sonho ou não,
Que cura a alma seu mal profundo,
Que o bem nos entra no coração.
É em nós que é tudo. É ali, ali,
Que a vida é jovem e o amor sorri.

(Pessoa, 1942, 158)

[I know not whether it is dream or reality,/or a mixture of dream and life,/that land of sweetness/which on an island far to the south is forgotten./It is the one we long for./There, there/life is youthful and love smiles./Perhaps inexistent palm-trees,/distant alleys unable to be,/shade or rest may they give to the believers/that that land can be had./Happy. We? Ah, perhaps, perhaps,/in that land, at that time./But once dreamt it loses value,/just to think of it has tired thinking,/under the palm-trees, in the light of the moon,/is felt the cold of it being moonlight./Ah, in that land also, also/evil does not cease, good does not last./It is not with islands at the world's end,/nor with palm-trees of dream or not,/that the soul cures its deep ill,/that good enters the heart./It is in us that everything is. It's there, there,/that life is youthful and love smiles.]

For the moment, the Pessoa word I choose to emphasise is 'mistura'. Why? Listen to Guimarães Rosa... and to a deferred translation:

Quando menino, no sertão de Minas, onde nasci e me criei, meus pais costumavam pagar as velhas contadeiras de estórias. Elas iam à minha casa para contar casos. E as velhas, nas puras misturas, me contavam estórias de fadas e de vacas, bois e reis. Adorava escutá-las. (Rosa, in Dantas, 1968, 1)
[When as a boy, in the Minas sertão, where I was born and grew up, my parents used to pay the old women story-tellers. They would come to my house to tell their tales...]

Listener worry not... if translation is as irresistible as it is impossible (or irresistible *because* it is impossible), I choose only now to hear (chafurdo?): 'And the old women, in pure mixtures, told me fairy-tales and Daisy-tales, ox-tales and Rex-tales. I adored listening to them'. *Et tu?*

Pessoa's 'Ansiamos', Rosa's 'adorava' – pressure points, conjunctures at and in which their respective oxymoronic 'se sonho... se realidade' and 'puras misturas' perform resistantly against the would-be causality effects of analysing poetry or narrative with a view to exorcising their spectralities. Desire and adoration – pleasure effects no less than pleasure texts – in these two instances occupy but one buffer of the shuttle-system which Freud, for one, named Eros-Thanatos. Yet just as the erotic pulsion is unendingly deferred in relation to the other – remember how, for Levinas, 'Nothing is further from *Eros* than possession' (Levinas, 1969, 265) – so deferred acceptance of any loss of other, whether by death, or disappearance, or abandonment, is expressed always in the relation which we have come to call the mourning-spectre.

For Derrida, the relation in question is evoked in one of the subtitles of *Specters of Marx*, namely, *The Work of Mourning*, and in his categorical 'there is no singular memory [...] all work is mourning' [...] 'Ego = ghost. Therefore "I am" would mean "I am haunted": I am haunted by myself who am (haunted by myself who am haunted by myself who am... and so forth). Wherever there is Ego, *es spukt*, "it spooks"' (Derrida, 1994, 133). For Rudolf Gasché, 'mourning [is] constitutive of philosophy [...] To "think" the absolutely contingent and singular, the irreducibly arbitrary, corresponds, indeed, to a mourning of another past that had to be forgotten for thinking to come into its own' (Gasché, 1989, 219). For me, more simply, my relations with Pessoa and Guimarães Rosa are inscriptions which I cannot categorize as deconstructive merely via post-scripts. Rather am I forced, always, to re-engage with them in ghost-scripts.

For a Portuguese reader, the forgotten island in the south might conjure up *Os Lusíadas* and the Island of Love. Veloso's cry no doubt re-echoes in Pessoa's poem but primarily to remind us of what Helder Macedo has identified as 'the vision of a golden age [that] is more of a wishful project than a prophetic affirmation [...] a modern sense of doubt which is central to [Camões'] complex vision of history, realistically understood as a composite of ambiguities' and an epic, 'finally, in the conditional mood, disclosing the empty space which only history could fulfil' (Macedo, 1983, 16). Pessoa's swerve away is not a mere anxiety of influence. 'É a que ansiamos' (an anxiety of *con*fluence) is expressed as affirmation but, though the construction of a convoked, never virtual, dreamland has been most fragile, the very effort of dreaming it has proved burdensome to thought. Previously comforting shade turns to shadow, the source of light is now the moon... a chilling moonlight, a chill realisation; there can be no permanent suspension of duration, the undermining of youth and well-being by age and ill. Mourning. Therefore, in the final stanza, the very idea of a *locus amoenus* as having any relevant external existence is dismantled. A series of negative particles ('não', 'nem', 'não') interrupts the flow of thought, obstacles to the construction of either palm-trees or dreams, hammer-blow reminders of the irrelevance of Utopianism... but only insofar as it is traditionally constructed, outside the self. The anti-dualist, full-blown existentialism of the final two lines performs a commentary on the tradition and the psychology of the *locus amoenus*. Camões' attempted re-integration of the fantastic, the erotic, the dreamt, into the principle of reality, political, temporal, mortal, is re-read, revised, revived but, at the same time, by no means has the *locus amoenus* been abolished. Rather does Pessoa's poem subject it to a process of deconstruction, whereby the metaphor is revealed as containing both a present and an absent term, existence (at the level of dream) and inexistence (at the level of experience). The interplay between the two levels constitutes the poem, the rhythm encapsulated in 'Talvez [...] inexistentes'. But the poem is kinetic, never static, indulging the trace and supplement of whichever term is momentarily absent. Might it be that Pessoa, in his poetic practice, has not so much intuited the – however sophisticatedly – formulaic Harold Bloom ratios (of swerve), but rather has anticipated a markedly different Derrida insight (of verve)?

> Play is the disruption of presence... Play is always play of absence and presence, but if it is to be thought radically, play must be conceived of before the alternative of presence and absence. Being must be conceived as presence or absence on the basis of play and not the other way round. (Derrida, 1978, 292)

The *locus amoenus* (or, never *hors-texte, Os Lusíadas*?) is still at – and in – play. 'It is' would mean 'It is haunted'... And what of the scandalously repressed term of negation which inhabits the *locus amoenus*, a dread of another other place, of an othered identity? That space which dare not speak its name? The 'rupture' text by which that space will be accessed, if not directly named, is often spoken as conjuration:

> One must, magically, chase away a specter, exorcise the possible return of a power held to be baleful in itself and whose demonic threat continues to haunt the century. Since such a conjuration today insists, in such a deafening consensus, that

what is, it says, indeed dead, remain dead indeed, it arouses a suspicion. It awakens us where it would like to put us to sleep. Vigilance, therefore: the cadaver is perhaps not as dead, as simply dead as the conjuration tries to delude us into believing. The one who has disappeared appears still to be *there*, and his apparition is not nothing. (Derrida, 1994, 96-97)

'...such a conjuration... the one who has disappeared'

History is the path, myth the trajectory. Not with the projected title *Portugal* but as *Mensagem*, the play begins, an interplay of direct reference to the events and personalities of Portuguese national consciousness and of an ever deferred, ever more diffuse 'message' which, in the final poem 'Nevoeiro', is subsumed into the spatio-temporal mist of its closing lines:

> Tudo é disperso, nade é inteiro.
> Ó Portugal, hoje és nevoeiro...
>
> É a Hora!
>
> (Pessoa, 1934, 104)

> [All is dispersed, nothing is entire,/Oh Portugal, today you are a fog.../It is Time!]

'It is Time'... Is that time (already and always) also out of joint? Without knowledge of Portuguese history, *Mensagem* does not begin to make sense. With knowledge of that same history, *Mensagem* re-defines sense. The inseparability of history from myth is never put to the question... it is the question.

The critical tradition of history-cum-myth-cum-history (the oscillation is where we begin to read, not the relationship between polarities of difference) knows, but has possibly moved away from, the key names and motifs of the founding of a nation, an identity, a tradition. For *Mensagem* is notable in its restraint, its concentration, its discipline, its division into three sections: 'Brasão' ('Escutcheon'), 'Mar Português' (Portuguese sea'), and 'O Encoberto' ('The Hidden One'). Much has been made of the nationalist content and trajectory of *Mensagem*, partly due to the contemporary circumstances of António Salazar's construction of the 'Estado Novo' which, from 1928, projected an image of Portugal as inward-looking, self-sufficient and 'free' of foreign interference. Undoubtedly, Pessoa's attachment to the idea of a 'poeticized Portugal' is worthy of critical attention, arguably, however, rather more in psychological than in political terms. For the search for a sense of identity, initially anchored in a given space though, conceivably, transcending time, informs *Mensagem*, demonstrably influenced by a Romanticism shot through by quasi-religious transcendentalism. Thus, in coming to terms with his Portuguese heritage, both historical and literary, Pessoa constantly brings to his treatment of national themes an ironic, metaphysical tone which, finally, implies attachment to a mystic 'Além' – a Beyond – rather than to a specific cultural nationalism. The force of *Mensagem*, therefore, derives from both the national and the metaphysical, since Pessoa's treatment of a set of authentically Portuguese preoccupations captures precisely that projection of frontiers characteristic of a consciousness habitually focussed, in the first instance, perhaps, 'overseas' yet, in the abstract, ever 'over there'. However, as Helder Macedo has asserted, 'epic poetry, even when it concerns real historical persons or events, always represents a metaphorical vision of history' (Macedo, 1983, 3). In more than one sense, then, does Pessoa subsume the tradition of Camões. Not simply in taking up lyrically the epic subject-matter of Portugal's geographic setting in the opening poem of *Mensagem*; nor even, subsequently, in echoing the myth of the founding of Lisbon by Ulysses, or the heroism of the legendary Viriathus; not even in the evocation of the glories of Prince Henry the Navigator or of the lost warrior – King Sebastian. The more resonant legacy is the poet's exploiting the metaphysical dimension of an already metaphorical vision.

In this respect, there is consistent evidence in Pessoa's contemporary prose-writings of his confronting History not as fact but as necessary fiction. That evidence attests time and again to the poet's own transcendentalism and, no less, to the alert ear of his Brazilian interlocutor's 'sei também quanto é preciso, pá /Navegar, navegar':

- Navegadores antigos tinham uma frase gloriosa: 'Navegar é preciso; viver não é preciso'.
- Quero para mim o espírito [d]esta frase, transformada a forma para casar com o que eu sou: Viver não é necessário; o que é necessário é criar.
- O conceito de Pátria é um conceito puramente místico.
- O erro político fundamental tem sido julgar que pode haver uma política verdadeira;
- Só a ciência busca a verdade e a quer
- [a ciência] é a primeira Nau que parte para as Índias Espirituais

- Desejo ser um criador de mitos.

(Pessoa, 1986, 156, 160-1)

[Navigators of old had a glorious phrase: 'To sail is a must; not so to live'/I wish for the spirit of this phrase, transformed to marry it with what I am: To live is not necessary; one must only create. /The concept of *Pátria* is purely mystical/The fundamental political error has been to think there can be a true politics/Only knowledge seeks truth/(knowledge) is the first Ship to sail for the Spiritual Indies/I wish to be a creator of myths.]

The trajectory of Pessoa's myth-creation in *Mensagem* follows a clear pattern, from Land, to Sea, to Mist. Taking the Portuguese coat of arms as the basis of a schematized presentation of the figures of an emerging patriotic glory, the poet weaves threads of enigmatic speculation on the tapestry-frame of received history. I choose but one strand for comment here, perhaps the most famous, that of Sebastião. Without some explanation of the significance of this promised redeemer of the nation, born in 1554 but lost, impetuous, his body never to be found, at the battle of Alcácer-Quibir in 1578, *Mensagem* loses much of its coherence, especially as Pessoa situates the figure of Sebastião in key-poems of each of the collection's three sequences:

Louco, sim, louco, porque quis grandeza
[...]
Sem a loucura que é o homem
Mais que a besta sadia,
Cadáver adiado que procria?

(Pessoa, 1934, 42)

[Mad, yes, mad because I wanted grandeur/[...] Without madness what more is man/Than the healthy beast,/The deferred corpse that procreates?]

Pessoa approaches the figures of Sebastião not *tabula rasa*, not even afresh but, consciously and unavoidably, as one of the great commonplaces of Portuguese history, politics and literature. The danger inherent in too generalized a reading of Sebastianism as a peculiarly Portuguese version of the perennial Quest motif, expressed elsewhere in the Grail, in Messianism or even in Utopianism, threatens and curtails many a critical interpretation of Pessoa's poetry. For it is as implausible to limit his trajectory to some lyrical mysticism as, in parallel, it has often been to restrict the enterprise of Stéphane Mallarmé to an exquisite angelism. If there is, indeed, a theological rhythm here it is certainly heterodox, tantamount to that negative aspiration which would detect in Otherness not the ultimately revealable but rather the forever unobtainable, the more 'purely' longed for in the knowledge of guaranteed failure.

In contrast with orthodox Christian theology, no solace is offered; hence, I would argue, the attachment, from the outset, to 'loucura' – a 'madness' which, however, raises human kind above compulsive animality. In an essay entitled 'Sobre o Mito Sebastianista', Pessoa is at pains to elaborate the *strategy* of his recourse to the figure of potencial national redemption:

> Que Portugal tome consciência de si mesmo. Que rejeite os elementos, estranhos. Ponha de parte Roma e a sua religião. Entregue-se à própria alma. Nela encontrará a tradição dos romances de cavalaria [...] a Tradição Secreta do Cristianismo [...] Expulsemos pois o elemento romano. Se há que haver religião em nosso patriotismo, extraiamo-la desse mesmo patriotismo. Felizmente temo-la: o sebastianismo. (Pessoa, 1979, 52)

> [Let Portugal become aware of itself. Let it reject extraneous elements. Let it put aside Rome and its religion. Let it give itself over to its own spirit. There it will find the tradition of the Romances of chivalry [...] the Secret Tradition of Christianity [...] Let us then expel the Roman element. If there is to be religion in our patriotism, let us extract it from that same patriotism. Happily we have it: Sebastianism.]

Far from constituting, then, a faith in certainty, the function of Pessoa's Sebastianism is to enshrine faith in doubt. The point is made never more clearly than in the second sequence of *Mensagem*, in the title poem of 'Mar Português':

> Deus ao mar o perigo e o abismo deu,
> Mas nele é que espelhou o céu.
> (Pessoa, 1934, 70)

> [God to the sea gave peril and the abyss,
> But in it he mirrored heaven.]

In a trope much used by Pessoa, an initially clear-cut statement of fact is simultaneously undermined by the form in which it is expressed. Here a chiasmus of equivalences in balance with their opposites (namely, God/heaven *versus* it/the perilous abyss of the sea) is prevented from operating as a figure of contrast by the fulcrum-term 'mirror'. At a stroke, presence becomes the projection of absence, plenitude a reflection of the void. Identity becomes non-identity under erasure... and vice-versa.

The lines quoted here immediately precede the poem 'A Ultima Nau', on which is borne El-Rei D. Sebastião:

> Não voltou mais. A que ilha indescoberta
> Aportou? Voltará da sorte incerta
> Que teve?
> Deus guarda o corpo e a forma do futuro,
> Mas Sua luz projecta-o, sonho escuro
> E breve.
>
> (Pessoa, 1934, 71)

> [It never returned. At what undiscovered island/Did it call? Will it return from the uncertain fate/It had?/God keeps the body and the shape of the future/But His light projects it, a dream dark/And brief.]

The epigrammatic formula of the question-and-answer structure is emphasized by the rhyme of 'teve' and 'breve'. While the sequence of questions contains the *facts* of Sebastianism, the sequence of answers only appears to entrust to God the content and form of the unknown. (Note, incidentally, the play on the unfound body and the unspecified shape of things to come.) What Divine light projects, however, is scandalously, not to say blasphemously, dark and short-lived.

And so, as we moved from Land to Sea, now we move from Sea to a light which is not light, a realm which is insubstantial and fleeting... to the final sequence of *Mensagem*. While it is true to say that Sebastianism pervades every line of 'O Encoberto', the traditional penetration of the mists which shroud Sebastião's imaginary location constitutes, in 'As Ilhas Afortunatas', a particularly poignant moment of Pessoa's insight:

> Que voz vem no som das ondas
> Que não é a voz do mar?
> [....]

São ilhas afortunadas,
São terras sem ter lugar,
Onde o Rei mora esperando.
Mas, se vamos despertando,
Cala a voz, e há só o mar.

(Pessoa, 1934, 85)

[What voice comes from the sound of the waves/That is not the voice of the sea?/[...]/They are fortunate islands,/They are lands with no place,/Where the King dwells, waiting,/But, if we go waking,/The voice falls silent, and there is only the sea.]

The construction of convoked, never virtual, dream-isles, arises from the (illusory) presence of voice – the over-arching guarantee that response will find an object where object is presumed to lie. To lie... *perchance to dream...*

Waking to the lie of voice as the underpinning lure of men, of seafarers, of hearers of sirens from Ulysses to Sebastião and beyond, Pessoa broaches the possibility that the desert(ed) island of the imagination is constituted only by the sound of breaking waves. That waves should break endlessly, one into the other, without the consoling *locus amoenus* of the beach (the soothing madness of identity), however remote, on which might be salvaged the shipwrecked hope of waiting, is the closing insight of *Mensagem...* before the mist. Knowledge – ever in the mist – might be the first ship to set sail for the Spiritual Indies but cannot perform in indifference to the writing of it: 'My death is structurally necessary to the pronouncing of the I' (Derrida, 1973: 91).

Out of space-ness

Yet, it is now of the spectrology of Guimarães Rosa that *I* shall speak.

Nonada [...] O sertão está em toda a parte. Do demo? Não gloso [...] Explico ao senhor: o diabo vige dentro do homem, os crespos do homem [...] é que não tem diabo nenhum. Nenhum! – é o que digo. O senhor aprova? [...] Tem diabo nenhum. Nem espírito. Nunca vi. O diabo na rua, no meio do redemunho...
(Rosa, 1978, 9, 11)

[*Nonada* [....] The sertão is everywhere. About the devil? No comment [...] I'll explain to you, sir: the devil is on the watch in

man, in man's curls [...] there is no devil. None! – that's what I
say. Does sir approve? [...] There's no devil. Not even a spirit.
I've never seen one. The devil in the street, amidst the
worldwind...]

And, lest *I* be accused of (mis)reading the opening shots of *Grande
Sertão:Veredas* through only (merely?) spectral obsessions, in haunted
performance of my shuttle-title, and indulging the interplay of
horizontal-material and vertical-transcendental appropriations, it is
worth listening to the Brazilian critic Alfredo Bosi:

> Riobaldo, o protagonista de *Grande Sertão*, é um homem que
> busca, no vaivém das suas memórias e reflexões, negar a
> existência real do demônio ('o que-não-há') [...] É certo que a
> crítica mais recente, escolhendo o ponto de vista técnico, no
> espírito do neoformalismo, tende a passar por alto a complexa
> rêde de estilos de pensamento que serviram de contexto e
> subjazem à ficção de Rosa. Uma leitura que ignore essas
> vinculações pode resvalar em uma curiosa ideologia, espécie de
> transcendentismo formal, não menos arriscada que o
> conteudismo bruto que lhe é simétrico e oposto. (Bosi 1973:
> 485, 487)

> [Riobaldo, the protagonist of *Grande Sertão*, is a man who
> seeks, in the toing-and-froing of his memories and reflections,
> to deny the real existence of the devil ('who-doesn't-exist') [...]
> Certainly, recent criticism, opting for the technical point of
> view, in the spirit of neo-formalism, tends to overlook the
> complex network of styles of thought which provide the context
> and underlie the fiction of Rosa. A reading which ignores those
> links can slip into a curious ideology, a kind of formal
> transendentalism, no less risky than the brute contentism
> which is symmetrically opposed to it.]

'Transcendentismo formal' and 'conteudismo bruto' will not always
operate so diametrically in a 'simétrico e oposto' pattern. Guimarães
Rosa's own delight in 'puras misturas', as Sandra Vasconcelos has
indicated with cryptic acuity, is both archaeologically and analytically
gestured at:

> Num gesto de bricoleur, Guimarães Rosa resgata [...] peças de
> um mosaico que, articuladas em novas relações, adquirem um

significado particular definido a partir de sua reatualização. (Vasconcelos, 1997, 11)

[In a *bricoleur*'s gesture, Guimarães Rosa rescues [...] pieces of a mosaic that, laid out in new relations, acquire a particular meaning defined according to their reworking.]

For, if Riobaldo indeed enacts a conjuration, attempts an exorcism, is vigilant, and resists the demon (and the 73 [72+1?] 'cognomes' attributed to this devil of a text), then it is perhaps in order to perform a desire, an 'ánsia', an *un*-death wish... though 'navigating' ill (or so he claims):

Sou só um sertanejo, nessas altas idéias navego mal. Sou muito pobre coitado. Inveja minha pura é de uns conforme o senhor, com toda leitura e suma doutoração. Não é que eu esteja analfabeto. Soletrei, anos e meio, meante cartilha, memória e palmatória. Tive mestre, Mestre Lucas, no Curralinho, decorei gramática, as operações, regra-de-trés, até geografia e estudo pátrio. Em folhas grandes de papel, com capricho tracei bonitos mapas. Ah, não é por falar: mas, desde do começo, me achavam sofismado de ladino. E que eu merecia de ir para cursar latim, em Aula Régia – que também diziam. Tempo saudoso! Inda hoje, apreceio um bom livro, despaçado [...] Eu quase que nada não sei. (Rosa, 1978, 14)

[I am but a *sertanejo*, through those high ideas I navigate ill. I'm a very poor soul. Mine is pure envy of some, according to you sir, with all the reading and high learning. It's not that I'm still illiterate. I spelled letter by letter, for years and a half, from primer, memory and ferrule. I had a teacher, Mestre Lucas, in Curralinho, I decorated grammar, operations, the rule of three, even geography and study of the nation. On big sheets of paper, at whim I traced pretty little maps. Ah, it's not to be spoken about: but, from the beginning, they thought I was a sophistricate *ladino*. And I deserved to go on to study Latin, in Aula Régia – they said so too. A nostalgic time! Even today, I appreciate a good book, unspaced out [...] I almost who don't know anything.]

A cliché of 'sertão-mar' equivalence is erased in the very instant in which it is broached: for 'navego mal' asserts and denies in inseparable measure the oral *presence* which, purportedly, takes precedence over a writing *absence*, in the confession of this 'pobre coitado' (or is it a poor devil's advocate?) My spectral obsessions force me to listen other-wise, to hear in difference. The arch *écriture* of an evasive ego is spooked by tensions the terms of which appear to locate the speaker in an *ersatz* Greco-Roman discourse ciphered by 'regra-de-três' (Three in One?); 'geografia e estudo pátrio' (Nation-State?); 'bonitos mapas' (seductive trace?); 'capricho' (supplement?); 'merecia de ir para cursar latim' (admission into Roman order(s)?); 'Aula Régia' (schooled and ruled?). Underwritten-undercut by 'palmatória' (discipline and punish?); 'decorei gramática' (an *other* – illuminated? – grammatology); 'nao é por falar' (a writing, then? a cryptology?); 'desde o começo' (in the Beginning was the Word... but spoken or written?); 'sofismado' (sophist[r]icate-Sophist?); 'ladino' (or crypto-Jew?).

'Eu quase que nada não sei'. Me neither. Mis(sed)-spell(ing)s or spells cast? I am just haunted by spectres... of Marx, of Freud, of Derrida, and of other rabbis... Reb Der < > Reb Ber? But what's in a name? Take Riobaldo. I am sorry, José Alves Pires, but your, albeit unconscious, lapse into a metaphysics *and* a metonymics of presence is just too temptingly dismantlable: 'Rio *baldo* é sinónimo de Rio baldeado (ou passado a vau), e não de Rio *baldado* (ou travessia fru-strada)' [Rio *baldo* is a synonym of Rio baldeado (or forded crossing), and not of Rio *baldado* (or passage frustrated)'] (Pires, 1993, 124).

To cross the river by fording the shallows is the easier passage. But to what promised land has access been granted? Certainly not to the transcendental. Not yet. Deferral or frustration? Or the 'impossibility of translation' both linguistically (*à la* Derrida) and theologically (*à la* Moses)? If we must return less to an *Ur*-text than to an *Ursprache* (and an illusory-originary dictat of Abraham), then 'o diabo', too, will be denied transcendence, kept in the here and now, 'na rua'. Not for nothing do 'redemoinho' and 'redemunho' operate interchangeably in a written-oral/oral-written scrambling effect. *Vortex*(t) of demon-sounds or *net*work of Script/ure?

If I have gone too far in order to arrive nowhere, if I have played (out) the obsessions of a spectrology too self-indulgently, I am none-theless still spooked by the closing words-cum-sign, and the re-opening *ad infinitem* of supplementary traces, of *Grande Sertão: Veredas*:

> Nonada. O diabo não há! É o que eu digo, se for... Existe o homen humano. Travessia. (Rosa, 1978, 460)[1]

---

[1] Aos leitores, e aos que escreverem sôbre êste livro, pede-se não revelar a

[*Nonada*. The devil there's not! That's what I say, if there were... Human man exists. A crossing.]

∞

Infinity ≠ unrepeatability ≠ untranslatability...

Tra(ns)vesty

'Foi bonito o texto, cara' – for by no travesty dare I utter 'pá' (as I must now, and always, respect cultural difference... before refusing it neo-hegemony). Guimarães Rosa's calculated (or Calculussed?) inscription of the sign of infinity, after the closing but never final word 'Travessia', prompts me to return to the broken spectrum of my initial thoughts on *arché-telos*. For the critic eager to complete the crossing, to move beyond structural imminence towards the representation of infinity, *Grande Sertão: Veredas* might hold out a possibility of closure. Thereby, such a reader might supplement the lexical gaps of deconstruction's sealed-off sign of erasure **(x)** by tying up the loose ends ∞. The novel's title, however, will (empirically?) fight back. For *Grande Sertão* posits thinking transcendentally – myth (or Nation)-making – only as a necessary move prior to the fragmentation of *Veredas*: multiple trails, plural traces of the differences within the confected nation (Brazil) *qua* construct.

Mourning lost plenitude, totality; exorcising possession, at-oneness; these are trajectories in tension but not at odds with each other. Re-appropriating Geoffrey Bennington's (*d'après* Derrida) 'Jewgreek is greekjew; but greekjew is Egyptian' (Bennington, 1994, 207), I shall risk thinking, in terms of Guimarães Rosa's mosaic disposition of the tiles (and his title) of (negative) theology and (affirmative) mourning (and, *d'après* Riobaldo), that ladinoromano is romanoladino; but romanoladino is Brazilian.

I claim no *trouvaille* – archaeological or otherwise – in excavating

---

sequência de seu enrêdo, a fim de não privarem os demais do prazer de descoberta do *Grande Sertão: Veredas*. [To readers, and to those who write about this book, it is requested that they do not reveal its plot sequence, in order not to deprive others of the pleasure of discovery of *Grande Sertão: Veredas*.] Back-matter of the first Livraria José Olympio edition, João Guimarães Rosa's *hors-texte* (*il n'y a pas de*) is (not) a midrashic imperative of non-revelation.

such a Mosaics from the text of Guimarães Rosa. On the contrary, to be sucked too easily into the fascination of mixings and hybridities or their (still 73?) 'cognomes' – as if they were some revelation – would be but to blind oneself to the insights of his 'puras misturas' as he both adores *and* indulges them.

Elaborating on my assertion that literature highlights the differences that cultural studies explore, I address but one of the operative differences between their respective discourses. The (im)possibility of translation, the (un)paraphraseability question, must be projected beyond the heavy veil of institutional paradigms at those professionally compromised practitioners of the sociology of literature and of its acolyte cognates. At what cost is the 'end' of literary criticism declared when literature's 'eschatological themes' are most polemically and subtly resistant to textual criticism's replacement by neo-hegemonies such as cultural studies? It cannot be a question of one *or* the other. The mutually feeding practices of creative critical thinkers working dialogically with critical creative writers are a necessarily tough intellectual challenge to purveyors of any transportable, transposable, translatable or paraphraseable blanket discourses.

There is a devilish humour – perhaps black – in the devices whereby literature speaks to would-be revealers of the meanings of cultural differences:

> Nem pensei mais no redemoinho de vento, nem no dono dele – que se diz – morador dentro, que viaja, o Sujo: o que aceita as más palavras e pensamentos da gente, e que completa tudo em obra; o que a gente pode ver em folha dum espelho preto; o Ocultador. (Rosa, 1978, 198)

> [I didn't think again about the whirlwind of the winds, nor of its owner – as they say – its inner dweller, the one that travels, the Devil: the one who allows bad language and thoughts in people, and completes everything while it's still being done; what people can see on the leaf of a black mirror; the Occulter.]

There may be an irresolvable tension between theological and sociological objectives, especially in that gnostic strain of turning against thought ('nem pensei'); of seeking not to reap the wind ('no redemoinho'), much less to confront its Patron ('o dono dele'); whether the latter take (the dominant metaphysical) positive or (the scandalously repressed) negative form ('o Sujo'). In any case, transparency will ever be denied in the 'espelho preto' of what literature accepts as its peculiar currency ('as más palavras e pensamentos da gente'). Much to the frustration of the literary *and* the social exegete, the differences highlighted (in a glass darkly?) will remain but untranslatable manifestations of... 'o Ocultador'. Alfredo Bosi grasps the issue and accepts both the enigma and the challenge:

> Outro problema seria o de situar a opção mitopoética do escritor na praxis da cultura brasileira de hoje. A transfiguração da vivência rústica interessa principalmente enquanto mensagem, ou enquanto código? (Bosi, 1973, 487)

> [Another problem would be that of situating the mytho-poetic option of the writer within the practice of Brazilian culture today. Is the transfiguration of rustic living of interest principally as message or as code?]

'Mensagem' or *Mensagem*? Code or goad? Riobaldo, and I, confronting the need to 'transfigure' our spectres, have come to learn that neither *message* nor *code* alone suffices; neither contemporary Brazilian cultural praxes nor earlier Portuguese mythopoetics resolve a predominant sense of loss, of need for contact with the ever-absent other.

In her seminal corrective to what she categorizes as the predominantly 'socio-economic', 'political' and 'oral discourse' emphases of Brazilian criticism on Guimarães Rosa, Kathrin H. Rosenfield, however un-explicitly, could just as easily have been referring to Hamlet as to Riobaldo when she claims:

> [His] grumbling is provoked by these enigmatic reversals of the purely apparent and 'mutative' values of all things or experiences [...] their reversal makes us perceive that we might have recognized their real significance had we been able to interlock the 'diverse' insignificant details involving their appearance. The gap between finite and infinite comprehension is what provokes the narrator's grumbling: telling the story of the *Grande Sertão* is an effort to re-articulate 'quicksilvery' reality, shaping and giving form to the 'devilish' ambiguities of experience [...] He sums up the precarious results of his grumbling in a paradoxical formula, saying that the devil – just like the *sertão* – does not exist even though both tend to reappear. (Rosenfield, 2000, 203-4)

For one critic, paradox; for another – Reb Ber – erasure: 'does[not]exist'; 're[dis]appear'; '[g]rumbling' narrativity; [non]*écriture*; non[orality]; [in]corporeality; [non]being:

> Sufoquei, numa estrangulação de dó [...] Não escrevo, não falo!
> – para assim não ser: não foi, não é, não fica sendo! Diadorim...
> [...] Uivei. Diadorim! Diadorim era uma mulher [...] O senhor
> não repare. Demore, que eu conto. A vida da gente nunca tem
> termo real [...] Fim que foi.
> Aqui, a estória se acabou.
> Aqui, a estória acabada.
> Aqui a estória acaba.
>
> (Rosa, 1978, 454)

> [I suffocated, in a strangling of pain [...] I can't write, I can't
> speak! – for it not to be so: it wasn't, it isn't, it won't be!
> Diadorim... [...] I screamed. Diadorim! Diadorim was a woman
> [...] Don't look, sir. Wait, while I tell you. A person's life never
> really ends [...] Here, the story ended. Here, the story is ended.
> Here the story ends.]

Diadorim is for Riobaldo 'the cadaver [but] perhaps not as dead, as simply dead, as the conjuration deludes us into believing' (Derrida 1994: 97). For mourning defers writing/ orality; being/non-being; gender/crossing; revelation/narration; terminology/termination; closure/aperture; time/tense... the real/intense.

Riobaldo might also have said, as could Hamlet, 'Cá estou carente'. I too. The time is out of joint so palpably as to oppose my conjoining of the Portuguese and Brazilian spectres which have haunted me throughout this nostalgia; I am as incapable of reading *Grande Sertão: Mensagem* as any less ludicrous than *Grande Sertão: Lusíadas*. Yet I resist, as excessive dislocation, such posturings as would separate, irremediably, an ex-colonizing Portugal from a formerly colonized Brazil. Spectrology, transcendentalism, historical materialism... all have left me, too, lacking. 'Cá estou carente'.

*

At the time of this re-writing, and twenty or more years on from the discovery of (my) lack, I re-discover the outstretched hand of Silviano Santiago:

Assim se constitui uma tradição de leitura do *Grande sertão: Veredas* que hoje nos incomoda e perturba [...] A qualidade selvagem [...] – sua *wilderness* – tinha sido domesticada pelos que recomendavam sua leitura pela mediação da prosa de *Os sertões* [...] Des/domesticar a monstruosidade do romance, eis uma nova proposta de leitura. O contemporâneo é o inatual. A fatura de *Os sertões* é histórica e simbólica. *Grande sertão: Veredas* pouco ou nada tem a ver com os acontecimentos históricos narrados com brilhantismo por Euclides da Cunha [...] Reparem. Não há uma única data no romance de Rosa [...] 'Viver é perigoso' — eis o *leitmotiv* da trama. Notável [...] é o fato de que, no mais profundo da vida miserável e autodestrutiva — na morte do humano, há lugar para o afeto e o amor. Ao compasso de espera, Riobaldo e Diadorim, os dois jagunços enamorados, dançam novos e felizes tempos [...] Remeto-vos às linhas finais do conto: 'voava a luzinha verde, vindo mesmo da mata, o primeiro vagalume. Sim, o vagalume, sim, era lindo! — tão pequenino, no ar, um instante só, alto, distante, indo-se. Era, outra vez em quando, a Alegria'. (Santiago, 2020, unpaginated)

[This is how a tradition of reading *Grande sertão: Veredas* now discomfits and perturbs us [...] Its quality of the *selvagem* [...] – its *wilderness* – has been domesticated by those who recommend reading it through the prose of *Os sertões* [...] To de/domesticate the monstrosity of the novel, *that* is a new proposal for reading. The contemporary is the unpresent. The craft of *Os sertões* is historical and symbolic. *Grande sertão: Veredas* has little or nothing to do with the historic events narrated with such brilliance by Euclides da Cunha. Notice. There is not a single date in Rosa's novel [...] 'To live is dangerous' – *that* is the *leitmotiv* of the plot. Noteworthy [...] is the fact that, in the very depths of miserable and self-destructive life – in the death of the human, there is room for affection and love. To the cadence of hope, Riobaldo and Diadorim, the two *jagunços* in love, dance new and happy rhythms [...] I take you back to the final lines of the short story: 'flying there in the faint green light, rising straight from the land, came the first fire-fly. Yes, the fire-fly, yes, it was beautiful! – so very tiny, on the air, just for an instant, high up there, distant, fleetingly. It was, every now and again, Delight'.]

Not for the first time, Silviano, the flickering brightness of your insight, in the words you cite from 'As margens da alegria' (*Primeiras estórias*, 1962), has *in-and-out* jointed the Time of a then with the now. The shuttling between the supposed time of one text and the moment of a subsequent analysis of other textuality disrupts the falsifying harmonizing proposed by a literary historical approach that looks for and then detects some putative thematics whilst overlooking the most egregious of genre distinctions. The structurings of da Cunha and Rosa are as distant from each other as to render disrespectful to both any collapse into oneness of their trajectories and effects. I reiterate: *Grande Sertão* {inseparable from} *Veredas*; singular overarching *with within* the fragmentation of plurality; multiple trails, plural traces pointing towards and away from each other – *différance* – within the confected nation *qua* construct.

*

And now? *Maintenant...* I repeat the opening word of *Specters of Marx*. The wedges driven between Portugal and Brazil by their respective histories – and why deny it? – by Fanon's criminal nationhoods, might indeed be said to have put their relation, now, 'out of joint'. But as *maintenant* splits into *main/tenant*, I am spooked again by Chico Buarque's inter-linking of fingers with Fernando Pessoa, by the would-be gesture, the reaching out, of 'Tanto mar', and by the way it exploits a complex literariness in order to resist, and even overcome, hand-in-hand recognitions of – or resignations to – historical and cultural differences as matters of *fact*... mere *faits accomplis*.

Un fait accompli? 'Tanto mar'... and, therefore, 'navegar'? But that is not what the song-text says. For it subjects the cliché to pressure, first, by repetition: 'navegar, navegar'. Poetry departs from history in this simple locution: the *question* of repetition is excessive with respect to the *fact* of repetition... Now an interpellatory Brazilian voice slips illusorily into the familiarity trope of a Portuguese 'sei que é preciso [...] pá'. Familiarity or defamiliarization? A 'making strange' of the passive acceptance of destiny? Or a reminder of '*quanto* é preciso' to re-read, re-write, re-live *H*istory (with a capital H) by constantly putting it under political and metaphorical pressures? An urgent making sense of the past in the present by looking to the future? In this case, even, the plea for a re-reading of colonial patterns whereby they might be strategically reversed?

'Tanto mar, tanto mar' and 'navegar, navegar' at once emphasize the separation of a Portugal in 'festa' from a Brazil in need – and a subjectivity 'carente' – and invoke a shuttle-effect which, culturally, might still have the power to realign relations and dependencies between them. To say 'I am dependent on you', for so long a taboo, is re-polarized by the fact that the utterance, in the political circumstances of its place and moment of enunciation, now breaks censorship. Here I swerve towards and (scandalously) away from the swingeing critic of Brazilian contemporary society, Phyllis Peres – and in a calculated misprision – her notion of the staging of negotiated identity. Peres might not be impressed that I choose to invoke in addressing such an internationally celebrated artist as Chico Buarque de Hollanda an analysis long since applied by her to 'Subaltern Spaces in Brazil':

> [T]he (utopian) ideal of a carnivalized Brazil [...] does not mean, however, that subalterns are silenced or silent [...] Nor does it mean, in [Eduardo] Galeano's terms, that they are condemned to suffer history rather than make it. What it does mean is that Brazilian subalterns are speaking in carnivals, but in dynamic elaborations of negotiated maskings and unmaskings, just as they have always done. (Peres, 1994, 119)

Just as Peres is concerned to go beyond, and to radicalize, limited notions of carnival as mere temporary, cyclical release, so I read the song-text's treatment of 'revolutionary' *festa*. It is just too simplistic to hear Chico's plea as saying: 'give us a little of the freedom you've already gained... and thrown away again'. Though that was perhaps enough for the Brazilian censors who banned the 1975 version of the song (which I shall shortly reveal). I suggest that the text never allows for the possibility of translation, linguistic, cultural, or otherwise; that the song takes *intraduzibilidade* for granted; that, in common with the tenor of the other texts I have referred to – and, indeed, of this meditation on (in)corporability itself – it is the *mourning* of untranslatability that constitutes the dynamics of the performance. 'Uma casa portuguesa' echoes, but 'com [in]certeza'... as *revenant*, as haunting, as *fado espectral*. And so, 'que fica'? The remainder, the supplement of any *N*ationalism will be not 'essa' but an ever-different 'fraqueza'; that shuttle between 'pobreza' and 'riqueza' all too empty of 'promessa' for a still expectant Brazil: 'For Marx has not yet been received [and] the subtitle of this address could thus have been "Marx [not] *das* [but has] *Unheimliche*"' (Derrida, 1994, 174).

Your *cravo* cannot be my *cravo*. Your red (blossom) and green (stem), momentarily stuffed into rifle barrels, cannot operate here. In *this* space, *that* flower will continue to adorn our cemeteries; if a *cravo* is put into anything here, it will surely be but another nail driven into our – *pace* Geisel – hardly closed wounds. Only emblematically – although in oblivion now ('esqueceram') – we might be said to have had some seed of common genealogy ('uma semente'). In whatever garden corner ('of some foreign field'?) or in whatever folk song (*canto/canto*), that seed is definitively lost... at least insofar as any possibility of origin, of ontology, is concerned. What remains is the knowledge of a separation ('Sei que há léguas a nos separar') so painful that the singer takes stock, reassesses. Out of repetition, the literal turns metaphorical; a pressurised 'navegar, navegar' is forced first into a two-way process, then into a repetition compulsion. Single syllables perform chiasmically: 'cá' >< 'pá'/me >< you... 'ca(nta)' >< 'ca(rente)'/you >< me... *fort* >< *da*. In short, the 'staging of negotiated identity' comes close to Theodor Adorno's negative dialectics: 'Objectively, dialectics means to break the compulsion to achieve identity, and to break it by means of the energy stored up in that compulsion and congealed in its objectifications' (Adorno, 1973, 157).

Staging the negative

Compulsive congealings of national consciousness – pre-figuring Chico Buarque's nostalgic compulsion to re-haunt *différance* – have been multiply done and undone by Pessoa in inexorable (dis)embodiments of the *fort-da* relation between subjective identities and objective framings; between the writ(h)ing of the self as non-self and the ship-wri(gh)ting of the nation as non-sense. Figures of *in*-capable imagination? Or the breaking of the vessels?

> Ó naus felizes, que do mar vago
> Volveis enfim ao siléncio do porto
> Depois de tanto nocturno mal –
> Meu coração é um morto lago,
> E à margem triste do lago morto
> Sonha um castelo medieval...
>
> E nesse, onde sonha, castelo triste,
> Nem sabe saber a, de mãos formosas
> Sem gesto ou cor, triste castelã
> Que um porto além rumoroso existe,
> Donde as naus negras e silenciosas
> Se partem quando é no mar manhã...

Nem sequer sabe que há o, onde sonha,
Castelo triste... Seu 'spírito monge
Para nada externo é perto e real...
E enquanto ela assim se esquece, tristonha,
Regressam, velas no mar ao longe,
As naus ao porto medieval...

(Pessoa, 1942, 206)

[Oh happy ships which from the fitful sea/Return at last to the silence of port/After so many a troubled night –/My heart is a dead lake/And at the edge of the dead lake/Dreams a medieval castle.../And in that, where she dreams, sad castle,/She knows not how to know, in her lovely hands/No life, no colour, the sad lady of the castle,/That beyond exists a bustling port/Whence the black and silent ships/Set sail upon the morrow.../She knows not even, where she dreams,/The sad castle stands... to her nun's spirit/Nought outside is near nor real.../And while she thus dissolves in dream, saddened,/The ships, far out to sea,/Sail back to the medieval port...]

The metaphor of 'meu coracão' conceived of as 'um morto lago', initially, functions as does the heart metaphor of 'comboio de corda' ['clockwork train'] in the keynote poem 'Autopsicografia', as an objective correlative. Here, however, the metaphor undergoes not only a process of development and interiorization but also, first, a dislocation and distancing effect ('à margem'), second, a spatial blurring (similar to the Proustian 'tremblement de contours') in 'sonha um castelo', and, third, a temporal shift to match in 'medieval'.

This carefully constructed process of penetration of the original metaphor brings an illusion of inhabitation, of life, to the original emotion of 'meu coração' and achieves that effect through the stylization of the 'fingidor' ['feigner']. In other words, the reader-response to the said metaphysical construction is to move away from 'a dor que deveras sente' ['of the pain he really feels'], namely, 'coração/lago morto' towards some feigned pain of the 'triste castelã'. Such a response, on the part of the reader, is the indulgence or *jouissance* proposed in such an 'Autopsychography' by the notion: 'E os que lêem o que escreve,/Na dor lida sentem bem,/Não as duas que ele teve,/Mas só a que eles não têm' ['And those who read what he writes,/In the pain that is read,/Feel not the two he had,/But only the one they have not']. It is an appreciation of that elaborate metaphorical interiorization which constitutes the poetic *effect,* or what the poem *does.*

As proof of the lull, the supposed departure from what the poem 'is' to what the poem 'does', comes the shock-realization that we as the reader, like the 'castelã, have forgotten or have become (momentarily) oblivious to the external ('além existe') existence of 'o porto rumoroso', the vivid reality evoked in the poem's opening three lines. These lines, in their relative simplicity and directness, constitute a recall to external life, to the coming and going of ships, a kinesis which contrasts starkly with the stasis, the frozen interior, of 'sem gesto ou cor'. Yet is the sequence, in its emphatic, apparently triumphant evocation of happiness in the transferred epithet of 'naus *felizes*', totally divorced from the subsequent process of metaphorical internalization? Despite the hyphen of separation, the answer is... *no*. Firstly, because the poem opens on a vocative, a mere convocation of the joyous reality 'effect' of the busy port. Secondly, despite the safe return of the ships after a long and troubled journey, the perception of the sea as 'vago' embryonically proposes the potential for blurring, vagueness and oblivion later to be exploited with reference to the lake (the inland, internal water to be juxtaposed with the off-shore, external sea). What the poem *does*, therefore, is to produce, in the reader, a pause (post-*jouissance*); after that pause comes the shock, the realization.

In the final stanza, 'Nem sequer sabe', reinforcing the earlier 'nem sabe saber', intensifies the process of removal from even a convoked, only wished-for reality. And the technique by which such a negation of an already inexistent reality is achieved is reminiscent of perhaps the greatest exponent of tightly constructed multi-negativity, Mallarmé. An aesthetic of intuition, a knowledge ('sabe', 'saber', 'sabe') is forever bracketed off, enshrined within particles of negativity ('nem', 'nem sequer') in typically Symbolist manner, a stylization of the purely feigned, the process of 'chega a fingir' ['com(ing) to feign']. Thus, when we ask 'what is the reality of which the 'castelã' is oblivious?', we begin to appreciate how that reality has been both constructed from a series of negatives and, in turn, as the poem nears its end, is also subject to a further process of fragmentation culminating in the final word of the text, 'medieval'. Is it a matter of surprise that the 'porto rumoroso' has been revealed, finally, to be as distant (or rather distanced) in time and space as is the 'castelã'? Perhaps. For we may have been seduced by the intricate detail ('seu 'spírito monge', 'esquece', 'tristonha') which would render her remote, explicitly, from all that is 'externo', 'perto' e 'real'; seduced, that is, into mistakenly juxtaposing her with an *external* 'perto' e 'real' port; seduced into a false binary of unreal versus real.

In fact, the poem has taken us through a double 'tremblement de contours', on a journey of evasion away from the inexistent lively reality ('rumoroso') into indulgently sad oblivion ('tristonha'). This journey, a reader's journey, might be construed as a metaphor of Portuguese historical or 'temporal' consciousness: evasion by dwelling 'tristonham-ente' on the maritime-associated glories of a mediaeval past, preferring the "spírito monge' of nostalgic waiting to even the illusion of external ('rumoroso') movement/life. I suggest further that the remarkable syntactic and metaphorical tortuousness of the poem delights poetically and heightens readerly sensitivity ('sentem [sent*imos*] bem') yet cont-ains a carefully hidden danger: the lure of an institutionalized national literary consciousness of 'saudade', of longing, of 'frozen' Sebastianism.

In summary, the poem seduces the fellow-traveller into indulgently opting for what it *does*, namely, the triggering of myriad associations of Portuguese literary consciousness, through its effect on the emotions – *saudade*, 'sadness', intimations of former maritime glory. But the poem *is* a juxtaposition of all that (the frozen, 'sem gesto ou cor') with life... namely, the port which might exist (which is longed for) but which is held back, prevented from existing, not least, by the indulgence of empathizing readers. Or even by an indulgence specific to the Portuguese... a nation of 'castelãs'?

Re-evoking momentarily 'Autopsicografia', while a nation of 'castelãs' 'na dor lida sentem bem', the castle (in Portugal's pain)-dwellers do not respond to the double-pain of the poet ('não as duas') as expressed in the poem. This nation, as readers, has opted for, and continues to opt for, 'só a que eles não têm', or the pain which is the effect of the poem. Rather than what it *is*, they read what it *does*.

In brief, the filtering of 'Ó naus felizes...' through 'Autopsicografia' highlights the limits and capacities of reading. It demonstrates the relationship of reader to text not only in the individual act of one reader to one text but also, demonstrably, in this instance, of a nation of readers to its national literature. In both cases, the danger of reading is the creation of a 'psychography'... *Luso-psicografia*.

Brazil... or *graphia*?

So what was all the fuss about? What *were* the words so dangerous in the earlier version that the song was banned in Brazil, as first performed, in 1975, in Portugal?

> Tanto mar
>
> Sei que estás em festa, pá
> Fico contente

E enquanto eu estou ausente
Guarda um cravo para mim

Eu queria estar na festa, pá
Com a tua gente
E colher pessoalmente
Uma flor do teu jardim
Sei que há léguas a nos separar
Tanto mar, tanto mar
Seí também quanto é preciso, pá
Navegar, navegar

Lá faz primavera, pá
Cá estou doente
Manda urgentemente
Algum cheirinho de alecrim.
                (Chico Buarque de Hollanda, 1975)

[So much sea/I know you're having a party, pal/I'm
happy/And, while I'm away/Keep a carnation for me/I wanted
to be at your party, pal/With all of you/And to pick for myself/a
flower from your garden/I know we are leagues apart/so much
sea, so much sea,/I know too how much we need, pal/To
navigate, navigate/There it's springtime pal/Here I am feeling
ill/Send me urgently/Some whiff of rosemary.]

Under pressure, the most telling change has been the substitution for
'eu estou ausente' of 'inda guardo renitente' – the shedding of a
dominant metaphysical, physical and political role of non-being, non-
participation; for onlooking and for the assumption of stubborn
resistance? The song operates less as an expression of identity, more as
a transmission of indemnity... a (hidden) transmitter both making
(codes) and breaking (censure). So what spectres have been raised by
the censors? What *revenants*?

First of all, mourning [...] It consists always in attempting to
ontologize remains, to make them present [...] Next, one cannot
speak of generations of [...] spirits [...] except on the condition
of language – and the voice in any case of that which *marks* the
name or takes its place. Finally, [...] the thing works. By 'Spirit'
here I mean a certain *power of transformation... the Spirit...
works.* (Derrida, 1994, 9)

These three spectrality effects are Jacques Derrida's categories for describing Hamlet's resistance to a sense of irremediable loss; initial bewilderment; resignation to the fact that 'the time is out of joint'. For my part, as at the outset, I have also looked to Hamlet for a strategy of literariness in the decomposition of any reading of the historical and cultural differences between colonizer and colonized as mere *faits accomplis*: 'The Play's the thing'.

Chico Buarque de Hollanda's song-text, as I hear it, and under the pressure of censorship, turns to effect literature's capacity to perform in opposition to both totalitarian (non-)readings of reluctant politicians and sectarian (under-)readings of reductive cultural historians. Constructing upon Derrida's earlier insight that 'play must be conceived before the alternative of presence or absence. Being must be conceived as presence or absence on the basis of play and not the other way round' (Derrida, 1978, 292), we can observe how 'Tanto mar', in its recast version, 'ontologizes the remains' of 'eu estou ausente'; inverts a non-participating absence into a provisional presence of that stubborn 'voice [...] which *marks* the name' and the 'place' of 'inda guardo renitente'; exploits 'a certain *power of transformation*' whereby neither going transcendental ('Spirit') nor historical materialism ('the thing works') suffice as readings of the ideological relationship between Brazil and Portugal. The toing-and-froing of the song-text's revised stratagems erases certainty ('Sei'); historicizes satisfaction ('Fiquei contente'); replaces desire ('queria') with solidarity against the reactionary forces of a *common* enemy ('Já murcharam'); and re-establishes a possible future of mutual interest ('Esqueceram uma semente'). New roots, new routes, new reflections are planted, mapped, convoked... invited.

Third(world)ness *spooks*

Is it necessarily paradoxical that the plea for a renewal of the Portuguese enterprise of pursuing new spice and herb routes, of catching favourable winds, and of singing afresh a strengthening of cultural relations, comes from Brazil? Far from necessarily; for there is the dilemma of the writer faced with the temptation, the desire, the need, or even the culturally inherited imperative to define the nation and its representation as, precisely, having – or pointing to – a 'rational historical pattern'. The very insight, supposition, claim, that there *are* deep structures, 'unpredictable metamorphoses', without the possibility of interventions for change, produces not only a Lévi-Straussian

231

'provocative silence' but also analogues, substitutes, metaphors of and for silence. In discursive, representational, terms, silence is masked by the wail of mourning, by the veil of regret; by the spectre of what never was. A double power of the ghost imposes both the enforced hearing of what it has not said and the silence of its having not spoken.

For Marxist critiques of such structural 'autonomies', or relative distance from any notional 'centring', to see only through the lens of structure is to situate the Other as different... but without any (over-arching) explanation of how, why, and with what agent(s) such difference might have come about. Not only is history elided to the extent of relegating cultures to a status of 'being there' but also, *pari passu*, and reflexively, the Self is rendered either incapacitated, or passive, certainly unentitled to the intervention of political action, in respect of its relation with the Other. Post-Rousseau, post-Lévi-Strauss, the stress has fallen on a rhetoric of the Other (including the Third World) as 'beauty, dignity and irreducible strangeness' but, given the reflexive relation between the irreducible Other and the striving but never arriving Self, an ever-lurking space-to-be-filled inhabits the Self and, or, its discursive representations.

Returning to the analogues, the substitutes, the metaphors which move in the place, the gap, of silence, it is possible, suggestive, even necessary, to examine such tropes and to see how they have come to occupy not only the place but also the power of supplementing silence. In the case of Portugal and Brazil, we have considered such dominant national discursive tropes as 'mar' and 'sertão' in the light of a Rortian 'going transcendental' whereby the figuration of the 'sertanejo' assumes proportions of the lost repository of the values of an *Além* comparable with Sebastianism but, also, in Spanish America, with the Argentine *Don Segundo Sombra* or, in North America, with the Western's frontier hero-idyll. Nostalgia for the loss of what never existed... In Portugal, 'mar' versus 'montanha'; in Brazil (Brasília?), 'sertão' versus 'a interiorização da Capital'; but further binary idealizations or transcendentalisms. A false consciousness which equates *inwards* with *upwards* emerges in myth-making treatments of the reality principle (refusal) and the pleasure principle (sublimation). The (desired) Other is inserted, enshrined, in a space reserved, epistemologically, for the non-contactable... It is as if every national expression has to invent itself *tabula rasa*; as if the rhythms of discursive self-representation were not always, already, imported, inherited. When the admission *is* made, it often takes the form of the transcendental, e.g. the substitution of terms ('sertão' for 'mar'), or of the (politically) unthreatening admission of a shared but inaccessible commonality. Justification can be sought, and found, in the reluctance even to admit the terms, the terminology, of colonization. The desire for separateness, autonomy, 'new' identity, difference (with an 'e'), is strongly, exclusively, *anti*-contact with the real other. The Other is preferred, because it does not have to be lived with (any more).

To hear again 'Tanto mar' is to shift towards an interpellation between never conceivably autonomous cultures evinced at moments of crisis, crucial, politico-historical, symptomatic, instances of resistance to the strong metaphors of uniqueness, autonomy, nation, identity. A turning inside out of such metaphors reveals not seamless but re-sewn, re-sewable, fabrics of assemblage, continuities, patch works.

Engineering *bricolage*

Pessoa's own assemblage, his heteronymy, can always also be read as instrumental. For, across the panoply of his (at least) seventy-two heteronyms, he is able both to enter and to keep a distance from a multiplicity of aesthetics, a plurality of postures, a heteroglossia of poetic experimentations. (*Caveat emptor/lector academicus*: overweening attention to any body might appropriate, re-incorporate, Pessoa *qua* person into readings of Pessoa persona/e). I refer to but a short text of Álvaro de Campos – 'O Engenheiro' – in order to illustrate how by machination (be it mechanical or affective), the exaltation of metaphor – or that metonymy that dares too readily to speak its name (*pro patria*) – ever betrays a strong sense of personal loss, of failure, of voicelessness behind the mask. Even of the would-be mechanical, latterly naval, but currently unemployed (extra) homo-diegetic (bored) constructor:

> Ah, um soneto...
>
> Meu coração é um almirante louco
> que abandonou a profissão do mar
> e que a vai relembrando pouco a pouco
> em casa a passear, a passear...
>
> No movimento (eu mesmo me desloco
> nesta cadeira, só de o imaginar)
> o mar abandonado fica em foco
> nos músculos cansados de parar.

Há saudades nas pernas e nos braços.
Há saudades no cérebro por fora.
Há grandes raivas feitas de cansaços.

Mas – esta é boa! – era do coração
que eu falava... e onde diabo estou eu agora
com almirante em vez de sensação?...

(Pessoa, 1993, 148)

[Ah, a sonnet/My heart is a mad admiral/who has left the profession of the sea/And who keeps remembering little by little/At home walking up and down, up and down.../In the movement (I myself shift in this chair, just imagining it)/the sea left behind remains in focus/in muscles tired of having rested./There is longing in the legs and in the arms./There is longing in the brain outside./There are great furies made of tiredness./But – that's a good one – it was of my heart/That I was speaking... and where the devil am I now/With an admiral instead of feeling?]

'Ah, um soneto...' performs in exemplary manner tensions detected by Octavio Paz:

> In modern times this great emptiness of the Western world has been expressed [...] but [...] poets have tried to fill something. I mean desperation, negation, emptiness is but one part of the picture. The other is creation. (Paz, in Bourne, 1987, 99)

The poem both performs and requires incompletion. For distancing and self-distancing, however controlled, however heteronymized, however dislocated through the ironic displacements of style, will barely conceal a self constructed both psychically and socially.

Familiarity with the history, politics, and literary consciousness of Portugal will at once prompt recognition in this sonnet of tensions similar to the tropes of 'Ó naus felizes...'. Contact with the Other entails both exaltation and loss of self. Here, additionally, there emerges a national context of *saudosismo*, of nostalgic, maritime yearning, of a longing to be both 'em casa' and 'além'; both here and there; rooted and uprooted; familiar and de-familiarized; in sadness and madness; in the Past and in the Future... Álvaro de Campos's version of the to-ing and fro-ing in question, here conveyed by 'a passear, a passear', focuses in this instance on a very Portuguese past, and on an admiral torn between *saudade* and *raiva*. The bracketing of subjectivity – in the distancing of me ('me desloco') from an illusory him ('louco') – cannot conceal a tension between 'coração' and 'sensacão', between emotion and sensation. Both remain distanced, however, from any socio-historical correlative, even the simple chair, the locus of enunciation of an irredeemably Lusitanian dreamer. Correlatives will ever be but subjectively objective – for 'Objects do not go into their concepts without leaving a remainder' (Adorno, 1973, 5). Excess? Poetics. Or perhaps psychology – if 'the ego is merely an onlooker who has identified himself with the man he is continually looking at' (Borges, in Barnstone, 1982, 47).

Navig(N)ations... *Ils ont changé ma chanson*

n times have the *revenants* of spectrology multiplied my Lusophone visit(ation)s. Each time, the *n* of indeterminacy has borne me to, through, and beyond the *N* of Nation. Poetry, too, passes through the gauze of History that has shrouded all paternities since this play began. *What have they done to my song, Ma*[r]*? What have they done to my song?*

Chico Buarque's doubled – censored or uncensored – reflections on the roots of the Revolution of the Carnations and of their putative ideological implications for the Brazil of his and of others' imaginary open up (again) already-existing other routes. 'Tanto mar' voices difference as potentially positive never more than in moments when it has come to be categorized as negative. However, the song-text also unsettles (again) the positive, not least when it can be revealed as naïve, superficial, clichéd. We have heard already how the simple polysemia of 'cravo' shuttles between carnation, clove and nail. For a (naïve?) moment, I even wondered whether, as Fernando had played with escutcheon, so Chico might have indulged a clichéd colour-play of national flags. He did, and I do... *now*. But, at first, I could see no Brazilian counterpart of a Portuguese red and green. The *Herbário Inglês* and the *Novo Dicionário da Língua Portuguesa* (edited by Aurélio Buarque de Hollanda Ferreira) confirmed what I knew, certainly, about rosemary/'alecrim': green and pale blue. But the facts, *les faits,* 'ain't necessarily so' *accomplis*. Literature, rather than that arch metaphysic of presence, the dictionary, was again to highlight for me a difference for cultural studies to explore:

> Aqui no Brasil – como você pode comprovar – outras espécies recebem o nome genérico de alecrim e seguem-se as sub-

espécies; e destas o alecrim-do-campo é de pétalas amarelas, é flor nativa nos cerrados e campos, e é considerada, poeticamente, pelos cantadores dos sertões, como singela, pura, inocente e bela. Existe até uma canção folclórica que diz assim:

Alecrim, alecrim dourado,
Que nasceu no campo sem ser semeado.
Ah! meu amor... ai meu amor,
Quem te disse assim que o alecrim é a flor do campo?

(Duarte, 1998)

[Here in Brazil – as you can check up – other species are given the generic name of *alecrim* and then there are the sub-species; and of these the *alecrim-do-campo* is one with yellow petals, its a flower native to the pastures and fields, and it is considered, poetically, by the singers of the *sertão*, simple, pure, innocent and lovely. There's even a folk-song which goes like this: 'Rosemary, golden rosemary,/Born in the fields without being sown./Ah! my love... alas my love,/Who told you so, that rosemary is the flower of the fields?']

This I was told by a Brazilian herbalist, expert in the *flora* and *fauna* of the *sertão*. But I would not venture to pursue primary colours as first terms in Chico Buarque's pressurizing of the metaphors of second navigations. In his discourse of third possibilities, and in his song, 'the Play's the thing'. National flags – and nations – are (also) but patchwork constructs to be sewn and re-sewn... never seamless. Like song-texts.

É tanto assim?... 'Tanto mar'? Myth(ography) *is* excess.

...nele é que espelhou o céu.
Fernando Pessoa

A vida da gente nunca tem termo real.
João Guimarães Rosa

Mar[x] remains an immigrant chez nous [...]
Between earth and sky.
Jacques Derrida

Coda

Je vous remercie d'avoir internationalisé ma spectrologie; d'avoir réhabilité des langues qui souffrent l'hégémonie de l'anglo-saxon. Des centaines de langues disparaissent chaque jour. Le poème, c'est l'une des langues qui résistent, à travers les – ces – spectres.

Jacques Derrida

Lire la littérature... c'est une spectrologie. Lire libère les spectres. Mes chants sont méchants.

Bernard McGuirk

Is there a Latin American [*hors-*] text... in this or any other class?

Afforded the opportunity to re-contextualize the notoriously mistranslated and consequently widely misread axial insight into the often mutually uncomprehending stances of specialists in the many disciplines that constitute Latin American studies, I recall the invitation received from Jon Beasley Murray to address the June 2002 Manchester colloquium on *The New Latin Americanism*. In the foregoing chapters, I have meditated on the implications of Terry Eagleton's necessary corrective to dismissive attitudes to deconstruction: 'The statement that "there is nothing outside the text" is not to be taken, absurdly, to suggest that, for example, Jacques Derrida does not exist, but to deconstruct empiricist or metaphysical oppositions between discourse and some "brute" reality beyond it'. Assuming rather that the French simply states that there is nothing that might not be read as already and always also textual whenever broached discursively, I take it as read, re-read, and re-writable, that *il n'y a pas de hors-texte* and that, inseparably, *il n'y a pas de hors-contexte*.

Prompted by Sergio Chejfec's 'Breves opiniones sobre relatos con imágenes', delivered at the Instituto Cervantes on the eve of my 'Response to Alberto Moreiras: on Deconstruction', I meditated then as now on location, time and text in context. Inverted commas had textualized the 'Manchester' of W. G. Sebald, in *The Emigrants*, just as they did on that Saturday in June, in the 'Manchester' rendered text as the locus of my private early awareness of the transatlantic that has ever since accompanied the class-room responsibilities, challenges, and pleasures, of the period two decades ago and a career enjoyed inseparably from performances shared.

X. POST-
On hospitality for *The Emigrants*
A response *d'après* W. G. Sebald to Alberto Moreiras on
Deconstruction

Could the story of *New Latin Americanisms* – or, under erasure, that of Manchester – be, like that of the universe, *pace* Borges, 'the history of but a few metaphors', or of their futile pursuit? Any generating of metaphors will invoke the risk of rapid exhaustion, but if 'we must begin wherever we are [...] in a text where we think we are' (Derrida, 1976, 162) whenever we invoke the buildings, the trains, the ship canals, the waves, of our collective imaginary, it is we – as agents – who exhaust the metaphors. Even when we listen to those scandalously repressed or suppressed metaphors underlying ideological hegemonies, we 'lend the ear', but briefly, otherwise; for example, to Alberto Moreiras and to his claim that 'that exhausted or worn-out but lethal mode of inhabiting non-belonging is belonging itself'. In locating the habitation of 'regional intellectuals, whose anomic law is the law of unconditional love for the other' (towards the end of his proposal), Moreiras has shadowed, re-configured, perhaps even sought to peg down, Jacques Derrida's deconstructed metaphor of hospitality. The tent-text, of ever-open flap, the tent-*tienda* (why not, too, the contentious *tienda* of the market-place?) of 'aporetic hospitality' will invite, but ever defer, homecomings.

In a classic deconstructivist's (re)turn, reminiscent of the frame or the pharmakon, Moreiras renders inside-out or outside-in the never-to-be always nor ever-already repressed or suppressed metaphor/s of hospitality: 'How can you be hospitable if you have no home you can properly call your own? [...] The regionalist intellectual [...] would be hard-pressed to show hospitality in the classic sense [...] It would have to be a form of hospitality that has renounced sovereignty'. Yet, and here comes the inversion – the lure of a deconstructive radicalization – he adds: 'But isn't hospitality precisely the renunciation of sovereignty?'

Post-structuralist practice will continue to be a (does it) matter of symptoms, risks, strategies; so (again) I shall have risked the strategic (re-)appropriation of a dominant metaphor symptomatic of a first day's reflections. Tea...

I locate myself and us all, provisionally, *not* as guests who have passed beneath the flap of the open tent/text; or been invited, in an initial gesture of hospitality, to take mint tea together with the hosts. But rather as accomplices, present, addressed, from Argentina by Sergio Chejfec or, from England by Jon Beasley-Murray and, as readers, in translation from the German, interpellated by W. G. Sebald, through writing and interjected images, from beyond the flap of his re-opened text, *The Emigrants* (1997); in Manchester, or in 'Manchester':

The Emigrants

three, when Mrs Irlam knocked at my door. Apparently by way of a special welcome, she brought me, on a silver tray, an electric appliance of a kind I had never seen before. She explained that it was called a *teas-maid*, and was both an alarm clock and a tea-making machine. When I made tea and the

steam rose from it, the shiny stainless steel contraption on its ivory-coloured metal base looked like a miniature power plant, and the dial of the clock, as I soon found as dusk fell, glowed a phosphorescent lime green that I was familiar with from childhood and which I had always felt afforded me an unaccountable protection at night. That may be why it has often seemed, when I have thought back to those early days in Manchester, as if the tea maker brought to my room by Mrs Irlam, by Gracie – you must call me Gracie, she said – as if it was that weird and serviceable gadget, with its nocturnal glow, its muted morning bubbling, and its mere presence by day, that kept me holding on to life at a time when I felt

◇ 154 ◇

What 'mere presence [...] kept me holding on'?

In that affective ambience of a first evening's hospitality, and in a but minimally *Institut*-ionalized *Cervantes*, I cupped my own *Thé –* post-Menardian – *Ear of the Other*. What grasp of cultural memory author(iz)ed my dialogue with so many Latin Americanists? How was I, come the morrow, to respond not only to Alberto Moreiras but also to his exhaustion of the indifference to deconstruction – already ostensible – of most of the area specialists present? Sebald's post-textuality, the supplement of his photographs, the trace of his own

240

performance, showed me a way; for I was moved as I heard, first, the orality of 'Tea's made'. The tone and the accent that I recalled were, in this my encounter with the textual 'Mrs Irlam' of the Sebald imaginary, with the 'Gracie' of his foreign fields, *not* that of the Urmston-near-Manchester landlady of his reality effects. It was simply the Cadishead-near-Irlam voice of my mother: 'Tea's made'... And years later: 'Bernard! I pour yer tea and you let it grow cold!'... 'I pour yer tea'/aporia-tea. This was the first time I ever heard the sound of *aporia*. Flooding into the orality of 'tea's made' poured associations of Empire, the East India Company, the labour intensive process of the shift from plant to product; my own subsequent West-East-West comings and goings and, no less, the constructs of gender politics.

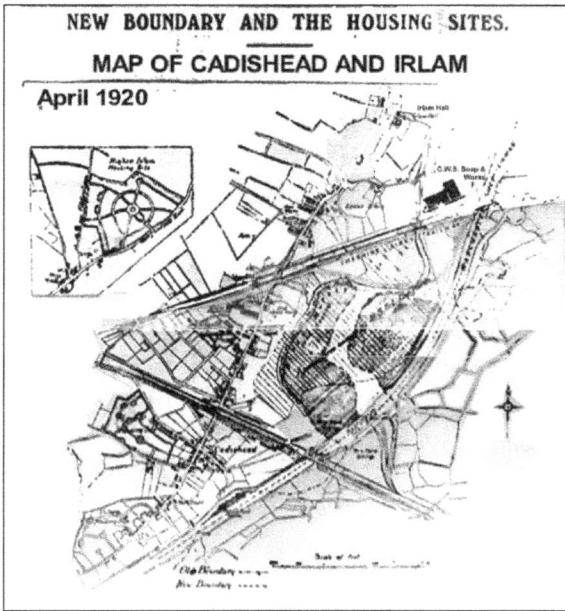

NEW BOUNDARY AND THE HOUSING SITES.

MAP OF CADISHEAD AND IRLAM

April 1920

Forty-eight years ago, in 3 Melville Road, my first childhood home, she made tea for Dad and, thereafter, for me; now I 'brew' for her. Pre-, post-Raj (pre-, post- Eros?); twenty-three flits on... or away. *I* grow cold (though still, 'I wear my trousers rolled').

No doubt the trans-lingual Ear of m(an)(y) (an)Other was hearing, at this moment, a voice perplexingly different from the discourses on *The New Latin Americanism: Cultural Studies* agenda. In my mind's ear, I could imagine the reaction to my performing *Beyond Borders*; unvoiced but inscribable: '¿Qué? Tea? 'E's mad, eh. ¿Oral... y té?'

And then there's *écriture*. You saw, I saw, the written play of/with (in)difference: Teas*maid* [m-a-i-d] ... and she's still there, *té*/there-d *criada*, serving-maid. She, maid. Me? Mad, eh? In the maddening shift from an irre*cuper*able, muted ('everything stops... for thee, mum'), personal, oral, history to slippery, excessive, supplementary, gone-cold (not easily swallowed) *técriture*, I find my location; amongst you, and unverifiably welcome. A guest has been received hospitably. But, in case you assume that deconstruction has been consigned, like Sebald's *teasmaid*, into a past still with us, as a mere instrument that has outlived its ever-waking usefulness, I must tell you that *I* still have one... Yes, a *teasmaid* (a mad one, in the attic, in 'stainless' steel). *And* I'm still a post-structuralist. Do you differ? *I* defer. *Et tu?* ... 'Brew t'tay!'

If I have over-run the risk of localizing, domesticating or personalizing a dialogics of Lancashire hospitality, might I suggest that *all* intellectuals dis/cover themselves to be regionalist – however provisionally – as they enter into or perform that hospitality which is precisely, as for Alberto Moreiras, the renunciation of sovereignty. The binary relations of periphery-centre, or region-globe, when pressured by a deconstructive practice that constitutes 'a political rather than [...] textual operation', when 'touching solid structures, "material" instit-utions, and not merely discourses or significant representations' (Eagleton, 1985, 5), betray a further lure. Like presence and absence, regionalist and non-regionalist must be pressured terms; 'thought radically' (*à la* Moreiras, *d'après* Derrida), conceived of 'on the basis of [an inter-] play [between them] and not the other way round' (Derrida, 1993, 12).

Coda

Alan Knight ('yesterday, -ay') made a helpfully frank admission when he spoke of his reading of Alberto Moreiras's *The Exhaustion of Difference*. He found it, 'in part, difficult because the language was either unfamiliar or abstract or discursively sophisticated'. He also remarked that, as part of that pragmatics whereby he prefers, as a historian, the knowledge of economics or politics, he reads literature but *not* literary criticism ('such an easy game to play'). Eric Hershberg subsequently reminded us of a further either/or – an option on the part of certain political scientists for 'a view from somewhere as distinct from a view from nowhere' ('man'), as a 'protection' against abstract theorizing. Mike González's echoing of the *Grundrisse*, 'To rise from the abstract to the concrete' – presumably in order to 'interrogate reality' (*ipse dixit*) – was again an option: opting *for* the concrete in order to interrogate the concrete ('in Blackburn, Lancashire', or near enough)? But what of Marx, of Marx's text, as a radical thinking that demands and practises a *play* of the abstract and the concrete that is conceived of before the alternatives of abstract and concrete; and not the other way round. Here, therefore, deconstruction is not, cannot purport to be, an alternative to Marxism. It is a reading practice that cannot but re-engage with Marxism... and other 'grand' theories. (And you; are *you* into texts? Do you cross-address?).

Alberto Moreiras – in a gesture of hospitality, of cross-disciplinary welcome – addresses Latin Americanists bent on interrogating not 'reality' but differential realities. And they will always and ever be identifiable not sufficiently in terms of who they are but, politically, of what they do and, no less, of *how* they speak and write. Moreiras engages with, operates on, not one *or* the other but the effects of one *on* the other... and vice-versa. And what has that got to do with deconstruction? Or with you? It's just that the place of an aporia is at the border, 'or the approach of the other as such.'

Post scriptum

'Throughout the nineteenth century, the German and Jewish influence was stronger in Manchester than in any other European city; and so, although I had intended to move in the opposite direction, when I arrived in Manchester I had come home, in a sense [...] I have realized more clearly than ever that I am here, as they used to say, to serve under the chimney' (Sebald, 1997, 192). Soot yourself. Rush in where even Engels feared to tread. But if to be a Marxist is 'Always [to] historicize', then no contemporary ideology can be traced other than post-structurally.

In the twentieth century, or for me as for W. G. Sebald in the s(w)ingin' '60s, 'Oh – oh, oh – oh, life goes on', ever indelibly, 'in the market-place'. Place? Or space? Shuttle space – 'the loading and unloading never stopped: wheat, nitre, construction timber, cotton, rubber, jute, train oil, tobacco, *tea*, coffee, cane sugar, exotic fruits, copper and iron ore, steel, machinery, marble and mahogany – everything' [my italics] (Sebald, 1997, 165).

It was at the always other end of the line, or the Ship Canal of my embryonic cartography – 'it's the leavin' o' Liverpool' – that *my* then imaginary was transported to Latin America; and, now, in the twenty-first, anew. *New* cultural studies?

21 June 2002

Coda: *Pardo*[n]... Is there a transatlantic class in this text?

> There where post-colonialism was – or is –
> will intra-colonialism be?

Via Atlântica, the São Paulo-based journal, re-published, in an admirably risk-taking translation by Emanuelle Santos, my 2010 essay on *O Vendedor de Passados/The Book of Chameleons* by the Angolan, sometime Brazil-based, J.E. Agualusa.[1] I was informed that Agualusa's novels have come to feature regularly on the syllabus of the Brazilian pre-university examination, the *vestibular*. As to why his Brazilian readers might be more trusting of the tale rather than of the less-than-diplomatic teller, we may consider his provocative meditation on Brazil's current status:

> In my opinion, Brazil is still a country moulded on slavery, the same as Africa. Brazil has an Africa inside itself and at times it pays no attention to it. Here, as in Angola, for example, there exists the figure of the black nanny who passes from one generation to another; there is the house boy brought up as if he was a son but, in truth, he works in the house, without remuneration. Black and poor are conditions which are confused in Brazil. A black élite has not grown up here, in contrast with Angola. People notice this inequality on a day-to-day basis, in the relations between individuals, and even in the culture. Today it is not possible to cite a great black or *mestiço* Brazilian writer. That is incredible because in the nineteenth-century there were great writers of African descent, such as Machado de Assis and Cruz e Sousa. What is worse, there is not a single great indigenous author, something that is the case throughout the Americas. Until it confronts the problem and as long as it does not give greater participation to black people, Brazil will not have decolonized itself. Brazil is a colony. (Agualusa, 2007, my translation)

On transatlantication, in respect of literary texts read in cultural contexts, Agualusa is emphatic:

---

[1] *Dossiê: Triangulações Atlânticas – Transnacionalidades em Língua Portuguesa*, *Via Atlântica*, São Paulo, N. 25, 15-46, July 2014. See this version for all original texts in Portuguese.

PP/AT: *The Book of Chameleons* recalls in many ways the work of the great Argentine writer Jorge Luis Borges. How important has Latin American literature been to your work? JA: I read a lot of Latin American literature when I was younger, especially Borges. His worlds are similar to mine. Gabriel García Márquez once said that when he arrived in Luanda, Angola, in 1977, he saw himself as an African. That part of Africa where he arrived – the old city of Luanda – is a mixed, creole Africa, not so different from the Latin America where he was born and grew up. Evidently, there are a lot of Africas, some of them remote and impenetrable. I found out that I'm a Latin American, too, reading García Márquez and Borges. And I found out that I'm also Brazilian, reading Jorge Amado as a teenager. PP/AT: The novel unfolds from the point of view of a chameleon. Why did you choose such a narrator? Does it owe something to Borges' work? JA: Yes, the book was written in honor of Borges. The chameleon is a reincarnation of Borges – all its recollections are related to actual events in Borges' life (Polzonoff and Tepper, 2007, 1).

Intra-Colonialism: Re(p)tiling the *azul* aegis
J.E. Agualusa's *O Vendedor de Passados*
The Book of Chameleons

> Sei que há léguas a nos separar
> Tanto mar, tanto mar
> Sei também quanto é preciso, pá
> Navegar, navegar
>
> Chico Buarque de Hollanda

A question of colour

In the canonical lineage of Fyodor Dostoevsky, and Franz Kafka and, in a swerve towards and away from his own Lusophone literary precursors, João Guimarães Rosa and José Saramago, the Angolan novelist José Eduardo Agualusa deploys in *O Vendedor de Passados/The Book of Chameleons* (2004) a narrator-protagonist prone to be less *porte-parole* than *animot*.[1]

> *Ecce animot*, that is the announcement of which I am (following) something like a trace, [...] assuming the title of an autobiographical animal, in the form of a risky, fabulous, or chimerical response to the question 'But me, who am I?' (Derrida 2002, 2)

Jacques Derrida's 'announcement' is here appropriated – and (following) 'an autobiographical animal' will glide across the surface cracks of my text – in order that I might trace and critically re-contextualize Agualusa's re(p)tiling of history in and on the mosaic of Angolan memory. The eponymous 'vendedor', the albino Félix Ventura (future happiness guaranteed?), 'is a man with an unusual occupation. If your lineage isn't sufficiently distinguished, he'll change that for you. If your family isn't quite as glorious as you'd like, Félix Ventura can make you a new one. Félix Ventura is a seller of pasts'.[2] But who is

---

[1] For instance, Fyodor Dostoevsky's mouse (*Notes from the Underground*), Franz Kafka's beetle (*Metamorphoses*), João Guimarães Rosa's jaguar ('The Mirror') and José Saramago's pachyderm (*The Elephant's Journey*).

[2] This teasing marketing line is provided for the reader of the English translation, *The Book of Chameleons*, by the cover-blurb writer of the Arcadia Books edition of the translation by Daniel Hahn.

watching him? Who is telling his tale? Who, or what, is on his tail? Who, or what, sets the plot in (ani)motion? *L'animot juste* or *juste l'animot*?

The title of the English translation rather lets the catalyst out of the bag, though problematically; for in the shift in the title's emphasis from narratee to narrator(s), there is also a transmogrification from Agualusa's original *lagartixa* or *osga*/gecko to Daniel Hahn's suggestive but translator-*traditore* shading into the perspectives of ever-traducing chameleons. *Il n'y a pas de (mot juste) hors-couleur*...

Intra-colonialism

The continued and continuing structuring of political thought and action in nation states that have gained their independence from former master powers in reaction to but never free from embedded mastering discourses cannot be other than controversial. For what is at stake in the reading and, more pertinently, or riskily, in the writing of, in, and from any supposedly post-colonial condition is the danger of slipping into a perilous repetition, even a misreading, understood as ideological *misprision*; that is, an anxiety-driven re-representation of, and still-terrorized swerve away from, the phantom-laden bin of lapsed imperial histories. If there is a determined or restless concern to escape from the discursive straitjacket of the implications, in a post-colonial context, of Derrida' s early insight that 'we can pronounce not a single destructive proposition which has not already had to slip into the form, the logic, and the implicit postulations of precisely what it seeks to contest' (Derrida 1978, 280), then the challenge for the novelist addressing an assumedly post-colonial society will be to write supplementarily – in the sense of both after and within – to the spectral discourses of any national literary heritage.

The winning of *The Independent* Foreign Fiction Prize for *The Book of Chameleons*, in 2007, has brought for its author a broader attention that at once highlights both his established reputation in the Lusophone world and the controversial nature of a writing that confronts the legacies of Portuguese colonial power in a manner not easily subsumed under the rubrics of the post-colonial. In Brazil, too, such is the symbiotic pull of the Atlantic relation with a westward-looking if still ostensibly northward-thinking Angola, there has been a noteworthy detection in Agualusa's fiction of pertinent challenges posed in a broader post-imperial southern hemispheric context. Let it be said, however, that it is not the person of the novelist, the figure who infuriates or provokes reaction in the Portuguese-speaking world, which will be the subject of further concern here. Any brouhaha surrounding a writer of growing international renown or notoriety will no doubt be heeded by those who grasp more readily at the context than the thorn-text of Agualusa's ever-prickly narrative relation with Angola's – and Portugal's and Brazil's – discursive histories; whence the option for a Derrida-derived instrument of access to the animotions of *The Book of Chameleons*. While it is to the gecko-voicing of the narrator of *O Vendedor de Passados* – cackler reincarnate of a dandy literatus – that critical attention will be addressed, noted already is the sly slippage from an economy of transformed pasts to the currency of exchanged identities; from the sound of colonizing coinage to the colours of chameleon disguise in the English title's rendering for an international market.[3]

Sic transit gloria (im)mundi as the base looker-on of a reptile/human-human/reptile sphere of action is exploited and explored. From the debased, the abject, might a re-forging of Angola's inheritances be alchemized... true currency or false; stable narrative or fool's gold in the selling of an emergent literature to a world-wide readership.[4] 'Tu m'as donné de la boue et j'en ai fait de l'or'[5] might be heard as one of the many precursor texts that Agualusa's intra-modern narrative echoes whilst the ceiling-seer gecko performs – a complicit *beau de l'air* – the role of mocking interlocutor-witness to the infelicitous ventures of the earthbound Félix:

---

[3] The lure of translation, in the case of the title of this novel, is one with which the author has colluded, as seen in his interview with Paulo Polzonoff, Jr. and Anderson Tepper:

> PP/AT: 'Do you participate in the process of translating your work from Portuguese?'
>
> JA: 'It depends a lot on the translator and the language it is being translated into. With the English translations by Daniel Hahn, I do participate a lot. But this collaboration between the writer and his translator is rare, I think [...] we met twice, and I helped him with a few things. We took a long time to decide on an English title for the book. But the rest was fairly easy. Daniel Hahn is an excellent translator, and also a sensitive creator in his own right – and that seems to me to be the most important quality in this whole process.' (Polzonoff and Tepper 2007, 4)

[4] 'Today', BBC Radio 4, 4 September 2008: 'Luanda is the most expensive capital in the world for expatriates. In oil revenues, Angola is beginning to rival South Africa in terms of regional influence.'

[5] The alchemy referred to, and to which I shall return, is the turning of base matter to gold of 'L'Invitation au voyage' (Baudelaire 1961, 253-4).

'I don't believe it – are you laughing?'

The creature's amazement annoyed me. I was afraid – but I didn't move, not a muscle. The albino took off his dark glasses, put them away in the inside pocket of his jacket, took the jacket off – slowly, sadly – and hung it carefully on the back of a chair [...]

'*Pópilas!*' he exclaimed. 'So I see Your Lowness is laughing?! That's quite a novelty...' [...] 'You've really got terrible skin, you know that? We must be related...'

I've been expecting something like that. It's like being able to speak. I would have answered him back. But my vocal abilities extend only to laughing [...] Until last week the albino had always ignored me. But since he heard me laughing, he's started coming home earlier [...] we talk. Or rather, he talks, I listen. Sometimes I laugh – this seems enough for him. I get the sense that there's already a thread of friendship holding us together. On Saturday nights – but not always – the albino arrives with some girl. Some of them are scared as they come in [...] trying not to look directly at him, unable to hide their disgust [...] they look around the bookcases for records.

'Don't you have any *cuduro* music, old man?'

And since the albino doesn't have any *cuduro* [...] they end up choosing something with a bright cover, which usually means it's some Cuban rhythm or other. They dance slowly [...] as the shirt buttons come undone, one by one. That perfect skin, so very black, moist and radiant, against the albino's – dry, rough, and pinkish. I watch it all. In this house I'm like a little night-time God. During the day, I sleep. (4-5)

The thread that is to bind the actantial fabric of the novel is not only the affective tug of friendship but also the structuring suture of inverse or inverted perceptions. Félix is seen by the gecko as 'the creature'; the gecko is, in an instant, though it will have to wait for Félix to grant it the dignity of a proper name, elevated to the sovereign albeit ironized status of 'Your Lowness', and demeaned by a non-essential but euphemistically expletive epithet, '*Pópilas!*'.[6] Bound together in their respectively perceived defectiveness – lack of colour, lack of speech, and a mutually acknowledged lack of status – the companions in mockery sardonically reconstruct the isolated, lonesome, outcast and

---

[6] 'Pópilas! Chissa! Possa! Arre! Porra!', undeletedly colonial, post-colonial and, no less, intra-colonial expletives.

oft-despised self-identity of the individual judged and thus situated, in a post-conflict Angola, according to perceptions of their skin.

Félix inspires disgust, in the series of black and *mulata* girls and women who pass – or dance – fleetingly through his LP collection, his bedroom and his boredom, as albino, as 'old man', and as a cultural throwback to an era prior to the perceived authenticity of the new-Angolan *cuduro*,[7] steeped (blanched?) in an outmoded taste in reading and in records – gaudily sleeved vestiges of a Cuban 'or other' cultural imprint of the now-to-be-forgotten anti-colonial wars. The voice of the complicit gecko may be heard to perform dialogically yet differently from those of the itinerant week-end sexual partners that Félix ventures to bring back to his antique book-seller's solitude. Its laughter supplements both Portugal's silence about the colonial wars (prior) and, for Angola, the cacophony (post-; in the 1990s boom) referred to by Mark Sabine as the 'potentially therapeutic' and 'unprecedented growth in popular publishing and e-publishing, popular music and theatre, television and filmmaking focused on lusophone African culture and history' (Sabine 2009, 254). The vision of the gecko may be seen to supplant the panopticon power of both the colonizing other (Portugal) and the anti-colonial agency of a subsequent, post-1974 alternative, Marxism, and its would-be principal instrument of conversion (Cuba).

Sabine's parallel meditation on Angola's ever-more-rapid shift away from colonizing efforts, literary and otherwise, 'to configure the white male in Africa as a transcendental subject' (Sabine 2009, 266)[8] through recent pop culture and cinema, is both echoed and subverted in Agualusa's exploitation of the albino function. A further inversion of a half-century-old shibboleth text, Frantz Fanon's *Peau noire, masques blancs* archiving of white and black as interdependent terms brought into discursive possibility by the binarizing moment of 'Empire', underlies the parodic first encounter of Félix Ventura with a mysterious stranger who presents himself as an eager *comprador de passados*, a man in the market for reincarnation. By-product or craft, Agualusa's

---

[7] *Cuduro* or *Kuduro* is dance of relatively recent vintage which has spread from Angola to Portugal, Brazil and beyond the Lusophone world. Apart from its Afro-rhythms and a characteristic emphasis on the movement of the bottom, the word plays on the Portuguese 'cu' and 'duro', 'ass' and 'hard'.

[8] See Mark Sabine's chapter on the act of forgetting and reconstructing the recent past in contemporary Angolan culture (Sabine, 2009, 250-77). Sabine, it will be recalled, was developing the arguments with respect to Tarzan and the 'white hunter' figure as deployed in *Images and Empires: Visuality in Colonial and Postcolonial Africa* (Landau and Kaspin, 2002).

portrayal of a defining male-to-male exchange will extend as it pastiches standard feminist objections to the gendering, in Africa, of compliant intra-colonialism as being an exclusive or predominantly female enterprise.[9]

Reincarnations... and introducing JB

'*Félix Ventura. Guarantee your children a better past.*' And he laughed. A silent laugh but not unpleasant. 'That would be you, I presume? A friend of mine gave me your card.'

I couldn't place his accent. He spoke softly, with a mix of different pronunciations, a faint Slavic roughness, tempered by the honeyed softness of the Portuguese from Brazil. Félix Ventura took a step back:

'And who are you?' The foreigner closed the door [...] Certain common friends, he said – his voice becoming even gentler – had given him this address. They told him of a man who dealt in memories, a man who sold the past, clandestinely, the way other people deal in cocaine [...]

Félix Ventura gave in. There was a whole class, he explained a whole new bourgeoisie, who sought him out. They were businessmen, ministers, landowners, diamond smugglers, generals – people, in other words, whose futures are secure. What these people lack is a good past, a distinguished ancestry, diplomas. In sum, a name that resonates with nobility and culture. He sells them a brand new past. He draws up their family tree. He provides them with photographs of their grandparents and great-grandparents, gentlemen of elegant bearing and old-fashioned ladies. The businessmen, the ministers, would like to have women like that as their aunts, he went on, pointing to the portraits on the walls – old ladies swathed in fabrics, authentic bourgeois *bessanganas* –, they liked to have a grandfather with the distinguished bearing of a Machado de Assis, of a Cruz e Souza, of an Alexandre Dumas. And he sells them this simple

---

9 In *Peau noire, masques blancs*, 1952 (*Black Skin, White Masks*, 1967), Fanon suggested that the categories 'white' and 'black' are interdependent, both emerging as such with Empire and conquest. He focused primarily on black men; feminist critics in particular have reviled and revised his depiction of the role of black women in the apparatus of colony and colonization.

dream.

'Perfect, perfect.' The foreigner smoothed his moustache. 'That's what they told me. I require your services. But I'm afraid it may be rather a lot of work...'

'Work makes you free...' Félix muttered [...]

'And might I know your name?' [...] Félix insisted [...] 'You're right. I'm a photo journalist. I collect images of wars, of hunger and its ghosts, of natural disasters and terrible misfortunes. You can think of me as a witness.' [...]

He needed a new name, authentic official documents that bore out this identity. The albino listened, horrified:

'No!' he managed to blurt out. 'I don't do things like that. I invent dreams for people, I'm not a forger... And besides, if you'll pardon my bluntness, wouldn't it be a bit difficult to invent a completely African genealogy for you?'

'Indeed! And why is that?!...'

'Well – Sir – ... you're white.'

'And what of it? You're whiter than I am...'

'White? Me?!' The albino choked. He took a handkerchief from his pocket and wiped his forehead. 'No, no! I'm black. Pure black. I'm a native. Can't you tell I'm black?...'

From my usual post at the window I couldn't help giving a little chuckle at this point. The foreigner looked upwards as though he was sniffing the air. Tense – alert:

'Did you hear that? Who laughed just then?' [...]

'It's a gecko, yes, but a very rare species. See these stripes? It's a tiger gecko – a shy creature, we still know very little about them [...] They have this amazing laugh – doesn't it sound like a human laugh?'

[...] They spent some time discussing me, which I found annoying – talking as if I weren't there! – And yet at the same time it felt as though they were talking not about me but about some alien being, some vague and distant biological anomaly. Men know almost nothing of the little creatures that share their homes. Mice, bats, ants, ticks, flees, flies, mosquitoes, spiders, worms, silverfish, termites, weevils, snails, beetles. I decided that I might as well simply get on with my life (16-18) [...]

'Angola has rescued me for life.' [...]

Félix looked up [...] he had an identity card, a passport, a driver's licence, all these documents in the name of José Buchmann, native of Chibia, 52, professional photographer. (38)

A markedly male bonding wreathes the dialogue (cum trialogue) that encourages the initially cautious Félix Ventura to peddle his reading – and his role in the re-writing – of modern-day Angola to an urbane foreign client (soon to be 'outed' as José Buchmann). In the post-colonial phase of reconstruction, 'a whole new bourgeoisie' must undergo decon-struction, must be de-binarized, must enter that aporia – instead of seeking any verifiable past – which will allow the supplementarity of a falsified story to forge a new Angola. A post-colonial state will play on that *différance* whereby no difference might be traced between inside-outside, intra- and extra-, after-before, pre- and post-, black-white, a blank page or an excess of history. Its trip – 'clandestinely, the way other people deal in cocaine' (16) – will consist of a journey into a past-free and timeless present, the chimera of a future construct-country – *un pays superbe/pays de Cocagne* – without ever having to leave home.[10]

Félix thrills and wallows in the 'great white trader' role that he plays behind his neither-white-nor-black mask; his skin. Antiquarian book-seller that he would be, albeit divested of the apparel of the economically dominant male of his father's generation, he traffics still in literary nostalgia amidst the sub-genre of *faux-monnayeur* documentation that has become his daily bread. Ah, would some intra-colonial power the gift but give us to see ourselves as others see us... then might Ventura recognize for what it is his own *branqueamento* – that peculiar brand of skin-lightening which translates the past from a colonizing *Heart of Darkness* to Félix the albino's Art of Lightness.[11]

---

[10] 'Un vrai pays de Cocagne', in the legerdemain of Félix Ventura's artful re-casting of a nation newly hooked on its hallucinogen-history, is re-packaged as a *true* country that can resemble *you*: 'Il est une contrée qui te ressemble, où tout est beau, riche, tranquille et honnête, où la fantaisie a bâti [...] C'est là qu'il faut aller vivre, c'est là qu'il faut aller mourir!' Baudelaire's exoticism in the prose poem 'L'Invitation au voyage' is played out, it will be recalled, within the confines of 'Le Spleen de Paris' (Baudelaire 1961, 253-4). His 'Pays singulier, supérieur aux autres, comme l'Art l'est à la Nature, où celle-ci est réformée par le rêve, où elle est corrigée, embellie, refondue' is but one of the precursor tropes to be pastiched by the splenetic fantasy, the Eros-Thanatos risk-taking, of *O Vendedor de Passados*.

[11] In a recent and seminal meditation on nationalism and identity, Roberto Vecchi begins with the striking image of 'a cartography of horror' and, with particular reference to Lusophone Africa, addresses the problem of events distant not only historically but also and above all spatially, 'transoceanic', and in some cases with more than an ocean in between. He speaks of an 'elsewhere' of horror that immediately recalls *Heart of Darkness*; an 'elsewhere' in which

253

His re-enactment of 'L'Invitation au voyage', as a seller of pasts for myriad upwardly mobile fellow citizens, updates the exotic trajectory of an unholy trinity of nineteenth-century *littérateurs* carefully chosen to accompany the cultural alchemy of a virtual if still Jeanne Duval-fixated Baudelaire – Alexandre Dumas, Machado de Assis, Cruz e Souza – because of their long-hidden black imprint on the blank page of a literature of exclusion, the textual apartheid of French, Brazilian... or any other canonic and colonizing culture.[12]

Fleetingly on a high in the artificial paradise of his far-from-simple dream of lineage-and-new-Empire building, Félix soon comes down; and, mutteringly, he ironizes his own racially doctoring enterprise by echoing the anti-*mot*, the obscene lie, the final collusion, of Auschwitz. No poetry... just confession; and the effect is to trigger in his mysterious – possibly East European (via Brazil) – visitor the blurting out of the identity-bereft role of the mere, but no less guilt-ridden, 'photo-journalist', the collector of 'images of war, of hunger and its ghosts, of terrible misfortunes'. Once a witness always a witness, however; and the reader is teased to anticipate that the self-dispossessed stranger, a burdened bearer of *animages*, has come to the new Angola in search of something old and in remembrance of things past... of some unfinished business no longer to be hidden from expression, from view, from memory or from representation.

The discomfited Félix ('Oh, the horror') is so plunged into the loss of

---

there dwell, however, a present and a proximity very close to home, very much our own and in no way improper or remote (Vecchi 2008, 187) .

[12] Provocation *à la* Agualusa... transparently fluid, possibly enlightening? In the vestibule of entrance (examination), the *entre-lugar* of aporetic transition, the rite of passage from secondary to tertiary education, have Brazilian educators, legislators, betrayed, consciously or not, a guilt-prompted awareness of exceptional lack? Vital to a curriculum of inclusion, a programme to be followed by pupils in, but not always of, a mixed-race economy comes a narrative ostensibly addressing that prior passage of transatlanticism, of a slave heritage yet to be rendered past, its traces to be expunged in a clarifying modernity. The importation of a seductively *lisible* cum *scriptible* textuality, one peppered with bridging references to Brazil from Angola, may prove to be but a lure. Framing *parergon* cannot contain; curative *pharmakon* leaks infection; symptomatic analogies proffer fake brother/sisterhoods. Wherever (re-)located, Àngela-Lúcia will embody the scars of transluciferation; again, intra-colonizing gesture conceals as it reveals a local-national Brazilian-appropriated grand narrative, a post-colonial placebo – to be misread (*à suivre*).

his self-possession that he momentarily loses, too, the plot of his own making, his own inventions, his certainty as to his own (perceived) colour. 'Can't you tell I'm black?' says the albino. And from within this tension the trialogue is rendered overt... via a chuckle; the 'amazing' laughter of identity-deconstruction made manifest. *Et homo faber est –* shaper, moulder, image-maker, factor, *hacedor...* fictionist? But that's another's (short) story; the legacy of one about to be reincarnated. As author, Agualusa will also create his precursors.

Pace animot... for 'men know almost nothing of the little creatures that share their homes'. Self-obsessedly lost in the game of 'But me, who am I?', they are meanwhile narrated by but one of that infinite series of autobiographical animals ('mice, bats, ants, ticks, flees, flies, mosquitoes, spiders, worms, silverfish, termites, weevils, snails, beetles'... and, here, why not?, *geckopidae*) who can say 'I might as well simply get on with my life' whilst tell-tailing the 'risky, fabulous or chimerical response', or responses, of a felicitous venturer into the company of another re-incarnate J(L)B. José. Bookman par excellence; with one 'L' of a difference.

In the actantial sphere of Félix Ventura, of José Buchmann and of the narrating tiger gecko, the possession of their textual status by the shades of Jorge Luis Borges will come ever more overtly to haunt the plot of *O Vendedor de Passados*. Buchmann has the acquired initials of the blind librarian precursor; 'Félix and I share a love (in my case a hopeless love) for old words' (25) muses the gecko; and Félix himself takes on the mantle of a revenant: 'The tightly curled hair, trimmed down now, glowed around him with a miraculous aura. If someone had seen him from out on the road, seen him through the window, they would have thought they were looking at a ghost' (23). Interviewed (but trust the tale not the teller; for the text betrays a less restricted, an uncontrollable, a more infectious re-inhabitation), Agualusa says that his gecko-'chameleon is a reincarnation of Borges'.[13] Perhaps:

> It's been nearly fifteen years that my soul has been trapped in this body, and I am still not used to it. I lived for almost a century in the skin of a man, and I never managed to feel altogether human either. To this day I have known some thirty geckos [...] But I'd gladly exchange the company of all the geckos and lizards for Félix Ventura and his long soliloquies. Yesterday he confided to me that he'd met an amazing woman. Though, he added, the

---

[13] Recall: 'The chameleon is a reincarnation of Borges – all its recollections are related to actual events in Borges' life' (Polzonoff and Tepper, 2007, 1).

word 'woman' doesn't quite do her justice.

'Ângela Lúcia is to women what humankind is to the apes.'

'I ought to be charging you overtime, damn it!. Who do you think I am – Scheherezade?...' (40-42) [...]

But excuse my digression – that's what happens when a gecko starts philosophizing... So let's get back to José Buchmann. I'm not suggesting that in a few days a massive butterfly is going to burst out of him, beating his great multi-coloured wings. The changes I'm referring to are more subtle. For one thing, his accent is beginning to shift [...] it has a Luandan rhythm to it now [...] to hear him laugh you'd think he was Angolan. (55)

Perhaps not or, at least, not alone.

A Borges-like sequence, a pastiched taxonomy not of the fantastic but of 'some alien being[s], some vague and distant biological anomal[ies]', is followed by the narrator's option for neither the shared lineage of the ex-human race (of gecko memory) nor the companionship of fellow lizards but for the role of silent witness cum laughing *animot*-interlocutor of Félix Ventura, of José Buchmann and, not least, of its own alter-ego. *Lagartixa* ('e eu'), too, turns maker of fictions: *castigat ridendo mores... et colores*. All three, albino-black animus, chrysalis-blanched yet potentially 'multi-coloured' Angolan, and a 'terrible skin[ned]' animator, inherit and re-perform the role of Borges's *El hacedor*: artificer, here, of adopted fictions *qua* the assumed identities of those who buy into the commerce of 'the seller of pasts' – a currency, an exchange mechanism (and rate) of memory conceived as coinage and counterfeit bills. All three? Sounds familiar; there where Hegel was will 'ipseity' be?

By means of the chimera of this singular word, the *animot*, I bring together three heterogeneous elements within a single verbal body. (Derrida 2002, 1)

Plus ça change... three in one. Amidst the emerging plurality of a 'new' tale of the nation, African, facing West, but resisting the behest of a too-homogenizing 'Black' Atlantic identity of popular jargon and populist appeal, echoes the heterogeneity of an intra-Angolan actant. The mixed economy of *O Vendedor de Passados* underwrites the fiction that, there where 'new bourgeoisie' peoples' 'futures are secure', it is via text, including sold 'diplomas', that 'a brand new past' will be. It is the happy venture of fiction that 'draws up their family tree'. Subjectivity *is* heterogeneity; *is* attributable to archi-texture. 'But me, who am I?' Anima? No. *Animot*:

> Autobiography, the writing of the self as living, the trace of the living for itself, being for itself, the auto-affection or auto-infection as memory or archive of the living would be an immunizing movement (a movement of safety, of salvage and salvation of the safe, the holy, the immune, the indemnified, of virginal and intact nudity), but an immunizing movement that is always threatened with becoming auto-immunizing, as is every *autos*, every ipseity, every automatic, automobile, autonomous, auto-referential movement. Nothing risks becoming more poisonous than an autobiography; poisonous for itself in the first place, auto-infectious for the presumed signatory who is so auto-affected. (Derrida 2002, 1)

O tempora, o mores... et colores

At this point a teller is permitted to enter the tale. In a dream sequence, the gecko imagines that Félix confides in him, flick-knife collector and man of inaction reincarnate; again via the gentlemanly intertexts, *à deux*, of JLB, authorizing creator of precursors... and of liars:

> 'You invented him, this strange José Buchmann, and now he has begun to invent himself. It's like a metamorphosis... A reincarnation... Or rather: a possession.'
> My friend looked at me with alarm:
> 'What do you mean?'
> 'José Buchmann – surely you're noticed? – He's taken over the foreigner's body. He becomes more and more lifelike with each day that passes and that man he used to be, that night-time character who came into our house eight months ago as though he'd come not from another country but from another time – where is he now?'
> 'It's a game. I know it's a game. We all know that.'
> He poured himself some tea and took two cubes of sugar, and stirred it. He drank, his eyes lowered. There we were, two gentlemen, two good friends, wearing white in an elegant café [...]
> 'So be it,' I agreed. 'Let's acknowledge that it's no more than a game. So who is he?'

I wiped the sweat from my face. I've never distinguished myself by my valour. Maybe that's why I've never been attracted (speaking of my other life, that is) by the stormy destiny of heroes and rogues. I collected flick knives. And with a pride of which I'm now ashamed I boasted about the exploits of a grandfather of mine who'd been a general. I did befriend some brave men, but unfortunately that didn't help me. Courage isn't contagious; fear is, of course. Félix smiled as he understood that my terror was greater, more ancient, than his:

'I have no idea. You?'

He changed the subject. He told me that a few days earlier he'd been at the launch of a new novel by a writer of the Angolan diaspora. He was an unpleasant sort of character, professionally indignant, who'd built up his whole career abroad, selling our national horrors to European readers. Misery does ever so well in wealthy countries [...] 'In your novels do you lie deliberately or just out of ignorance?' Laughter. A murmur of approval. The writer hesitated a few seconds. Then counter-attacked: 'I'm a liar by vocation,' he shouted. 'I lie with joy! Literature is the only chance for a true liar to attain any sort of social acceptance.' Then, more soberly, he added – his voice lowered – that the principal difference between a dictatorship and democracy is that in the former there exists only one truth, the truth as imposed by power, while in free countries every man has the right to defend his own version of events. Truth, he said, is a superstition. He – Félix – was taken with the idea. (67-68)

Ah would some intra-colonial power... It did. JEA as others (his readers, the critics) see him? 'But me, who am I?' 'Agualusa and I'? 'Borges y yo'? 'I do not know which of the two is writing this page'.[14] 'Tiger, tiger'? No. 'El otro tigre'? Yes... ('a very rare species'). 'It's a *tiger* gecko' and 'we *still* know very little about them' [*animot* italics];[15] 'this amazing laugh – doesn't it sound like a human laugh?', an anxiety-of-influence, a JLB-echolalic, an other, a nervous, laugh? Laughter that

---

[14] 'No sé cual de los dos escribe esta página'/'I do not know which of the two is writing this page', in 'Borges y yo' (Borges 1980, 69-70); my translations of Borges *passim*.

[15] A *tiger* gecko? Leopard gecko, panther gecko, yes, but tiger... 'a very rare species' indeed; read between the lines from *El hacedor*'s 'El otro tigre'/'The other tiger' (Borges 1980).

cannot hide that I, geck(anim)o, am also 'destined to perish, definitively, and only some instant of myself can survive in him. Little by little, I am giving over everything to him [...] Spinoza knew that all things long to persist in their being: the stone eternally wants to be stone and the tiger a tiger. I shall remain in Borges, not in myself (if it is true that I am someone)' (Borges 1980, 69-70). And the tiger a gecko...? Reincarnation? Or animosity burning bright? Perhaps the funereal dread of the curse of having to remember? Memory as metamorphosed gecko-echo of 'Funes el memorioso': 'Courage isn't contagious; fear is, of course. Félix smiled as he understood that my terror was greater, more ancient, than his.' *Comparationem fingere*: 'I was numbed by the fear of multiplying superfluous ge [cko] stures.'[16]

Behold the son of man; progeny, too, of *In principio erat verbum*. An inheritor of transcendental 'Colony' swerves towards self-identity inseparably from the cadences of intra-colonial discourse, that genre of testimony, in which the *apud*-Ventura performs. The 'me who am I?' of the post-colony necessitates not the post-theological echo of proselytizing mono-culture – *Ecce homo* – but the risky, fabulous, or chimerical response *Ecce animot*. There where dictatorship was will democracy, 'by vocation', be. Lies must go on. *C'est la vie...*

Just prior to the calculatedly Borges-riddled dream of the differential nineteenth- and twentieth-century 'stormy destiny of heroes and rogues', respectively military and literary, in a single-page chapter, 'My first death didn't kill me' – a text that mirrors as it distorts the doubling 'Borges y yo' original on which it draws – the other 'otro tigre' gecko confesses to having considered an alternative to the lie that is life ('woven superstition'), only to be interrupted by the greater lie that is fiction (not 'bad at all'):

> Once, when I was in human form, I decided to kill myself [...] I hoped that reincarnation, all that stuff, was no more than slowly woven superstition [...] I thought that the gin in combination with the tedium of a pointless plot would give me the courage to put the gun to my head and pull the trigger. But it turned out the book wasn't bad at all, and I kept reading to the last page [...] I put the pistol to my head, and I fell asleep. (63)

The textual gap after the comma is deliberate; the aporia is unavoidable in the circular ruins of any and all attempts to think from

---

[16] *D'après* 'me entorpeció el temor de multiplicar ademanes inútiles', 'Funes el memorioso'/'Funes the Memory Man' (Borges 1988).

within the post- without acknowledgement of the intra-, the impossibility of not 'living', in the new Angola, to spin the yarn, to bear as *animot* the tell-tale tail of witness to that afterlife that is the voice, the voicing, of mocked and mocking memory. The coda-imperative of 'reading to the last page' is to be the supplement to ever-failing memory as slowly woven fiction comes to the rescue of all-too-fast and irrecuperable history.

The counter-attack

That 'literature [might be] the only chance for a true liar to attain any sort of social acceptance' is a perception shared by all who require the services of Félix Ventura; by any who would seek *within* a post-colonial life a fictive identity to be appropriated *from* a preferred colonial memory. Yet the desire that is staged by individuals is played out at a national level not only in the arch-defensive attack on the truth-seekers who, affianced to Plato, would expel fiction-makers from the new Republic of Angola, wishing for an answer to the (1934 or *1984*) provocation – 'In your novels do you lie deliberately or just out of ignorance?' – *boutade* of either socialist realist recividism or dystopian *dirigisme*.[17] 'One truth' ideology, confronted with the globalizing falsehood that 'every man has [...] his own version', seeks an outlet less transcendental, less religious, than that 'the Truth' be 'a superstition' – however 'taken with the idea' might be a nostalgic and disingenuous Félix.

And so to the unfinished business no longer to be hidden from expression, from view, from memory or from representation. In the overtime of Scheherezadian deferral, the interweaving of her story with his story will divulge why 'Ângela Lúcia is to women what humankind is to the apes' not only for Félix but also for the inseparably male plotting that is the actantial tangle of Ventura, Buchmann and the gecko. Seek the supplement. *Cherchez la fff...fiction.*

When Ângela and José come together, the seller of pasts, Félix, prompts in her response to his insouciance a prejudiced reptile-narrator's *apartheid*-adjectival, nay, politically correct, interference:

---

[17] The 'writer of the Angolan diaspora [...] selling our national horrors to European readers' – be it in sly reference to Agualusa himself or to any other unveiler of intra-colonial social structures – will, classically, have to face, and face down, attacks from either post-colonial critics of an unreconstructed 1934 Soviet Writers' Congress bent or Orwellian post-modern gloom-mongers. Amidst the laughter, the timid murmurs of approval.

'Do you two know each other?'

'No, no!' said Ângela, her voice colourless. 'I don't think so.'

José Buchmann was even less certain:

'Oh, but there are so many people I don't know!' he said, and laughed at his own wit. 'I've never been so popular.' (73-74)

'I don't think' therefore I am not who I was. 'I don't know!' therefore I resist any populism that would hide behind the identity labels of instant recognition. Ângela presses Buchmann not as to *who* he has been but as to 'Where?':

> 'I've spent the last ten years without any fixed home. Adrift across the world, taking photographs of wars. Before that I lived in Rio de Janeiro, and before that in Berlin, and earlier still in Lisbon. I went to Portugal in the sixties to study law, but I couldn't stand the climate. It was too cold. *Fado*, Fátima, football [...] One day a friend gave me a Canon-1, the one I still use today, and that's how I became a photographer. I was in Afghanistan in 1982, with the Soviet troops... in Salvador with the guerrillas... in Peru, on both sides... in the Falklands, again on both sides... in Iran during the war against Iraq... in Mexico on the side of the Zapatistas... I've taken a lot of photos in Israel and Palestine – a lot – there's never any shortage of work there.'
>
> Ângela Lúcia smiled, nervous again:
>
> 'Enough! I don't want your memories to pollute this house with blood...' [...] The two guests remained [...] Neither spoke. The silence that hung between them was full of murmurings, of shadows, of things [...] dark and furtive. Or perhaps not [...] and I merely imagined the rest. (74-75)

'I am not there where I am the plaything' ['le jouet'] of... my camera.[18]

'But me, who am I?' Am I but my camera? Mere *animage*? If only I could get a shot in sideways... before I am re-narrated, 'merely imagined', ani(de)moted to my camera-always-lies reputation, the freeze-frame climate, the bloody pollution, of my photo-reportage, my unwanted memory. Must I, too, become a bookman reincarnate in order to persist in *my* being, to compete with the digressions, the interventions, the mediations, the mocking testimony, the authority of

---

[18] Cf. 'Je ne suis pas là où je suis le jouet de ma pensée' ('I am not there where I am the plaything of my thought') (Lacan 1966 , 136).

that benighted gecko? '*Pópilas!*' No eyelash! I am aware that its eyes are protected by a transparent membrane, cleaned of debris by its long tongue. Not a forked tongue. And when it's caught, it releases its tail, which twitches for a while, allowing it to escape capture... no doubt while, later, it will grow another *tale*. 'Little by little, I am giving over everything to him.' I don't even know which of us two is writing this page. Damn Spinoza! Damned gecko... whatsisname?

No name? Omniscient but anonymous narrator? Perhaps Félix can help. He sold one to me, 'Buchmann'... so why not bequeath an appropriate name, now, to a friend, the confidant of his soliloquies, to a gecko who reincarnates the man who laughs? (Who goes there, Victor?) *Victor ludorum*? ... 'Jouet'... Lui, Borges?

As compassion shades the dream-conversation with the Angolan seller of pasts of the reptile pining in reincarnation for the youthful venture to Europe and the dialogical eloquence of its Argentine precursor, let us listen in:

> 'I'm a man with no colour,' he said. 'And as you know, nature abhors a vacuum.' [...]
> I felt sorry for him:
> 'In cold countries people with light skin aren't so troubled by the harshness of the sun. Maybe you ought to think about moving to Switzerland. Have you ever been to Geneva? I'd rather like to live in Geneva.' [...]
> Félix looked at me carefully:
> 'Sorry to ask – but could you tell me your name?'
> 'I have no name,' I replied quite frankly. 'I am the gecko.'
> 'That's silly. No one is a gecko!'
> 'You're right. No one's a gecko. And you – are you really called Félix Ventura?'
> My questions seemed to offend him [...]
> 'Is this madness?'
> I didn't know how to answer him. (79-80)[19]

The companionable laughter of His Lowliness, sovereign though nameless and wordless, convinces Félix of what happens when one 'starts philosophizing' about a nonetheless articulate gecko. In an

---

[19] Jouer, lui? Donc moi aussi. Agualusa's text is littered with JLB jokes, not least in the chapter entitled, 'Dream No. 4' in which the dream conversation of the Borges of the Geneva period (1914-1921) provides the intertext for the gecko's tongue-in-cheek advice to Félix.

Apuleian, Erasmian, Bergsonian and particularly felicitous swerve, Ventura geckoes a Roland Barthes's *bon mot*; in the *animot* discourse of Agualusa's novel, his chit-chatting interlocutor demands, deserves, a proper name: 'Rire c'est lutter pour être nommé.'[20]

I, Eulálio

The following night Félix asked Ângela Lúcia the same question. First, of course, he'd told her that he'd dreamed of me again. I've seen Ângela Lúcia say very serious things laughing or, on the contrary, adopting a sombre expression when joking with her interlocutor. It's not always possible to tell what she's thinking. On this occasion she laughed at the anxiety in my friend's eyes, greatly increasing his disquiet, but then right away turned more serious and asked:

'And his name? So did the guy tell you who he is?'

No one is a name, I thought forcefully...

The reply took Ângela Lúcia by surprise. Félix too. I watched him look at her as though looking into an abyss. She was smiling sweetly. She lay her right hand on the albino's left arm. She whispered something in his ear, and he relaxed.

'No,' he whispered back. 'I don't know who he is. But since I'm the one who dreams about him I think I can give him any name I want, can't I? I'm going to call him Eulálio because he's so well-spoken.'

Eulálio?! That seems fine to me. So Eulálio I shall be. (83)

Subjectivity ('eu') and the speaking voice ('lalia'); whence the articulator is caught but not captured in the act of becoming... never being a fixed form, always potential, ever prone to generate a new tale (trust the tail not the teller?). Eulálio's tap-tapping – between sleeping watchfully and his devouring of multiple little *animaux* – draws Félix into that wisest of friendships which is the echolalia of coming (to laugh) together. Therein, babelic *ridere* and *ride* wrinkle inseparably into the laughter lines, the ageing skin, the wisdom, of mockery; and the infinite ludics of the mosaic, of tiling, assume the *animot* form of the re(p)tiling:

---

[20] Cf. 'Lire c'est lutter pour nommer' ('To read is to struggle to name') (Barthes 1974, xi).

It would not be a matter of 'giving speech back' to animals but perhaps of acceding to a thinking, however fabulous and chimerical it might be, that thinks the absence of the name and of the word otherwise, as something other than a privation. (Derrida 2002, 2)

Otherwise, I speak (laugh) therefore I am (not) brackets Félix and Eulálio as one and (not) the same: *Ecce homo et animot factus est.*

Out of habit, and out of genetic predisposition (because bright light bothers me), I sleep during the day, all day. Sometimes, however, something will wake me up [...] Perhaps I was dreaming about my father. The moment I awoke I saw the scorpion. He was just a few centimetres away. Motionless. Closed in a shell of hatred like a medieval warrior in his armour. And then he fell upon me. I jumped back, climbed the wall, in a flash, until I was up at the ceiling. I could hear quite clearly the dry tap of the sting against the floor – I can hear it still.

I remember something my father said once when we were celebrating – with only pretend joy, I like to think – the death of someone we disliked:

'He was evil, and he didn't know it. He didn't know what evil was. That is to say, he was *pure* evil.'

That's what I felt at precisely the moment as I opened my eyes and the scorpion was there.

[...]

After the episode with the scorpion, I wasn't able to get back to sleep. This meant that I was able to witness the arrival of the Minister. A short, fat man, ill at ease in his body [...] To watch him you'd think he'd been shortened only moments earlier and hadn't yet become accustomed to his new height... He was wearing a dark suit, with white stripes, which didn't really fit and which troubled him [...] [His] sudden camaraderie irritated my friend even more [...] [He] went off to fetch the file he'd prepared. He opened it on the little mahogany table – slowly, theatrically – in a ritual I'd observed so many times. It always worked. The Minister, anxious, held his breath as my friend revealed his genealogy to him:

'This is your paternal grandfather, Alexandre Torres dos Santos Correia de Sá e Benevides, a direct descendent of Salvador Correia de Sá e Benevides, the famous *carioca* who in

1648 liberated Luanda from the Dutch...'

'The fellow they named the high school after?'

'That's the one.'

'I thought he was Portuguese! Or a politician from the capital or some colonial; otherwise why did they change the name of the school to Mutu Ya Kevela?'

'I suppose it was because they wanted an Angolan hero – in those days we needed our own heroes like we needed bread to feed us. Though, if you'd rather I can fix up another grandfather for you. I could arrange documents to show that you're descended from Mutu Ya Kevela himself, or N'Gola Quiluange, or even Queen Ginga herself. Would you rather that?'

'No, no. I'll keep the Brazilian. Was the fellow rich?'

'Extremely. He was cousin to Estácio de Sá, founder of Rio de Janeiro.' [...]

The Minister was astonished:

'Fantastic!'

And indignant:

'Damn! Whose stupid idea was it to change the name of the high school?! A man who expelled the Dutch colonists, an internationalist fighter of our brother-country, an Afro-antecedent, who gave us one of the most important families in this country – that is to say, mine. No, old man, it won't do. Justice must be restored. I want the high school to go back to being called Salvador Correia, and I'll fight for it with all my strength, I'll have a statue of my grandfather cast to put outside the entrance. A really big statue, in bronze, on a block of white marble [...] So I'm descended from Salvador Correia – *caramba*! – and I never knew it till now. Excellent. My wife will be ever so pleased.' (105-11)

Following scripture into *écriture*, the Minister is confronted by an intra-historical conundrum. 'Can a man, merely by taking thought, add one cubit to his...' statue? Can an Angolan (as he spots a different *animot*) change (into) his stripes?

The black-and-white suited politician, ill at ease in his attire but at home in his skin and in his new-found past (post... post-), has many an antecedent in his discovery of the extent to which History with a capital(ist) H inscribes reality with excess... and profit. The sewing into the fabric of memory of the best-fitting minutiae of 'historical facts' – in the case of the Fascist Portugal of António Salazar – is replicated in the post-colonial era by an intra-colonialist ploy of writing – or having written for him – that fiction which will be called *The Real Life of a Fighter*. There where History was will his story be; that is, his lie. 'Real', 'life', 'fighter', sobriquets all, 'The Minister', 'writing his book with a hired hand – the hand of Félix Ventura' (127) – is the butt of Agualusa's set-piece satire of post-colonial intra-colonialism, namely, the appropriation not of the past but rather of the power of the past via mobilized memory. Ventura's sleight of hand, rendered explicit in his amorous boast to Ângela Lúcia, will soon further unveil the Angolan author's unremitting fascination both with Borges as text and with 'Borges y yo'. Meanwhile, the white rabbit that comes out of the inter-textual hat is more evocative of Lewis Carroll:

> 'If you ask me, whenever I hear about something completely impossible I believe it at once. And don't you think José Buchmann is impossible? Yes, we both do. So he has to be for real.' (116)

> 'You know, that's the first time I've kissed an albino'.
> When Félix explained to her what he did for a living – 'I'm a genealogist' – which is what he always says when he meets strangers, she became interested at once.
> 'Seriously? You are the first genealogist I've met.' (117)

Queer egg as he may be perceived to be, the albino's misprision of Humpty Dumpty allows him to perform, in a West African wonderland, the re-writing of history as fiction, genealogy as ingenious ingenuousness, that representation whereby form *is* content. Echoing perhaps the fact that the blind Argentine librarian was once mischievously designated 'Ministro de gallinas y conejos' ['Minister of hens and rabbits'] by President Juan Perón, Ventura overtly rewrites Angolan politics as caricature of the exemplary *Buchmann*'s legacy. And so, to bed in 'The Minister'... as History beckons:

> Félix would sew fiction in with reality dexterously, minutely, in such a way that historical facts and dates were respected [...] We remember other people's memories as though they were our own – even fictional ones.
> 'It's like the Castle of São Jorge in Lisbon – Do you know it? It has battlements, but they're fake. António de Oliveira Salazar ordered that some crenellations be added to the castle to make it more authentic. To him there was something wrong with a castle without crenellations – there was something monstrous

about it – like a camel without humps. So the fake part of the Castle of São Jorge is today what makes it realistic. Several octogenarian Lisboans I've spoken to are convinced the Castle has always had crenellation. There's something rather amusing about that, isn't there? If it were authentic, no one would believe in it.'

As soon as *The Real Life of a Fighter* is published, the consistency of Angolan history will change, there will be even more History. [...]

That is the truth that the Minister told Félix. The story Félix had the man tell in his true History [...] He wanted to give the people our-daily-bread. And that is exactly what he did [...] In just two years he himself was named Secretary of State for Economic Transparency and Combating Corruption [...] Today he is Minister for Bread-Making and Dairy Produce. (127-29)

Give 'em this day their daily bread and lead us into temptation – a.k.a. plenty of dough while we milk the system – 'driven exclusively by great and serious patriotic motives' (129).

Food for thought? Or just meat and drink to the sick transit of another gravy train *africanus*? *Plus ça* change here for the next station in life on the up-line. 'Memory is a landscape watched from the window of a moving train' (139). Intra-colonialism would rattle along, discursive lapses on track, halting not at some recuperable or necessary past (via a Truth Commission, for example) but forever in a present which has moved on, re-tracing, re-mapping, that History in which rewriting is a norm. Until José Buchmann intervenes. When he re-emerges, towards the end of the novel, it is to lift the stone of Angola's recent past. And out crawls Edmundo Barata dos Reis – fetid embarrassment to a post-colonial state that has already forgotten him and his deeds because of pressing and overwhelming needs: to live the post-ideological, intra-economic, 'new' nation(alism) that is the globalized (or un-'Black' Atlanticized) actuality of the *cuduro*... hard-assed, hard-headed, hard-faced.

When JB appeared tonight he was accompanied by an old man with a long white beard and wild braids, grey and dishevelled, cascading over his shoulders. I recognized him at once as the old tramp the photographer had been pursuing, for weeks on end, showing him – in that extraordinary image – emerging from a sewer. An ancient, vengeful God, wild-haired, with suddenly lit-up eyes.

'I'd like to introduce my friend Edmundo Barata dos Reis, an ex-agent of the Ministry of State Security.'

'Not ex-agent, say rather 'ex-*gent*'! Ex-exemplary citizen. Exponent of the excluded, existential excrement, an exiguous and explosive excrescence. In a word, a professional layabout. Very pleased to meet you.' [...]

'I thought you'd enjoy meeting him. This man's life story could almost have been made up by you...' [...]

'I'm-All-Ears. That's what they used to call me. It was my fighting name. I liked it. I liked hearing it. And then – in a flash! – the Berlin Wall collapsed on top of us. *Pópilas*, old man! Agent one day, ex-gent – ex-person – the next.' [...]

Two years in Havana, nine months in Berlin (East Berlin), another six in Moscow; his steel tempered, he returned to the solid trenches of socialism in Africa [...] 'I used to be a communist...' And he'd keep yelling out – 'Yes, I'm a communist, I'm really very Marxist-Leninist!' Even at a time when the official version has begun to deny the country's socialist past [...]

Edmundo Barata dos Reis shrunk back in his chair. He didn't remind me of a God anymore, he didn't remind me of a warrior – he was a dog, humiliated. He stank [...] And instead of replying to Félix's question he addressed himself to José Buchmann, pointing at him... 'That laugh – when I hear that laugh, old man, it's as though I'm face-to-face with someone else, from long ago. From another time, an old time. Don't we know each other?' [...]

'And now I wouldn't be able to take it off even if I wanted to. Like a skin to me – you see? I've got a hammer and sickle tattooed on my chest now. That won't come off.' (143-46)

To lift the lid on the sewer in which (the cockroach) Barata has been dwelling, ostensibly undetected under the cover of this era of the 'official version', restores to *animotion* but one more of that infinite series of 'autobiographical animals', the 'little creatures that share [men's] homes' and of whom they 'know almost nothing' (18). Recall, too, that 'nothing risks becoming more poisonous' (Derrida 2002, 1). 'But me, who am I?'... In the late chapter, 'Love, a crime', 'I, Eulálio' delights in narrating the new-found bliss of Félix and Ângela Lúcia:

Félix turned back to Ângela, and kissed her on the lips. I saw her – with some surprise – closing her eyes and accepting his kiss. I heard her moan. The albino tried to undo her shirt, but she stopped him.

'No. No not that. Don't do that.'

She raised her legs elegantly, and slipped off her shorts. Through the shirt that clung to her body you could make out the roundness of her breasts, her smooth belly. Then she turned her body, till she was kneeling over Félix. Her broad shoulders – lovely swimmer's shoulders – made her waist look even slimmer. My friend sighed:

'You're so beautiful...'

Ângela took his head in her hands and kissed him. A long kiss.

It took my breath away.

She takes off the t-shirt. She washes her face, her shoulders, her armpits. I notice a group of dark, round scars on her back, which stick out like insults on her golden velvet skin. I think I can see – in the mirror – just the same marks on her breasts and stomach. (153-54)

But... even indirectly, via the mirror of geckobservation, that 'auto-affection' which operates, narratively, 'as memory or archive of the living' and would be 'an immunizing movement (a movement of safety, of salvage and salvation of the safe, the holy, the immune, the indemnified, of virginal and intact nudity) [...] is always threatened' (Derrida 2002, 1):

José Buchmann bursts into the room. There's a pistol in his right hand. He's trembling. His voice trembles even more:

'Where is the son of a bitch?'

'You're not coming in!' She explodes: '*Poças*! Where the hell did you come from?'

I can hear the voice of Edmundo Barata dos Reis, shrill, desperate, but only then do I see him [...]

'Girl, this creature has appeared from hell! From the past! From the place the damned come from...' [...]

'Yes, that's right – I've come from the past! And who am I? Well? Tell them who I am!...'

All of a sudden he throws himself forward, knocking Ângela over while lunging for Edmundo – he grabs his neck with his left hand and forces him to his knees. He pushes the end of the pistol-barrel into his neck:

'Tell them who I am!'

'A ghost. A demon...'

'Who am I!'

'A counter-revolutionary. A spy. An agent of imperialism...'

'What's my name?'

'...Gouveia. Pedro Gouveia. I should have killed you back in '77.'

José Buchmann kicks at him. One. Two. Three. Four. Five. [...] Edmundo doesn't cry out. He doesn't even try to avoid the blows. The kicks find his stomach, his chest, his mouth. The boots turn red.

'Shit! Shit!'

José Buchmann – or Pedro Gouveia, as you prefer – puts the pistol down on the table [...]

'I never forgot you. I never forgot her either – Marta – young Marta Martinho – passing for some sort of intellectual – poetess, painter and God knows what else. She was pregnant, almost at term, a huge belly. Round. So round. It's as though I can see her now...'

[...] 'It happened a long time ago, didn't it? During the struggles...' He gestures towards Ângela – 'The girl hadn't even been born. The Revolution was under threat.

'I went off to interrogate the girl. She held out for two days. Then she gave birth to a little girl [...] When I think about it all I see is blood... And Mabeco, a mulatto from the South – he died a while ago, a stupid way to go, stabbed twice in cold blood in a bar in Lisbon, they never found out who did it – Mabeco cut the umbilical cord with a penknife, then he lit a cigarette and began to torture the baby, burning it on the back and chest. And the blood! Masses of blood, and the girl that Marta – her eyes wide like moons – it pains me to dream about it – and the baby screaming, the smell of burning flesh. Even today when I lie down to sleep, the spell is still there, the sound of the child crying...'

'Shut up!'

Félix, a rough shout, a voice I didn't recognize in him [...]

From where I'm watching, from here on top of the cupboard, I can see the top of his head lit up in rage [...]

'Now I'm absolutely certain. It really is you – Gouveia – the factionalist. The other day your laugh almost gave you away. You used to laugh a lot in the faction meetings, before the business with the consul, when your own countrymen handed you over to me. Not in prison, though – you just cried in prison.

You cried all the time – boohoo, like a girl... I watch you crying now and I see that nobody Gouveia. Revenge – is that what you wanted?

'No, you need passion for that. You need courage! Killing a man, that's a man's job'. And then –

      as

           in

                a

                      slow

                            dance...

Ângela crosses the kitchen,
Comes to the table,
her right hand picks up the gun,
her left hand pushes Félix away,
she points at Edmundo's chest –
and fires. (157-59)

If revenge – *sans animosité* – is a dish best eaten cold, then Ângela's *sang froid* is still performed in a deferred, a scar-traced, pharmakon-driven, choreography:

> Why should a new 'idea' of woman [...] be subjected to the urgency of this topo-economical concern? [...] This step only constitutes a step on the condition that it challenge a certain idea of the locus [*lieu*] and the place [*place*] and that it dance otherwise [...] the dance changes place and above all changes women's movements [...] has actually brought with it the chance for a certain risky turbulence in the assigning of places [...] to bring the dance and its tempo into tune with the 'revolution' [...] always deprived of insurance [...] Each man and each woman must commit his or her own singularity, the untranslatable factor of his or her life and death. (Derrida and McDonald, 1982, 68-69)

It is Ângela Lúcia, challenging Angola's urgent topo-economical concern, in the very market place of private life and institutions where the nation essays its tentative steps of rewriting history – choreographed by Félix as seller of pasts and outed as residence under surveillance by Gouveia alias Buchmann – who makes the decisive move. *Pas... pas.* She it is who brings the dance and its tempo into tune with the 'revolution'... and markedly not with the *cuduro* of intra-colonial compromise. Ângela Lúcia, as deprived of insurance in committing her own singularity – her ipseity – as the Archangel Lucifer whose pride her name echoes and her action reflects, triggers a risky turbulence by taking justice into her own hands. Truth without reconciliation... and, certainly, without remedy; but in and with the pharmakon.[21] Félix is left to bury 'the narrow body' of the *barata*, latest embodiment of that *'pure evil'* so feared by the gecko since his father's ani-*mot juste* had alerted him to the supplementarity of 'celebrating – with only pretend joy – the death of someone we disliked' (105). There where scorpion was will cockroach be?

Et mundus regum...

Edmundo [Barata] dos Reis is dead. Long live Ângela. Viva Angola. Via Ventura. Via Eulálio. Via all bookmen and their [intrusive] *animots*...

> 'And did you know that Ângela was your daughter?'
> 'Yes, I knew. I left prison in nineteen-eighty [...] That son of a bitch – Edmundo – had derived great pleasure telling me every time he interrogated me of how he'd killed my wife. He told me they'd murdered the baby too. But it turned out they hadn't killed her. They'd handed her over to Marina, Marta's sister, and she had brought her up [...] I became obsessed [...] I thought that if I killed him I'd be able to look my daughter in the eye [...] I returned to Luanda [...] on the table of my hotel I found a business card of our friend Félix Ventura. *Give your children a better past* [...] Then one evening I waited for him to leave the sewer where he used to hide out, and I slipped down into it. And there, in that filthy hole, I found a mattress, dirty clothes, magazines, Marxist literature and – would you believe it? – a set of archives containing the State Security reports for dozens of people [...] when all of a sudden Edmundo appeared [...] knife in hand. He was laughing [...] He said:
> *The two of us, face to face again, comrade Pedro Gouveia – but this time I'm going to finish you off...* – and he lunged at me [...] The rest you know.' (172-74)

In a pastiche of 'and the rest you know' predictability of socialist realist stereotyping presumptions, Agualusa plays with the campaign-

---

[21] 'The *pharmakon* is the movement, the locus, and the play [...] The translation by remedy can thus be neither accepted nor simply rejected' (Derrida 1981, 127; 99).

poster typicality of Edmundo Barata dos Reis – 'I'm the very last communist south of the Equator'. His T-shirt is inseparable from his skin, from his tatooed hammer and sickle (146). The easy eponymy of a fallen sovereignty interrupted by the *animot* abjection cockroach of the punning *barata* is a cheap shot at a no-less failed Soviet expansionism. Out of the sewer, with updated notes from the underground, emerges that subverted Marxist other, demon-creature of cyclically Dosto-evskian animation:

> the antithesis of the normal man [...] feels insulted [...] and wants to revenge itself [...] There in its nasty, stinking, underground home [...] insulted, crushed and ridiculed [...] absorbed in cold, malignant and [...] everlasting spite [...] incognito [...] it will suffer a hundred times more than the one on whom it revenges itself. (Dostoevsky, 57-58)

The depiction of the fallen ideologue's ends-and-means, criminal, axial role in the plot of *The Book of Chameleons*, at micro-level, stands in contrast to the macro-economic failure of the nation and the success as fiction-maker and host to Ângela as vehicle of justice of '*o vendedor de passados*', Félix. A venture performed, in collusion, via the silences and the voicings of the albino black and his *animot* interlocutor... but one which still requires a woman to commit her own singularity, the untranslatable factor of her life and death:[22]

> 'And what about Ângela – did she know you were her father?'
> She became a photographer, like me; and, like me, she

---

[22] For recall: 'Ângela Lúcia is to women what humankind is to the apes' (40). Not every critic has seen the characterization, or its function in Agualusa's text, as so strongly layered: 'Told in short, ironic scenes, *O Vendedor de Passados* is consistently taut and witty. Unfortunately, the novel's violent conclusion, which re-enacts the gruesome fate of the couple who staged the 1977 coup attempt, does not emerge organically from events in Ventura's bookshop; the story's final twists feel imposed' (Henighan 2008, 219). Such a reading of the relationship between fact and fiction, betraying no little animosity towards the mediations that national bookmen bring to international bookshops, hinges on the novel's oblique references (José *et al.*) to the events of 27 May 1977 and a MPLA purge after an attempted coup. Nito Alves, José Van Dúnem and a legendarily beautiful Cita (or Sita) Vales were victims of a prison atrocity still raw in the public conscience of the intra-Angolan national imaginary. Which, *pace* tale-trusters everywhere, is not to say that the thorn-text of another José – E. A. – might not further prick that conscience.

became a nomad.

A drowsiness came over me, I wanted to shut my eyes and sleep, but I resisted it, sure that if I fell asleep moments later I would awake transformed into a gecko.

'Have you had news from Ângela?'

'Yes, I hear from her. At this moment she should be going down the Amazon on a big, lazy, slowboat [...] I hope she's happy?' (174-75)

A journey and an escape that Félix and Eulálio already had news of, too. Via a photograph... and an inscription – 'In the margin, Ângela Lúcia had written in blue ink: *Plácidas Águas, Pará*' – for, in Brazil now, she is lost to Félix and Eulálio but for her *carte postale*... the missive that, always, may not arrive but that, in this instance, contains a clue to the framing of an inter-continental, intertextual, movement. 'And what about Ângela?' Her? Gone to Pará – *Parergon* – as 'accessory, foreign or secondary object, supplement, aside, remainder. It is what the principal subject must not become'. *Plácidas Águas*, placid waters whereby:

> memory or archive of the living would be an immunizing movement (a movement of safety, of salvage and salvation of the safe, the holy, the immune, the indemnified, of virginal and intact nudity), but an immunizing movement that is always threatened with becoming auto-immunizing, as is every *autos*, every ipseity, every automatic, automobile, autonomous, auto-referential movement'? Or, a cover story for 'a certain risky turbulence in the assigning of places'? (Derrida, 1987, 54)

After the crime, 'the crossing'; Ângela has fled, accessory after the fact, supplement to Angola-Brazil relations, remainder to and reminder of a mosaic of transatlantic shifts, re-enacting toings and froings, emigrations, forced or otherwise, retaking the soundings of an echo chamber of already multiple 'crossings', of past and present enslavements in selves journeying towards ipseities (becoming only for principal subjects). The 'Black' Atlantic still bears her trace (without signature) but in blue. A binary is diluted, yet an ever-framing Félix still opts for a pin, 'a bright, ludicrous green [one], and fixed the photograph to the wall'. An ethereally ever blue and green Brazil flags convenient escapism, ostensibly, but Ventura knows, better than most, that any game of colours masks the difference between searching for identities as distinct from ipseities. It's what you do... and she has done. His 'eyes filled with tears [...] "I know you want me to forgive her. I'm so sorry my friend, but I can't. I don't think I can do it'" (164). The *pardo*-ing of the sphere of action – a shade of grey – is too much for the African albino's black and white, entrenched, polarity to withstand. Ângela Lúcia's sin of pride, inseparable from revenge, has lost her, to him, forever.

The Borges-haunted Eulálio – 'I imagined myself sinking into that silence, blindly, like I used to' (152) – will soon have served, outlived, his purpose in Félix's narrowly superannuated, assigned, residence. After the explosive dénouement, the anxiety-influenced narrator, resisting sleep lest he dream, and wake, as a real gecko, settles for his terminal role of being – and penetrating – the animottled skin of Angola and the scarred body of national memory. In echo of 'Borges y yo', the narrator, 'Eu' and 'lália', wills his own and his other's oblivion, a release from the burden of further testimony, from re-narration. 'My whole life was an attempt to escape' (172-73), J [L] Buchmann had explained. I wish I had said that...

You will *osga*, you will

'Give your children a better past' had been the slogan of the seller of pasts. Only at the end of the novel, in a newly started diary, does Félix Ventura address his need of a living interlocutor cum witness to his writerly role in the recon/deconstruction of his nation's plausible story. Without an echolalic corroborator, his only resort will be to the painfully less-than-dialogical written or pictorial evidence of a diary or of postcards from afar.

Mythologized sub-Saharan animism will be supplemented by a new Angola-focused anim(ot)ism whereby a haunting if not-so-pure evil catches up with the narrative-for-sale of *O Vendedor de Passados*. 'Scorpion' – 'I ought to be charging you overtime, damn it! Who do you think I am – Scheherezade?...' – is always, *mot et parole*, already there, sting in the tale of a past that the *osga* Eulálio has heard tap-tapping – and has survived once before. It catches up with (and perishes with, no Scheherezade, *he*) the gecko *animot* that 'died in combat, like a hero – who'd never thought of himself as courageous' (179). He got his teeth into the 'horrible creature' of the past; the ever-present lurking past and its relationship with the chameleon-coloured laughing witness of a narrative, a dream, constructed, counterfeited before his very eyes.

> This morning I found Eulálio dead. Poor Eulálio. He'd fallen
> at the foot of my bed, with an enormous scorpion, a horrible

creature, also dead, clamped between his teeth. I decided to start keeping this diary today, to maintain the illusion that there's someone listening to me. I'll never have another listener like him, though. He was my best friend, I think. I suppose I'll stop meeting him in my dreams now. And indeed with every passing day, every passing hour, my memory of him becomes more and more like a figure made of sand. The memory of a dream. Maybe I dreamed it all: him, José Buchmann, Edmundo Barata dos Reis.

I'm an animist. I've always been an animist though I've only lately realized it. The same thing happens to the soul as happens to water [...] Eulálio will always be Eulálio, whether flesh (incarnate) or fish.

I'm reminded of that black and white picture of Martin Luther King speaking to the crowd: *I have a dream...* he really should have said 'I *made* a dream'. If you think about it there's a difference between having a dream and *making* a dream.

Yes, I've made a dream.

Lisbon, February 13th, 2004. (179-80)

'Finally, I learn to live', as a writer and cultural critic, as 'an autobiographical animal'. To write, no less than to read, frees us from our spectres.[23]

> *Ecce animot – that is what I was saying*
> *before this long digression.*
>
> Reb Der

Em teu seio formoso retratas
Este céu de puríssimo azul
A verdura sem par destas matas
E o esplendor do Cruzeiro do Sul

Pardo nem tem...
Na bandeira auriverde

Reb Ber

---

[23] The echoes from Jacques Derrida's meditations on 'Je suis en guerre contre moi-même' and 'Donner la mort' are taken from *Apprendre à vivre enfin* (Derrida, 2004) and from the last, short, digression I heard from him, in Rio de Janeiro in August 2004, and in Brazil to pursue and to lay some of the ghosts of my past and present – *pardo* – undertaking.

Au bas-relief:

L'instant singulier où la trace n'est pas
encore laissée, abandonnée, quand elle ne
se distingue pas encore de la surface ou du
lieu d'origine.

Jacques Derrida

Das verlieh ihr, ein flugartiges Schweben
mit festem Auftreten verbindend, die
eigenartige Anmut. Hatte er es für sich
benannt 'die Vorschreitende'.

Wilhelm Jensen

J'empruntais, dans cet enthousiasme
factice, les formules mêmes qui, si peu de
temps auparavant, m'avaient servi pour
peindre un amour véritable et longtemps
éprouvé. La lettre partie, j'aurais voulu la
retenir...

Gérard de Nerval, *Aurélia*

From April to September 2020, this
book emerged; from beneath the
protective shield of lockdown, in
isolation but never in solitude. 'Who is it
for, grandad?', asked Beatrice. It is for
you, Toodles, too...

Bibliography

Adorno, Theodor. *Negative Dialectics*, New York: Seabury Press, 1973.

Agard, John. 'Listen Mr Oxford Don', in *The New British Poetry 1968-1988*, ed. Gillian Allnutt, London: Paladin, 1988.

Agualusa, José Eduardo. *O Vendedor de Passados*, Lisbon: Booket, Publicações Dom Quixote, 2004.

Agualusa, José Eduardo. *The Book of Chameleons*, London: Arcadia Books, 2006.

Agualusa, José Eduardo. *Época* interview, www.afirma.inf.br/htm/colunistas/sueli/colunistas2.htm, 2007.

Agualusa, José Eduardo. Interview with Polzonoff, P. and Tepper, A., *Words Without Borders*, www.wordswithoutborders.org, 2007.

Andahazi, Federico. 'El dolmen', Bar La Academia, Buenos Aires, 1986, in *El oficio de los santos*, Madrid: Editorial Planeta, 2012.

Andahazi, Federico. 'El dolmen', *Blanco y Negro*, 50-55, 28 March 1999.

Anderson, Perry. *In the Tracks of Historical Materialism*, Chicago: Chicago University Press, 1984.

Anderson, Perry. 'The Cardoso Legacy', *London Review of Books*, 24 (24), 12 December 2002.

Barnstone, Willis. *Borges at Eighty*, Bloomington: Indiana University Press, 1982.

Barthes, Roland. 'Style and Its Image', in *Literary Style: A Symposium*, ed. Seymour Chatman, New York: Oxford University Press, 1971.

Barthes, Roland. *S/Z*, trans. Richard Miller, New York: Hill and Wang, 1974.

Barthes, Roland. *Roland Barthes par Roland Barthes*, Paris: Éditions du Seuil, 1975.

Barthes, Roland. *Image-Music-Text*, Glasgow: Fontana, 1982.

Baudelaire, Charles. *Oeuvres complètes*, Paris: Pléiade, 1961.

Bemberg, María Luisa. *De eso no se habla*, Buenos Aires: Mojame S. A./Oscar Kramer/Aura Films SRL, 1993.

Benjamin, Walter. *Illuminations*, ed. and with an introduction by Hannah Arendt, trans. Harry Zohn, London: Pimlico, 1999.

Benn Michaels, Walter. 'The Interpreter's Self: Pierce on the Cartesian "Subject"', in *Reader-Response Criticism from Formalism to Post-Structuralism*, ed. Jane P. Tompkins, Baltimore and London: Johns Hopkins University Press, 1980, 185-200.

Bennington, Geoffrey. *Legislations*, London: Verso, 1994.

Betto, Frei. 'Receita para matar um sem-terra', in *Landless Voices in Song and Poetry*, eds. Else R. P. Vieira and Bernard McGuirk

(2007), Nottingham: Critical, Cultural and Communications Press, 2002, 77-78.

Bhabha, Homi K. 'The other question', *Screen*, 24 (6), 1983, 18-36.

Bollig, Benjamin. *Néstor Perlongher: the Poetic Search for an Argentine Marginal Voice*, Cardiff: University of Wales Press, 2008.

Boone, Linda R. '"Si tú te llamaras Babel...": Love Poetry, Parody and Irony in *Tres Tristres Tigres*', in *Siglo XX/20th Century*, 8 (1-2), 1990-91, 31-40.

Borges, Jorge Luis. 'Funes el memorioso', *Ficciones*, Madrid: Alianza, 1988.

Borges, Jorge Luis. 'Kafka y sus precursores', *Otras inquisiciones*, Madrid: Alianza, 1995.

Borges, Jorge Luis. 'Juan López and John Ward', *The Times*, 18 September 1982.

Borges, Jorge Luis. 'Juan López y John Ward', *Clarín*, 26 August 1982.

Bosi, Alfredo. *História concisa da literatura brasileira*, São Paulo: Cultrix, 1973.

Bourne, B., Eichler U., and Herman D. (eds.), *Modernity and Its Discontents, Voices*, Nottingham: Spokesman/Hobo Press, 1987.

Bowie, Malcolm. *Mallarmé and the Art of Being Difficult*, Cambridge: Cambridge University Press, 1978.

Branco, Joaquim. 'Grande Sertão: Lusíadas (De como o vaqueiro Riobaldo encontra o velho Gama, nos mares bravios do sertão-linguagem)', Belo Horizonte: *Suplemento Literário de Minas Gerais*, 36, Secretaria da Cultura de Minas Gerais, 20-21 April 1998.

Buarque de Hollanda, Chico. Chico Buarque's lyrics: http://w.3.impa.br/-nivaldo/all-chico.html.

Buñuel, Luis. *My Last Breath*, London: Vintage, 1994.

Campbell, Duncan. 'The US is learning its Latin lesson', *The Guardian*, G2, 1, 2 October 1999.

Campos, Haroldo de. 'On Mephistofaustic Transluciferation', in *Haroldo de Campos in Conversation*, eds. Bernard McGuirk and Else R. P. Vieira, trans. Bernard McGuirk, London: Zoilus Press, 2009, 233-36.

Campos, Haroldo de. 'o anjo esquerdo da história', in *Mais!*, *Folha de São Paulo,* 28 April 1996.

Campos, Haroldo de. 'o anjo equerdo da história', in *ptnotícias*, São Paulo, Diretório Nacional do Partido dos Trabalhadores. n.d. Reproduced in: *Crisantempo: no espaço nasce um*, São Paulo: Perspectiva, 1998, 69-72,.

Campos, Haroldo de. 'Europe under the Sign of Devoration', in *Latin American Literary Review*, 25, 1986, 42-60.

Campos, Haroldo de. '*Iracema:* A Vanguard Archaeography', in *Tropical Paths. Essays on Modern Brazilian Literature*, ed. Randal Johnson, New York: Garland Publishing, 1993, 11-28.

Campos, Haroldo de. 'Ode (explícita) em defesa da poesia no dia da são Lukács', in *Educação dos cinco sentidos*, 1979-84, in *Melhores poemas*, selected by Inês Oseki Dépré, São Paulo: Global Editora, 1992.

Chanan, Michael 'The changing geography of Third Cinema', *Screen* 38 (4), 1997, 372-88.

Charter, David. 'Children in London share more than 300 languages', *The Times*, 22 January 2000, 18.

Collins, Merle. 'No Dialects Please', in *NEAB Anthology 1999 English Literature*, London: Heinemann. First published in *Watchers and Seekers: Creative Writing By Black Women in Britain*, eds. Rhonda Cobham and Merle Collins, London: Women's Press, 1987.

Dantas, Paulo. 'Sagarana emotiva', in *O Estado de São Paulo, Suplemento Literário*, 12, 583, 29 June 1968.

de Andrade, Oswald. *Manifesto Antropófago*, in www.agencetopo .qc.ca/carnages/manifeste.

Derrida, Jacques. *Writing and Difference*, trans. A. Bass, London: Routledge and Kegan-Paul, 1978.

Derrida, Jacques. 'Plato's Pharmacy', *Dissemination*, trans. B. Johnson, London: The Athlone Press, 1981.

Derrida, Jacques. 'Choreographies', interview with Christie McDonald, *Diacritics*, 12, 1982.

Derrida, Jacques. *The Truth in Painting*, trans. G. Bennington and I. McLeod, Chicago and London: University of Chicago Press, 1987.

Derrida, Jacques. Excerpt from 'The Animal That Therefore I Am (More to Follow)', trans. David Wills, *Critical Inquiry*, Winter, Volume 28, Number 2, 2002, http://criticalinquiry.uchicago. edu/issues/v28/ v28n2.derrida.html.

Derrida, Jacques. 'The Supplement of Origin', in *Speech and Phenomena, and Other Essays*, Evanston: Northwestern University Press, 1973.

Derrida, Jacques. *Of Grammatology*, trans. Gayatri Spivak, Baltimore: Johns Hopkins University Press, 1976.

Derrida, Jacques. *Specters of Marx. The State of the Debt, the Work of Mourning, & the New International*, trans. Peggy Kamuf, New York and London: Routledge, 1994.

Derrida, Jacques. 'Women in the Beehive: A Seminar with Jacques Derrida', in *Subjects/Objects,* 2, 12, 1984.

Derrida, Jacques *Le monolinguisme de l'autre*, Paris: Galilée, 1996.

Derrida, Jacques. 'Speculations on Freud', trans. Ian McLeod. Oxford: *The Oxford Literary Review*, 3:2, 1978, 78-97.

Derrida, Jacques. *The Other Heading: Reflection on Today's Europe*, Bloomington & Indianapolis: Indiana University Press, 1992.

Derrida, Jacques. 'Finis', *Aporia. Dying – awaiting (one another at) the 'limits of truth'*, Stanford, California: Stanford University Press, 1993.

Derrida, Jacques. *Speech and Phenomena, and other Essays on Husserl's Theory of Signs*, trans. David B. Allison, Evanston, Ill.: North Western University Press, 1973.

Derrida, Jacques. *The Ear of the Other*, trans. Peggy Kamuf, Bison Books, Lincoln: University of Nebraska Press, 1988.

Dostoevsky, Fyodor. *Notes from the Underground*, trans. Constance Garnett, New York: The MacMillan Company, 1918.

Drummond de Andrade, Carlos. *Antologia Poética*, Lisboa: Ática, 1965.

Duarte, Cabral. Private letter to author, 1998.

Eagleton, Terry. 'Marxism, Structuralism and Poststructuralism', in *Diacritics* (Winter), 1985.

Eagleton, Terry. *Literary Theory: An Introduction*, Oxford: Blackwell, 1983.

Eagleton, Terry. *Saint Oscar*, Derry: Field Day, 1989.

Eco, Umberto. 'Of Mice and Men', *The Guardian Review*, 1 November, 8, 2003.

Faiola, Anthony. 'Figures to die for in Argentina', *The Guardian*, July, 14, 1997, 5.

Fanon, Frantz. *Black Skin, White Masks*, New York: Grove, 1967.

Fanon, Frantz. *Black Skin, White Masks*, London and Sydney: Pluto Press, 1986.

Featherstone, Simon. *War Poetry: An Introductory Reader*, London: Routledge, 1995.

Fiedler, Leslie A. *Freaks: Myths and Images of the Secret Self*, New York: Simon & Schuster, 1978.

Fogwill, Rodolfo Enrique. *Los pichy-cyegos: Visiones de una batalla subterranea*, Buenos Aires: Ediciones de la Flor, 1983.

Forgacs, David. 'Marxist Literary Theories', in *Modern Literary Theory. A Comparative Introduction*, eds. Ann Jefferson and David Robey, London: Batsford, 1982, 166-203.

Fusco, Coco. *English is Broken Here. Notes on Cultural Fusion in the Americas,* New York City: The New Press, 1995.

Fussell, Paul. *Killing in Verse and Prose*, London: Bellew Publishing, 1990.

Fussell, Paul. *The Great War and Modern Memory*, Oxford: Oxford

University Press, 1975.

García Márquez, Gabriel. 'An Interview with Gabriel García Márquez', (a translation by D. Cole of an original *El País* interview), *Cencrastus*, 7, 1981, 6-7.

García Márquez, Gabriel. 'La tercera resignación' (3 September 1947); 'Eva está dentro de su gato' (25 October 1947); 'Tubalcaín forja una estrella' (18 January 1948); in *El Espectador*, Bogotá.

García Márquez, Gabriel. *Chronicle of a Death Foretold*, trans. G. Rabassa, London: Jonathan Cape, 1982.

García Márquez, Gabriel. *Crónica de una muerte anunciada*, Barcelona: Bruguera, 1981.

Gasché, Rudolf. 'Edges of Misunderstanding', in Walter Hamacher, Neil Hertz and Thomas Keenan, eds., *Responses: on Paul De Man's Wartime Journalism*, Lincoln: University of Nebraska Press, 1989.

Giles, Steve. *Theorizing Modernism: Essays in Critical Theory*, London: Routledge, 1993.

Gilman, Sander L. 'Black Bodies, White Bodies: Towards an Iconography of Female Sexuality in Late Nineteenth-Century Art, Medicine and Literature', in *Race, Writing and Difference*, ed. Henry Louis Gates Jr., Chicago and London: University of Chicago Press, 223-61, 1986.

Gilroy, Paul. *There Ain't No Black in the Union Jack*, London: Unwin Hyman, 1987.

Gledson, John. 'A Historic Landmark', in Schwarz, Roberto. *Misplaced Ideas: Essays on Brazilian Culture*, London and New York: Verso, 1996.

Gómez-Peña, Guillermo. *Warrior for Gringostroika*, Minnesota: Graywolf Press, 1993.

Gómez-Peña, Guillermo. *The New World Border*, San Francisco: City Lights, 1996.

Grossman, Edith. 'Truth is Stranger than Fact', *Review*, 30, 1981, 1-9.

Grosfoguel, Ramón and Chloe S. Georas. 'Latino Caribbean Diasporas in New York', in *Mambo Montage*, eds. Agustín Laó-Montes and Arlene Dávila, New York, Chichester, West Sussex: Columbia University Press, 97-106, 2001, 97-106.

Hall, Stuart. In conversation with Melvyn Bragg, *In Our Time*, London BBC Radio 4, 13 May, 1999.

Henighan, Stephen. *Times Literary Supplement*, 23 September 2005.

Irigaray, Luce. *Spéculum de l'autre femme*, Paris: Minuit, 1974.

Jameson, Fredric. *The Political Unconscious: Narrative as a Socially Symbolic Act*, London: Methuen, 1981.

Kantaris, Elia Geoffrey. 'The last snapshots of modernity: Argentine cinema after the "Process"', *Bulletin of Hispanic Studies* 73, 1996, 219-44.

King, John. *Magical Reels*, London and New York: Verso, 1990.

Kon, Daniel. *Los chicos de la guerra. Hablan los soldados que estuvieron en Malvinas*, Buenos Aires: Galerna, 1982.

Krog, Antjie. *A Change of Tongue*, Johannesburg: Random House, 2003.

Lacan, Jacques. 'The Insistence of the Letter in the Unconscious', *Yale French Studies*, 36-7, 1966, 112-47.

Ladipo, David. 'Imprisoned America', *New Left Review*, January-February, 2001, 109-23.

Landau, Paul and Kaspin, Deborah. D. *Images and Empires: Visuality in Colonial and Postcolonial Africa*, Berkeley: University of California Press, 2002.

Laviera, Tato. *AmeRícan*, Houston: Arte Público Press, 1985.

Leitch, Vincent B. *Deconstructive Criticism: An Advanced Introduction*, London: Hutchinson, 1983.

Lejeune, Philippe. 'The Autobiographical Contract' in ed. Tzvetan Todorov, *French Literary Theory Today*, Cambridge: Cambridge University Press, 1982, 192-207.

Levinas, Emmanuel. *Totality and Infinity*, trans. Alphonso Lingis, Pittsburgh: Duquesne University Press, 1969.

Levinas, Emmanuel. *A Levinas Reader*, ed. Sean Hand, Oxford: Blackwell, 1989.

Luis, William. 'Culture as Text: The Cuban/Caribbean Connection' in *Translating Latin America: Culture as Text/Translation Perspectives*, Binghampton: State University of New York Press, 1991, 7-19.

Macedo, Helder. 'The Purpose of Praise: Past and Future in *The Lusiads* of Luis de Camões', An Inaugural lecture in the Camões Chair of Portuguese, London: King's College, 15 November, 1983.

McGuirk, Bernard. 'Free play of fore-play: speculations on *Crónica de una muerte anunciada*', in *Gabriel García Márquez: New Readings*, eds. McGuirk, Bernard and Cardwell, Richard A., Cambridge: Cambridge University Press, 1987.

McGuirk, Bernard. *Latin American Literature. Symptoms, Risks and Strategies of Post-structuralist Criticism*, London & New York: Routledge, 1997.

McGuirk, Bernard. 'Est-ce bien de cela qu'on parle? En deçà et au-delà du surréel féminin en Argentine', in *La Femme s'entête. La Part du féminin dans le surréalisme,* eds. Jacqueline Chénieux-Gendron and Georgiana Colvile, Paris: CNRS, 1998, 323-45.

McGuirk, Bernard. 'Latin America – Interventions/Border Lines', in *Interventions. International Journal of Postcolonial Studies* 2 (3), 2000, 392-408.

McGuirk, Bernard. 'On Hospitality for *The Emigrants*: a response *d'après* W. G. Sebald to Alberto Moreiras on Deconstruction', in *The New Latin Americanism*: *Papers*, Manchester: University of Manchester, 2002. http://www.art.man.ac.uk/Lacs/seminars_events/newlatam/papers.htm, n.p.

McGuirk, Bernard. 'Triálogo/s con Guillermo Gómez-Peña y/en la poesía-frontera: ¿Es la traducción una (in)curable enfermedad (ir)repetible?', in *De Signis*, Barcelona: Gedisa, ed. Cristina Peñamarin, 2005a, 139-52.

McGuirk, Bernard. 'Dos *espectros de Marx* aos espectros do mar...', in *Jacques Derrida: Pensar a desconstrução*, ed. Evando Nascimento, São Paulo: Estação Liberdade, 2005b, 233-43.

McGuirk, Bernard. 'Derrida trans(at)l(antic)ated. Spectres of *mar...* Mythology as Excess in Fernando Pessoa and João Guimarães Rosa', *Versus: Quaderni di studi semiotici*, gennaio-agosto, 2006, 41-73.

McGuirk, Bernard. *Falklands-Malvinas. An Unfinished Business*, Seattle: New Ventures, 2007.

McGuirk, Bernard. '*Animot* liberation or oh! what a beastly war: the Falklands-Malvinas conflict in the political cartoon, from *Humor* to *The If... Chronicles*', *Journal of Romance Studies*, vol. 8, n. 2, 2008, 73-94.

McGuirk, Bernard and Else R. P. Vieira. (eds.) *Haroldo de Campos in Conversation: In Memoriam 1929-2003*, London: Zoilus Press, 2009.

McGuirk, Bernard. 'Intra-colonialism or *L'animotion* of the Black Atlantic: J. E. Agualusa's *O vendedor de passados*', *Hispanic Research Journal*, 13.2, 2010, 165-87.

McGuirk, Bernard. 'Intra-colonialismo ou *L'animotion* do Atlântico Negro: *O vendedor de passados* de J. E. Agualusa', *Dossiê: Triangulações Atlânticas – Transnacionalidades em Língua Portuguesa*, *Via Atlântica*, São Paulo, 25, July 2014, 15-46.

McGuirk, Bernard. *Latin American Literature and Post-structuralism*, London: SPLASH Editions, 2018.

Melo Neto, João Cabral de. *Morte e vida severina e outros poemas para vozes*, Rio de Janeiro: Editora Nova Fronteira, 2000.

Mendoza, Plinio Apuleyo. *El olor de la guayaba*, Barcelona: Bruguera, 1982.

Moreiras, Alberto. 'Ten Notes on Primitive Imperial Accumulation. Ginés de Sepúlveda, Las Casas, Fernández de Oviedo'.

Interventions. International Journal of Postcolonial Studies 2 (3), 2000, 343-63.

Moreiras, Alberto. *The Exhaustion of Difference. The Politics of Latin American Cultural Studies*, Durham, N. C.: Duke University Press, 2001.

Moser, Walter. 'Haroldo de Campos's Literary Experimentation of the Second Kind', in *Experimental – Visual – Concrete: Avant-Garde Poetry since the 1960s*, ed. K. David Jackson, 1998, 139-49.

Nascimento, Evando. (ed.) *Jacques Derrida: Pensar a Desconstrução*, São Paulo: Editora Estação Liberdade, 2005.

Nouzeilles, Gabriela and Graciela Montaldo. (eds.) *The Argentina Reader: History, Culture, Politics*, Durham, N.C.: Duke University Press, 2002.

Peres, Phyllis. 'Subaltern Spaces in Brazil', in *Dispositio/n* XIX, 46, Ann Arbor: University of Michigan, 1994, 113-26.

Perlongher, Néstor. 'Las tías', *Alambres*, *Poemas completos 1980-1992*, Barcelona: Seix Barral, 1997.

Perlongher, Néstor. 'Todo el poder a Lady Di: Militarismo y anticolonialismo en la cuestión de las Malvinas' (1982), 'La ilusión de unas islas' (1983), and 'El deseo de unas islas' (1985). *Prosa plebeya*, Buenos Aires: Ediciones Coluihue, 1997.

Pessoa, Fernando. 'A Nova Poesia Portuguesa no seu Aspecto Psicológico', III, *Obras em Prosa*, ed. Cleonice Berardinelli, Rio de Janeiro: Editora Nova Aguilar, 1974.

Pessoa, Fernando. 'O menino da sua mãe', *Poesia-1: 1902-1929, Obra Poética*, Lisboa: Publicações Europa-América, 1987.

Pessoa, Fernando. *Álvaro de Campos. Livro de Versos*, edição crítica, introdução, transcrição, organização e notas de Teresa Rita Lopes, Lisboa: Estampa, 1993.

Pessoa, Fernando. *Mensagem*, Lisboa: Parceria António Maria Pereira, 1934.

Pessoa, Fernando. *Obra Poética de Fernando Pessoa. Mensagem*, ed. António Quadros, Mira-Sintra: Publicações Europa-America, 1986.

Pessoa, Fernando. *Poesias*, nota explicativa de João Gaspar Simões e Luiz de Montalvor, Lisboa: Ática, 1942.

Pessoa, Fernando. *Sobre Portugal. Introdução ao Problema Nacional*, recolha de textos de Maria Isabel Rocheta e Maria Paula Morão, introdução organizada por Joel Serrão, Lisboa: Ática, 1979.

Phillips, Mike and Trevor Phillips. *Windrush. The Irresistible Rise of Multi-Racial Britain*, London: Harper & Collins, 1998.

Shaw, D. L. '*Trilce* I Revisited', in *Romance Notes* 20, Winter 1979-80), 167-71.

Pires, J. A. *João Guimarães Rosa – uma literatura amada*, Lisbon: Editorial AI Braga, Edicões Brotéria, 1993.

Poniatowska, Elena. 'Women writing and living in Latin America', in *Contemporary Women Writing in the Other Americas: Latin America*, ed. Georgiana Colvile, Lewiston, Queenston, and Lampeter: Edwin Mellen Press, 1996, 145-62.

Pratt, Mary Louise. 'Linguistic Utopias', in *The Linguistics of Writing*, ed. Nigel Fabb *et al*, Manchester: Manchester University Press, 1987, 48-66.

Pring-Mill, Robert. '"*Gracias a la vida*". *The Power and Poetry of Song*', The Kate Elder Lecture, Queen Mary University of London, 1990.

Ray, William. *Literary Meaning*, Oxford: Blackwell, 1984.

Reed, Henry. 'Naming of Parts', *New Statesman and Nation*, 24, 598, 8 August 1942, 92.

Reid, Anna 'Disintegration, dismemberment and discovery of identities and histories: searching the "gaps" for depositories of alternative memory in the narratives of Diamela Eltit and Carmen Boullosa', *Bulletin of Latin American Research*, 17:1, 1998, 81-92.

Rimbaud, Arthur. *Oeuvres complètes*, ed. Antoine Adam, Paris: Gallimard, Pléiade, 1972

Rosa, João Guimarães. *Grande Sertão: Veredas*, Rio de Janeiro: Livraria José Olympio Editora, 1978.

Rosenfield, K. H. 'Devil to Pay in the Backlands and João Guimarães Rosa's Quest for the Univeral', *Portuguese Literary and Cultural Studies*, 4/5, Spring/Fall, 2000, 197-205.

Roth, Michael S. *Psychoanalysis and History: Negation and Freedom in Freud*, Ithaca: Cornell University Press, 1987.

Rowe, William, in ed. John King, Cambridge: *The Cambridge Companion to Modern Latin American Culture*, 2004, 136-70.

Sabine, Mark. 'Killing and Nostalgia: Testimony and the Image of Empire in Margarida Cardoso's *A Costa dos Murmúrios*', in eds. Cristina Demaria and Macdonald Daly, *The Genres of Post-Conflict Testimonies*, Nottingham: Critical, Cultural and Communications Press, 2009, 250-77.

Safka, Melanie. 'What have they done to my song Ma?', on *Candles In The Rain*, London: Buddah Records, 1970.

Salgado, Sebastião. *Terra*. Prefácio de José Saramago. Poesia de Chico Buarque, São Paulo: Companhia das Letras, English edition (1998) published as *Terra: Struggle of the Landless*, London: Phaidon, 1997.

Santiago, Silviano. *Glossário de Derrida*, Rio de Janero: Livraria

Francisco Alves, 1976.

Santiago, Silviano. 'O entre-lugar do discurso latino-americano', in *Uma literatura nos trópicos*, São Paulo: Perspectiva, 1978, 11-28.

Santiago, Silviano. *Pernambucano, Suplemento Cultural*, 16 June 2020.

Schwarz, Roberto. *Misplaced Ideas*: *Essays on Brazilian Culture*, London and New York: Verso, 1992.

Sebald, W. G. *The Emigrants*, London: Harvill, 1997.

Sequeira, V. M., Ferreira, R., and Fonseca, A. *Uma casa Portuguesa*, popular fado (first performance), 1952.

Sharman, Adam. *Tradition and Modernity in Spanish American Literature*, New York and Basingstoke: Palgrave, 2006.

Shields, David. *Reality Hunger a Manifesto*, London: Hamish Hamilton, 2010.

Spivak, Gayatri. 'criticism feminism and the institution' interview with Elizabeth Gross, *thesis 11* No 10/11 (November/March), 1984-5, 175-87.

Tanner, Anthony. *Adultery in the Novel*: *Contract and Transgression*, Baltimore and London: The Johns Hopkins University Press, 1979.

Thénon, Susana. *Ova completa*, Buenos Aires: Editorial Sudamericana, 1987.

Todorov, Tzvetan. 'The Typology of Detective Fiction', *The Poetics of Prose*, Ithaca, NY: Cornell University Press, 1977.

Triquell, Ximena. 'Del cine-testimonio al cine-testamento', in *Changing Reels: Latin American Cinema Against The Odds*, eds. Rob Rix and Roberto Rodríguez Saona, Leeds: Trinity and All Saints University College, 1997, 59-74.

Valéry, Paul, 'Poetry and Abstract Thought: Dancing and Walking', in Lodge, David, ed. *Twentieth Century Literary Criticism: a Reader*, Harlow: Longman, 1972.

Vargas Llosa, Mario. 'Staring into the Abyss', in *The Sunday Times*, London, 24 April 1994, 8-9.

Vasconcelos, Sandra. *Puras Misturas*, São Paulo: Editora Hucitec, Fapesp, 1997.

Vecchi, Roberto. 'Maudsley e i crimini delle nazionalità', *Conflitti. Strategie di rappresentazione della guerra nella cultura contemporanea*, eds. Fortunati, V., Fortezza, D. and Ascari, M., Roma: Meltemi, 2008.

Veríssimo, José. *Estudos de Literatura Brasileira*, Belo Horizonte: Itatiaia, 1976.

Vieira, Else R. P. and McGuirk Bernard. (eds.) *Landless Voices in Song and Poetry: The Movimento dos Sem Terra of Brazil*, Nottingham:

Critical, Cultural and Communications Press, 2007.

Vieira, Else R. P. 'Postcolonialisms and the Latin Americas', *Interventions: International Journal of Postcolonial Studies* 1 (2), 1999, 273-81.

Vieira, Else R. P. 'Epistles of Possession, Epistemologies of Liberation', *Interventions: International Journal of Postcolonial Studies*, 2 (3), 2000, 309-27.

Vieira, Else R. P. 'Pos-Colonialismos e Teoria Literária', in *Caminhos e horizontes da teoria da literatura contemporânea*, Braga: CEH, Universidade do Minho, 2002.

Walsh, Rodolfo. *Operación masacre*, Buenos Aires: De la Flor, 1957.

Williams, Raymond. *Marxism and Literature*, Oxford: Oxford University Press, 1977.

Williams, Raymond. *Resources of Hope: Culture, Democracy, Socialism*, London: Verso, 1989.

Index

289

291

www.ingramcontent.com/pod-product-compliance
Lightning Source LLC
Chambersburg PA
CBHW022005080426
42733CB00007B/478